THE
SEXUAL
CREATORS

An Ethical Proposal for Concerned Christians

André Guindon

UNIVERSITY
PRESS OF
AMERICA

LANHAM • NEW YORK • LONDON

Copyright © 1986 by

University Press of America,® Inc.

4720 Boston Way
Lanham, MD 20706

3 Henrietta Street
London WC2E 8LU England

Library of Congress Cataloging in Publication Data

Guindon, Andre, 1933-
    The sexual creators.

    Bibliography: p.
    Includes index.
    1. Sexual ethics. 2. Sex—Religious aspects—
Christianity.   I. Title.
HQ32.G85   1986   261.8'357   85-31453
ISBN 0-8191-5239-0 (alk. paper)
ISBN 0-8191-5240-4 (pbk. : alk. paper)

All University Press of America books are produced on acid-free
paper which exceeds the minimum standards set by the National
Historical Publications and Records Commission.

For Benoit and Michèle

CONTENTS

CONTENTS

PART II

Moral Experiences

FOREWORD

> The perfection of the effect
> demonstrates the perfection of
> the cause since a greater
> power produces a more perfect
> effect. But God is the most
> perfect agent. It follows that
> things created by him obtain
> perfection from him. To
> detract, therefore, from the
> perfection of creatures is to
> detract from the perfection of
> divine power.
>
> THOMAS AQUINAS[1]

The extraordinarily beautiful idea that God's own perfection can only be exalted by recognizing his creature's perfection led me to entitle this book The Sexual Creators instead of The Sexual Creatures. More than a title, this insight commands a whole understanding of God's intervention in this world of ours and, therefore, a certain way of doing theological ethics. If God is seen as the competitor of human beings in some Promethean power struggle, "to detract from the perfection of creatures" is indeed the logical way to magnify his omnipotence. As a consequence, a theologian will hold that God not only creates human beings but controls every aspect of their activity. God will be thought of as having a minutely detailed plan in which human creatures are free to choose either to follow courses of action in conformity with this plan and thereby please the divine Designer, or to act contrary to this plan and thus provoke divine wrath. Christian ethics, therefore, becomes the juridical science which spells out this divine master plan and its breakdown into a vast number of subsidiary plans (for the individual, for the child, for the parent, for the family, for the judge, for the physician, for the nation, for sexuality, for economy, for war and peace, etc.). Christian ethics interprets these plans and weighs each of their obligations. It searches for all the loopholes (for creatures too must have some fun) and calculates every penalty God will inflict on those who interfere with the fulfillment of the divine blueprint.

If, on the contrary, God is seen not as the competitor of his human creature but as the creator of his creature's freedom - a freedom which makes man and woman share in God's perfection and creative energy – then, "to detract from the perfection of creatures is to detract from the perfection of divine power." God manifests his greatness through the perfection of this being that freely creates its own human interactions in accordance with an ongoing historical discernment of what humanizes. He has given man and woman the potential to liberate their own humanity so that they may stand in truth in His presence and be open to His loving and redemptive Mystery. Based on this conviction that ethics is primarily a discourse on our humanity, the reflections proposed here are open to all men and women.

Sexual human beings are seen, in this book, as intelligent and free persons, that is to say, persons who enjoy the ability to make sense of their concrete existence and who are responsible for creating a sexual language which expresses and structures meaningful human relationships. In other words, human persons are seen as sexual creators. The question this book wishes to address is the following: What do the sexual creators create out of this sexual fecundity of theirs? This, in my opinion, is the most crucial issue in sexual ethics today. Until this question is resolved, the heated debate over sexual ethics taking place in most Christian Churches will not subside.

For eons of history, Christian ethicists have assumed that fecundity is the hallmark of virtuous sexual activity. When, prompted by the Reformation, apologetical concerns led Roman Catholic theologians to consider human sexuality as choice material for confession,[2] fertile sex became a Catholic ideological bulwark. As one mulls over the textbooks written for future confessors in the first half of this century, one is struck by this overarching context of sexual ethics. All the key difficulties raised against sexual fantasies, masturbation, homosexual acts, pre-marital, extra-marital or post-marital sex, contraception and all other forms of sexual activity cluster about the concept of fecundity.

After more than a quarter century of virulent controversy among Roman Catholic theologians over the sensitive issue of sexual fecundity,[3] moralists seem to be regrouping in two parties: one which advocates that fecundity concerns sacramentally married, heterosexual couples carrying out their duty and privilege to bear children; and another which does not consider reproductive fertility to be synonymous with sexual fecundity. Theologians who voice the views of the fecundity-fertility party claim to be the champions of orthodoxy and preface their every intervention with the "Be fertile" of Genesis 1: 28. Those who speak for the fecundity-more-than-fertility party allude to sexual values other than reproductive fertility. But, as John Giles Milhaven rightly points out, the latter have yet to spell out what these values really are.[4]

Since this point is of capital importance for a theology of sexuality, the current dilemma cannot be resolved until the notion of sexual fecundity has been clarified. How, in effect, does one choose between a notion of reproductive fecundity which is gradually becoming even more rigid than the mildly progressive views expressed in <u>Humanae vitae</u>,[5] and another notion which purports to be more <u>integrally human</u>, but which is at best only suggestive?[6] I am convinced that their tradition offers Roman Catholic moralists the possibility of making a serious contribution toward the resolution of this dilemma. This work is offered to the Church as a contribution towards the construction of an alternative to the unsatisfactory fecundity-fertility view.

Ethics is not a theoretical science of truths to <u>behold</u> but a practical science of truths to <u>be made</u>. A sexual theory which is not structured on a sexual practice is, therefore, devoid of normative value. Only a reflection on the lived experience of sexual fecundity will validly lead to a renewed formulation of human sexual fecundity. Such experience has been the starting point of my own ethical enterprise. For pedagogical reasons, however, this experience will be presented last. The general theory which was gradually elaborated from observation of the data and the reflection on it is introduced in the first part of the book (chapter 1-4). Some of the characteristic moral experiences of sexual fecundity on which the theory is based are examined in the second part (chapters 5-8). The disadvantage of this presentation is that the basis for suggesting a new theory is less immediately conspicuous. The advantage is that, with a theory with which to start, the reader can make sense of the moral experiences described and test the validity of the proposed theory. In the theoretical part, the same pattern of moving from the more theoretical to the more concrete has been followed. A reader could, therefore, read this book from chapter eight to chapter one. This would enable him or her to reflect personally on some typical ways of experiencing sexual fecundity (chapters 8-5), to judge whether the proposed renewed notion of sexual fecundity is adequate (chapter 4) and the criticism of other notions justified (chapter 3) and, finally, to evaluate the significance of the theory of sexual ethics (chapter 2) and of the global ethical paradigm in which this renewed notion is inserted (chapter 1).

I wish to express my deepest gratitude to all those who have helped me in preparing this volume. In particular, to the students and professors of the Faculty of Theology of Saint Paul University for the intellectually stimulating community which they represent for me; to my Oblate confreres of Champagne House for their warm friendship and unfailing support; to Rosaire Bellemare, Hubert Doucet, Denise Doyle, Joseph Lazor, Maureen LaPlaca, Kenneth Melchin, Thomas Novak, and Denise Russell for their critical reading of the first draft of this volume and for their judicious remarks; to Kenneth Russell for reading the consecutive drafts of this book, correcting the writing and making other invaluable suggestions; and to Viviane Robidoux for her typing assistance.

NOTES

1. ScG, III, 69 (Vol. III, p. 96, n. 2445) (my translation).
2. See T. N. TENTLER, Sin and Confession on the Eve of the Reformation (Princeton: Princeton University Press, 1977).
3. The "official approval" of the rhythm method of birth control by Pius XII in 1951 (AAS, 43 [1951], pp. 835-854) marks the beginning of it. Two other official documents kept it alive and thriving during the 1960's and well into the 1970's, namely, Vatican II's Gaudium et Spes in 1965 and Paul VI's encyclical letter Humanae vitae in 1968.
4. "Conjugal Love and Contemporary Moral Theology," Theological Studies, 35 (1974), p. 693.
5. See, e.g., J. M. FINNIS, "Natural Law and Unnatural Acts," Heythrop Journal, 11 (1970), pp. 365-387; J. O'REILLY, The Moral Problem of Contraception (Chicago: Franciscan Herald Press, 1975); W. MAY, "The Liberating Truth of Catholic Teaching on Sexual Morality," Homiletic and Pastoral Review, 83 (1983), pp. 21-28.
6. Thus, my own chapter on sexual fecundity which is, nevertheless, more explorative than anything else published at the time: The Sexual Language. An Essay in Moral Theology (Ottawa: The University of Ottawa Press, 1976), pp. 173-178. See, again recently, P. AUDOLLENT et al., Sexualité et vie chrétienne. Point de vue catholique (Paris: Le Centurion, 1981), pp. 26-29, 60-61.

Part I

ETHICAL THEORY

CHAPTER ONE

PARADIGMATIC PRELIMINARIES

1. PARADIGMATIC TRANSITION

The scene takes place in 1929. A group of Roman Catholic physicians ask their Bishop whether they would be justified in having a patient suspected of having contracted the deadly and contagious infection, gonorrhea, masturbate in order to obtain sperm for a medical examination. Though they are well educated, these adult Catholic laymen cannot assume the elementary responsibility of resolving this moral dilemma.[1] Their reflex is to "seek permission" from their Pastor.

If consulted on most other moral issues, the good Bishop would have offered at least an educated guess. Faced with the simplest issue of sexual ethics, he feels he is not qualified to make a decision. He writes, therefore, to the Holy Office and asks: "Is it licit directly to produce a pollution to obtain a semen specimen for the purpose of medical diagnosis of gonorrhea and medical treatment?" On July 24th, 1929, the Roman Congregation decrees the following ethically and theologically enlightening answer: "Negative."[2]

This true-life story is as good an illustration as any of the state of Christian, and specifically Roman Catholic, sexual ethics in the first half of the twentieth century. The good Christians mentioned above - the medical practitioners, the Bishop, the Officers of the Curia as well as the commentators - were all thinking and functioning within the largely prevailing paradigm of theological sexual ethics of the time, one which imposed a standardized mindset on the whole Roman Catholic world. Anglicans and Protestants were also theologizing, in ethics, within a similar pattern of thought. Responsibility for a wise decision-making in sexual matters was transferred, one way or other, to an exterior "authoritative" agency.

Any attempt at renewing the crucial problematic on human sexual fecundity must start by addressing the question of ethical theories and, more fundamentally, that of ethical paradigms. The expression "ethical paradigm" is not meant here as a synonym for a specific ethical system. In the latter, the different elements composing the discourse of ethics (goals, principles or values, human acts, conscience, virtues, law, grace, etc.) are organized in a certain fashion' and their interconnectedness and functioning are explained with more or less ability and coherence. An ethical paradigm implies much more than organizing the ethical discourse somewhat differently while adhering to a common understanding of human realities. During periods of broad cultural shifts, a community of Christian ethicists may be calling upon a similar ethical theory. Yet diverging global world views may have created an unbridgeable gap between two camps. Although the words the protagonists use for arguing their case remain the same, the symbols, meanings, and values have become substantially different. As Thomas Kuhn puts it, their language has become incommensurate. They approach the same topic from incompatible viewpoints.[3]

This, in the judgment of many (including my own), is the present-day situation in theological sexual ethics. Before we set out to investigate a new, emerging notion of human sexual fecundity, it is important that we situate this analysis within the backdrop of the contemporary paradigmatic transition in which renewed Christian patterns of sexual ethics are being proposed. These revitalized models challenge the prescriptive systems which arose from a very different ethical paradigm in the sixteenth century and flourished well into the twentieth century...,[4] systems which denied Catholic medical doctors and even their local Church's Catholic Pastor the right to assess by themselves the morality of very specific acts of masturbation for medical purposes.

There are, in my judgment, two very basic problems with this former way of moralizing on human sexuality. One lies with the ethical pattern in which this discourse is couched. The other has to do with its lack of properly Christian meaning. The grievances against a "jurisprudence of sex" which emerged from the former ethical paradigm will, therefore, be exposed briefly. How these methodological problems can be understood and dealt with in another mindset will be suggested in a second part entitled "Sexual Action in Faith". These paradigmatic preliminaries will set the scene for the second chapter in which a contemporary theory of sexual ethics for concerned Christians will be propounded.

2. A JURISPRUDENCE OF SEX

The sexual ethics taught in many reputable theological institutions well into the first half of the twentieth century was generally tailored on a juridical methodology. Most textbook writers majored in law and produced what amounts to a jurisprudence of sex. Contrary to their treatment of other domains of morality, these moralists did not start by raising questions on the meaning, structure, and purpose of human sexuality. They seemed to assume that human beings knew and ought to know very little about this aspect of their lives. God, through his messengers (Biblical hagiographers, Church Fathers, or Ecclesiastical Authorities), was expected to spell out for us the whole gamut of moral do's and don'ts. Written Tradition is, therefore, understood as the definitive and fully stocked arsenal of precepts and interdictions providing answers for every conceivable and, sometimes, hardly imaginable concrete action. As a consequence, manuals of sexual ethics open up every discussion by reciting Biblical, traditional or magisterial positive and negative precepts. Manualists assume that these moral regulations apply basically for all times, all societies, all cultures, all age groups, and all individuals alike.

The list of grievances which can be raised against this ethical model and its paradigmatic assumptions is endless. Among other things, this fundamentalist reading of Biblical sources and of Revelation itself,[5] apart from being intellectually puerile, simply does not work[6] because God as lawgiver has "forgotten" to legislate on all sorts of sexual activities. Code moralists must, therefore, make Him say what they need to hear, since they and not God have, in fact, decided through other unconscious criteria that certain actions ought to be condemned. Thus, the injustice of Onan (Gn 38) will be transformed into a prohibition of contraceptive practices and (why not?) of masturbation;[7] the condemnation of porneia will include, against what can be conclusively drawn from Scripture, all coital relationships before the legal celebration of marriage;[8] homosexuality and pederasty will be covered by the Sodom incident;[9] conjugal coital positions in which a wife assumes an active role will be reproved with the help of Rm 1: 26, "their women have turned from natural intercourse to unnatural practices;"[10] the list of fictitious Biblical interdictions is endless.

The psychological mechanism which pushes the advocates of this model to place their every moral judgment under divine endorsement is so strong that they rarely even bother to check their sources. Recently, one of them wrote in a Canadian Catholic newspaper that masturbation, premarital sex, and adultery are condemned in the Decalogue, in Mt 5: 21-43, and in Vatican II's Gaudium et Spes.[11] Adultery, perhaps! But masturbation and premarital sex? Other writers refer more subtly and vaguely to non existent or unestablished sources. Through a series of vague allusions, we are made to believe that God legislated sex more than He actually did.

When, on the other hand, Yahweh's sexual ethics are at odds with prescriptive ethics, its supporters do not hesitate to

justify their lack of Biblical literality. If God shows too much
indulgence for the moral taste of later custodians of an allegedly
pre-established and immutable divine order, they justify their new
moral rigour by explaining away Biblical tolerance: such crude
behaviour, we are told, was linked with out-dated customs. Similar
explanations are brought forward where Yahweh proves, on the
contrary, to be harsher than need be. However, most code moralists
never formulate hermeneutical rules for discriminating between the
legitimacy of the developments which they support and the
illegitimacy of those which they refuse. Why do they not support
Biblical law prescribing capital punishment in the case of
adultery (Lv 20: 9-10), of incest (Lv 20: 11-12, 14,17), of
homosexual intercourse (Lv 20: 13), of bestiality (Lv 20: 15-16)?
Why, on the contrary, should some form of adultery not be
permitted for the sake of stimulating private family economy,
since this seems to have been allowed in the Bible? Crafty Onan is
punished for refusing to impregnate his sister-in-law to frustrate
her right to the family patrimony (Gn 38). Sarai, on the contrary,
gives an example of domestic virtue by arranging the reproductive
relationship of her slave-girl Hagar with Abram, Sarai's own
husband (Gn 16).[12]

To call upon "divine permissions" for all such
embarrassing instances of contradictions between divine moral
regulations and later "Christian" moral regulations only
contributes to manifesting how much, in this paradigm, the
arbitrary Power, freed from any ethic of means, grounds the
discourse of a prescriptive moral theology. Such a crude position
calls for an equally crude comparison. God, because He enjoys
absolute Power, could follow a Watergate model of morality: as
First Executive of the moral order, He could give the "good guys"
permission to do evil to prevent the "bad guys" from taking over.

Recently, attempts have been made in some Catholic
moral theology forums, to formulate hermeneutical rules for
discerning between legitimate and illegitimate developments in
moral teaching. Joseph Jensen maintains, for instance, that
Biblical arguments concerning issues such as prostitution,
homosexuality, or bestiality should not be disqualified on the
grounds that such practices were linked with heathen cults. After
all, Jensen argues convincingly, would we not consider the
sacrifice of children intrinsically immoral even if we did not
know of the Biblical denunciation of this practice as part of
ancient pagan rites?[13] But how does one decide, through Biblical
criteria, that such practices, whether they are linked with
heathen cults or not, are intrinsically immoral? If we must call
on extra-Biblical criteria to decide this point (and I am
convinced that we must do so), then quoting Biblical prescriptions
and interdictions is redundant: we are merely calling upon
Biblical words to voice what we already know from another source.
If this is the case, then this "other source" ultimately grounds

6

ethics, not Biblical authority.

If the criteriology of this ethical pattern is unsatisfactory on intellectual grounds, [14] what it does to people who internalize it is, in addition, morally objectionable. It does not empower them to make free, and freeing, moral commitments. The subjectivity needed for committing oneself responsibly is lacking. Individuals who behave in certain ways merely because they are told to do so never leave their own mark on their deeds. They cannot honestly append their signature to such works because they have turned out copies instead of originals. The rule of their action is not what they think, discern, and will to do, but what someone else thinks, discerns, and wills them to do. They are prevented from discovering moral values in their far-reaching goal, namely their own becoming who they ought to be, their success as human beings, their fulfillment. How then will their ensuing commitments be in line with their human vocation? "After all," pondered Saint Paul, "the depths of a man can only be known by his own spirit, not by any other man..."(1 Co 2: 11). How, in other words, will they and their performances be moral? Moral life requires that the very truth of the act be matched as closely as possible to the intention which devises it.

In point of fact, there is no such thing in the ethical pattern we are criticizing as a specific sexual goodness, one which, actualized, would become a special power (called aretè by the Greeks and virtus by the Romans) enabling a person to create well-adapted sexual acts. The only virtue encouraged by all brands of prescriptive ethics is obedience, and, for that matter, a patriarchal brand of blind obedience to the commands of an authoritative figure. But, as Beverly Harrison observes judiciously, the very notion of obedience - at least the notion described above - is antithetical to what we mean by ethics. Without underrating the nobility and sometimes the heroism of the attitude which conceives moral life as a series of acts of obedience to divine diktats, this attitude, nevertheless, often prevents one from personally and actively grasping moral values which are always found encased in their historical packaging. Obedience may well serve, then, to justify the abdication of personal conscience. On the practical level this means that the individual surrenders what is essential for the living of a moral life. [15]

Even in an ethics where obedience is ascribed as [16] restricted a place as it is in the theology of a Thomas Aquinas, the legitimate goals of obedience always run the risk of being falsified. When an individual has been infantilized by a constant denial of personal discernment and decision-making, we cannot expect him or her to be motivated by "common good" objectives. Instead, he or she is looking for answers which will enable him or her to perform sexually with a "good conscience." Seeking

permissions from law-givers or from law-interpreters is a strategy
which is meant to alleviate the fear of punishment in those who
function on this pre-moral level.[17] The moral protocols of
children whom Jean Piaget would classify as heteronomous[18] or even
of subjects whom Lawrence Kohlberg would score in his first four
stages of moral development[19] demonstrate that a lack of
self-identity and a good dose of anxiety-producing insecurity
constitute the psychological backdrop of all forms of code
morality.

To suggest that the shift in contemporary sexual
ethics amounts to an attitude of indulgence and leniency towards
the lax mores of the times is, in my opinion, a lack of
perceptiveness. Just as children who function on a preconventional
level have been shown by Kohlberg to be young utilitarians who
begin to develop the art (at Stage 2) of dodging punishments by
learning how to manipulate authority figures, the juridical ethic
of adults betrays the very same penalty-evasion strategies through
casuistry. It is well-known that, within the framework of
prescriptive ethics, the extremes of rigorism and of laxism were
ever present. A look at Pope Alexander VII's condemnation of some
Probabilist moral propositions,[20] for instance, will convince
anyone that, with a jurisprudence approach to sex, one can get
away with murder since the ethical problem itself can easily be
left unconsidered and unsolved. The moral agent's whole
preoccupation is to get rid of his burden of anxiety or guilt and
to be reinstated in his "good conscience." And the success of this
operation depends on how skillful one becomes at finding juridical
loopholes or at pleading the attenuating circumstances with
oneself. Let us not be deceived by appearances: the abuses of
obedience far outweigh the abuses of power. Indeed, it is moral
immaturity that makes these latter abuses possible.

Systematized and taught to adults, this childish
pattern represents an inadmissible lack of respect towards men and
women. For this very reason, the moral fabric of society is
jeopardized when it becomes the overarching ethical model. Instead
of liberating individuals from the blind determinisms which impede
them from freely answering God's call to loving fellowship in
Christ, it molds uncritical conformists who place conventional
order above everything else. When the Sabbath is no longer viewed
as made for people, but people for the Sabbath (Mk 2: 27), a
society's moral fiber has deteriorated dangerously. When this
prescriptive ethics is dominant the morality of official
statements (including ecclesiastical ones) cannot be questioned.
In her devastating criticism of obedience, Dorothee Sölle shows
how the ethics of obedience leads inevitably to the support of
oppression.[21] She calls upon the Nazi experience. But Stanley
Milgram's notorious obedience experiment has also shown bewildered
North Americans how far "good citizens" addicted to prescriptive
ethics will go in harming their neighbour at the command of any

8

legitimate authority.[22]

Once the moral arbitrator is construed by legalistic
ethics as an exterior instance, the whole moral order is,
logically enough, exteriorized and materialized. Moral objects are
no longer the acts of a subject who is necessarily pregnant with
his or her subjectivity but, first and foremost, exterior
accomplishments which can be measured and quantified. This view
enables juridically trained moralists to apply a law methodology
to the field of ethics. In the realm of sexual ethics, this
practice leads to biologism. In biologism, the body is divided in
parts (decent, less decent, indecent).[23] Sins of "impurity" are
said to be complete or incomplete depending on whether or not
orgasm is produced.[24] Described in its physical mechanics,
masturbation becomes the name of a sin.[25] The elements of the
consummation of a Christian marriage are determined in terms of
erection, penetration and insemination,[26] with some astounding
determinations of "real semen produced in the testicles."[27]
Disputes over the means of birth-control eclipse all other
intelligent discussions concerning responsible parenthood.
Biologically reproducing a human organism becomes, as will be seen
in the third chapter, an ethical goal. There is no end to the
evidence which can be brought forward to back up this allegation
of biologism.

Because it functions out of ready-made answers
allegedly handed down by some authoritative figure, this ethical
model cannot assume the new knowledge we have been acquiring on
human sexuality from over a century of ongoing research. This
noble endeavour of men and women to understand what lies in our
experience of humanity has to be considered by code moralists as
an exercise in futility.[28] This model does not and cannot take
seriously findings relative to phases of development with their
respective, necessary apprenticeships, cultural and subcultural
differences, diversified genetic heritage, ecological balance,
psychological and social laws, and so forth. Prescriptive ethics
has been left with a discourse which has become detached, to a
great extent, from any scientifically identifiable sexual reality.
As a consequence, fewer and fewer of our contemporaries can make
sense of their sexual experience within the definitions and
criteria of prescriptive sexual ethics.[29] It is an ethical pattern
which simply raises, for any critical mind, too many
insurmountable theoretical and practical difficulties.

The second basic problem with the manual tradition of
sexual ethics in theology is its conspicuous lack of properly
Christian meaning. While this model calls so readily upon
Christian "sources" to tell the faithful what their sexual conduct
ought not to be, it tells them practically nothing about the
relevance or the irrelevance of their sexual conduct to their life

9

of faith.

When it is felt that explanations should be added to the authoritative pronouncements that have been rightly or wrongly reported, this tradition invokes, it is true, "natural law." But the insights which are gained by this recourse to what it understands natural law to be are, in general, disappointingly vacuous. This is so because the natural law argument, rather than serving an intelligible function, seems to work as one more "authority," the authority of a given philosophical or theological tradition (e.g., Aristotelian, Augustinian, Thomist, etc.). This is so much the case that most manuals do not even explain why the position they have presented makes sense. They would sooner call upon the authority of the Church magisterium to interpret the authority of natural law, a law which, by definition, is supposed to be intelligible to right reason. For the authority of evidence, therefore, this model substitutes the evidence of authority; for the authority of reason, the reason of authority.

As heirs to impoverished traditions of natural law, prescriptive moralists understand this law not as the rational exigency of justice, truth, courage, etc., which, in a concrete historical situation, imposes itself upon reasonable minds, but as a kind of universal code which is preformed in every mind and effectively acknowledged in every society. In such sexual ethics, therefore, natural law is conceived as an abstract codification of unalterable biological functions. Little do the champions of this model suspect that their idea of "immutable biological laws" does not pass the test of biological knowledge and that it is alien to contemporary biological theory.[30] Be that as it may, code morality never even tries to explain seriously why or how biological determinisms (those determinisms which are operative today) constitute absolute ethical imperatives.

If Christian Churches claim that they have a vested interest in human sexuality and if Christian ethicists claim that sexual ethics is at home in the theologian's house, it should be because our faith in God is at stake, one way or other, in the sexual experience. If a prescriptive moralist does not explain what sexual action means in terms of Christian faith, he has not done his homework. For the Good News of the liberation of our humanity through the life, death, and resurrection of Christ, he has substituted a set of regulations which, out of his own unchristianized fears, he arbitrarily attributes to a terrifying and punitive God. Indirectly, he does speak of his God. But is this God, encountered in and manifested through his moral life, the Father of Jesus of Nazareth? This is the question which moral theologians, as theologians, should ponder in sexual ethics.

3. SEXUAL ACTION IN FAITH

Fortunately, Christian practical wisdom can thrive in an ethical paradigm which is totally different from the one in which sexual ethics has been entangled in the course of recent history. This other paradigm postulates and takes seriously the fact that being is first and comes before all its reverberations in us by way of law or of desire, let alone of precepts or of pleasures. Before prescribing or condemning sexual activities, therefore, moral theologians must start at the beginning. And the beginning of any discourse on sexuality is the knowledge of what a sexual self is and how a sexual self functions in a given society. Before suggesting any global and life-giving interpretation of the sexual experience, a moral theologian must, then, learn from sexology how the sexual script is correctly read. If a moralist forgoes this necessary step, his or her own discourse has no normative value whatsoever because it is detached from any identifiable sexual reality. This is not to imply that one can draw moral, let alone theological conclusions deductively from scientific findings and theories. When the best available knowledge of science concerning an issue in need of ethical assessment has been ascertained, we still do not have a moral judgment. However, we do have grounds for assurance that a moral judgment based on this knowledge is consonant with reality.

While paying lip service to the importance of scientific knowledge for an ethical discourse on human sexuality, some moralists are prone to add that "moral principles" (the exact meaning of which is seldom explained) are not affected by scientific data.[31] This is a shrewd way of avoiding their obligation to learn sexology before dabbling in sexual ethics. Theirs would be the lofty discourse on "moral principles," on the numerous "principles" and the multitude of "rules" deduced therefrom, which, for all practical purposes, would resolve most sexual perplexities without any sexological knowledge. Let empirically-minded ethicists, those who are more at ease with pragmatic findings than with moral speculation, fill in the fact!

The problem with most alleged moral principles is that, upon close examination, they prove to rest on a time-bound understanding of human nature or of God's will. Generations of moralists have deduced all sorts of moral consequences from such "moral principles": for instance, the principle of the headship of men based on unacceptable biological data;[32] the principle "no smallness of matter in sexual morality" grounded on sexual fears and on an ignorance of the non-biological functions of sexuality;[33] the principle of usury based on unawareness of modern economics;[34] the principle of autocratic government dependent on historical and sociological ignorance (as well as on a contestable epistemological theory) of the origin and structures of political power;[35] the principles of "just wars" and of "no conscientious objections" premised on historically dated notions of limited wars and feudal patriotism.[36]

There is no doubt in my mind that very fundamental moral principles can be formulated which transcend, at least in their intent, all historical and cultural expressions. Notwithstanding the diversity of cultures, of religions, of races, of economic, social, and political circumstances, the same ideals of truth, of justice, of freedom, of peace summon up all men and women of good will. This common human aspiration toward the good is, indeed, what makes ethics possible. Because ethics is a "quest for humanity," a search for that which makes human beings human, its project is universal. Ethics addresses all issues under the aspect of the human good as such, of the "good of humanity" in us. However, this ethical quest is undertaken by women and men who, because they are rooted in a material existence, can only live this universality in the particular. Good or evil are always contingent realizations. When, therefore, moral principles are formulated which have the same degree of universality as the transcendental aspects of human "beinghood" (e.g., "do good and shun evil," "be truthful," "respect life," etc.), they are inoperative at the level of activity. Instead of describing, even in general terms, the action to be undertaken, they move away from it. They transcend real performance, ignoring its coordinates, its rapport to history, its particular features. Even when they avoid the trap of becoming historically-loaded, as in the examples quoted above, principles are always formal, lacking content; that from which, therefore, nothing concrete can ever be deduced. Their application to reality grasped as totally as is humanly possible requires another moral judgment from which will emerge an obligation in keeping with the principle.[37]

The fact that the ethical discourse on human sexuality, as on any other human activity, cannot be reduced to scientific measurements is, nonetheless, indisputable. The scientifically measured sexual self is not a free subject who is reaching out, through his or her sexual behaviour, for that which lies beyond the results of mere mechanistic forces. If a person wishes to pull away from the magnetic field of biological, psychic, and social determinisms which, by undercutting any real initiative and liberty, impede him or her from becoming morally of age, then this person must be able to appropriate the meaning of his or her sexual project. It is by this appropriation and by the capacity of freely acting upon it that he or she becomes the creator of an original version of human sexuality, a version which goes far beyond hereditary and social imperatives.

The ethicist is one who reflects on the experience of those men and women who seek to make sense of their sexual life. Ethics can be neither taught nor learned like mathematics or physics. It presupposes a lived experience, a personal, immediate, and eventful grasp of moral values, without which all ethical discourse is meaningless and ineffective. It is against the very nature of the good to be known without being experienced. No one knows the good and values it if one does not "live" it. Listening attentively and with empathy to the community of purposeful men and women living sexual lives, the ethicist articulates the meaning inherent in the experience, proposes a sexual anthropology which, while passing the test of scientific knowledge, is in line with this meaning, and, from these premises, works out, without ever losing touch with the sexual experience and its scientific analysis, a coherent sexual ethics.

Is the task of the moral theologian different from that of the ethicist? First, she should recognize that there is, for her as well as for a magisterium meant to be instrumental in the process of human liberation, the very same obligation to hear men and women. She must understand the reality of their sexual experience, the demands they must meet, during the course of their life, to fulfil their human vocation. Human beings and their reasons for living have a consistency of their own. Christian faith refers to an anthropology and to an ethics which are not of its own making.[38] To acknowledge that much in honesty and humility is already a redeeming attitude. For, as Maxim the Confessor observes, to live the world's own truth is to already hear a silent revelation of God.[39] To dwell in God's presence, a human being must dwell in truth in his own self and in his own human world. It is with this truthful man, this truthful woman, that God walks "in the garden in the cool of the day" (Gn 3: 8).

French theologian Maurice Bellet remarks that the great task of sexual ethics which confronts us all today is to understand that, after Freud, we cannot ignore human sexuality without compromising Christian faith with its worst enemy, the fear of truth.[40] Without this human understanding of sexuality, in effect, no one can correctly discern the course of action to be undertaken in this domain in order to stand before God in truth. The reasons for believing must acknowledge completely the human reasons for living fully, and this includes the full living of our sexual lives.

Beyond this acknowledgement, however, - and this is my second point - the reasons for believing manifest the ultimate meaning of life. Because it experiences God's redemptive and revealing presence in the world, a Christian faith which is alive identifies the liberating Pull, that which definitively frees us from the realm of insignificance and alienation. Characteristic of the ongoing relation between God and human beings, the disclosive activity of God occurs as long as God's redemptive activity occurs in our midst. Revelation and redemption are necessarily concomitant activities. They represent the way in which the God of love and of mercy relates to his beloved but weak and sinful sons and daughters. To experience this relation in faith is to find one's ultimate meaning and the path to one's core freedom.

If this is the way God relates to us in faith, it is the task of moral theologians to bring this living faith of ours to bear on the sexual anthropologies which we construct with our reason and on the rules of conduct which we give ourselves in our daily lives. Does our sexual morality foster the unveiling in us of the image of God? To speak as if two ethics existed, one of which would be Christian, is inexact. What is true is that the ethics we share with others must be well coordinated to the experiential evidence and the authentic proclamation of faith.

Is this not what we have done, in point of fact, throughout the history of Christian experience? From its outbreak and throughout its historical manifestation, Revelation has been tuned-in to the world, as it were, assessing it, choosing among the many and discordant voices which are being heard in it. This is the way it has asserted itself.[41] In every period of Judeo-Christian history, prayerful women and men dwelling in God's presence have, out of their regenerating experience, meditated inquisitively on their Tradition, on this "History of listening" to the voices of those who are searching for their humanity. They have done so with their questions, their culture, their language, their problems, their aspirations, their hesitations and resistances. The only real-life location of Revelation has always been the human experience of liberation.

This has also been the case for the direct witnesses of the Jesus movement. What the disciples of Jesus handed down to us has been filtered through their own concrete understanding of the redemptive happenings. This meaning-ful and commitment-ful experience of Christ that was theirs and now is ours serves as a framework for perceiving the fundamental thrust of human realities. This, if I am not mistaken, is what Charles Curran calls "Stance,"[42] John Shea, "Story,"[43] and John Paul II, "Orientation."[44] This Christian "Posture", a faith perspective or horizon, does not provide solutions to our sexual dilemmas. By this Christian Posture, though, our excessively narrow questions are unremittingly displaced as we are summoned to invent the unedited truth of our liberated humanity created in God's image. For this truth, this harmony, is pre-established neither in humanity itself, nor in culture, nor in society, nor in the Christian community. In all of them, peace or harmony or truth is a reconciliation: it is always something yet to be achieved.[45]

Summing up, I would say that, like all ethics, theological ethics is, at least directly, language about human agency and not about Deity. It is language about ourselves and about our action in the world.[46] But this language is so

14

ultimately informed by our faith in God and by our symbols of Deity that, indirectly, it speaks about the God in whom we experientially believe. In fact, the indirect speech Christians deliver on God through their concretized Christian Posture, the one which molds their own truth in everyday practice, reveals much more the God with Whom they are in touch than do their formal discourses on God. To know God is not to have an idea about God. It is to be in His presence.[47] Only those who have the liberating experience of God's love can hope to know the Living God. Not unlike the truth of faith, the truth of morals lies in our becoming. Both are truth-happenings. It is for this reason that moral commitment is the meeting place between human beings and the God of the Covenant.

For a theory of sexuality to be theologically plausible in this second ethical paradigm, it must, therefore, be intelligible from a Christian Posture as well as from a human stance. Where such is the case, a theologian is not entitled to claim, it seems to me, that his or her theory of sexuality holds universal validity and that it should be universally imposed and accepted. However, those whose own human experiences are enlightened by it should be able to recognize in it a way to get in touch with their God and, through their sexual commitments, celebrate Her fecund presence among us. The theory of sexual ethics put forward in the following chapter makes no other claim.

NOTES

1. In English, the words "ethic" and "moral" mean the same thing. Following a widespread practice today, the word "ethic" will normally be used, here, to designate a scientific, coherent approach to the norms of human conduct and to their foundation; the word "moral" will serve to indicate concrete behaviour as qualified by those norms. This distinction is obviously relative.
2. AAS, 21 (1929), p. 490. In the Latin commentary of the decision published in Periodica, 18 (1929), pp. 215-219, the answers of officially approved moral theologians are quoted to show that the answer of the Holy Office is the right one. The authority is right because the authorized moralists say it is right. The authorized moralists are right because the authority says they are right.
3. See, on the notion of paradigm, the basic work of T. S. Kuhn, The Structure of Scientific Revolutions (Chicago: The University of Chicago Press, Second enlarged ed., 1970). In order to determine and assess the influence of paradigms specifically on sexual ethical theories, Kuhn's grid of analysis has been applied to the writings of twelve

contemporary American Catholic and Protestant theologians by J. M. LAZOR, Convergence in Sexual Ethics? Roman Catholic and Protestant Approaches in the United States Today (Unpublished doctoral dissertation, Saint Paul University, Ottawa, 1983).

4. See essential historical landmarks concerning these systems in F. L. CROSS and E. A. LIVINGSTONE, "Probabilism," in The Oxford Dictionary of the Christian Church (London: Oxford Univeristy Press, Second ed., 1974), pp. 1127-1128. - I am using the word "prescriptive" in the sense explained by E. L. LONG, Jr., A Survey of Christian Ethics (New York: Oxford University Press, 1967).

5. See the excellent contribution of G. BONNET, Au nom de la Bible et de l'Évangile, quelle morale? (Paris: Le Centurion, 1978), and Au nom de l'Église, quelle morale? (Paris: Le Centurion, 1980). For an analysis of Biblical fundamentalism, see J. BARR, Fundamentalism (London: SCM Press, 1977).

6. See the commonsensical remarks of J. M. GUSTAFSON, Ethics from a Theocentric Perspective. Theology and Ethics (Chicago: University of Chicago Press, 1981), p. 339.

7. See P. ARIES, "Interprétation pour une histoire des mentalités," in H. BERGUES et al., La prévention des naissances dans la famille. Ses origines dans les temps modernes (Paris: Presses Universitaires de France, 1960), p. 313.

8. Biblical scholars generally believe that the proof of this use of the word porneia cannot be established: W. G. COLE, Sex and Love in the Bible (New York: Association Press, 1959), pp. 243-244; L. M. EPSTEIN, Sex Laws and Customs in Judaism (New York: Ktav, 1967), pp. 126 and 167; A. HUMBERT, "Les péchés de sexualité dans le Nouveau Testament," Studia Moralia, 8 (1970), pp. 155-159; B. MALINA, "Does Porneia Mean Fornication?," Novum Testamentum, 14 (1972), pp. 10-17 [the refutation of J. JENSEN, ibid., 20 (1978), pp. 161-184, is not, in my judgment, very convincing]; M. DUMAIS, "Couple et sexualité selon le Nouveau Testament," Église et Théologie, 8 (1977), p. 47-72.

9. References to the criticism of proof-text Biblical references concerning homosexuality are found in chapter 7 of this book.

10. J.-L. FLANDRIN, Le sexe et l'Occident. Évolution des attitudes et des comportements (Paris: Seuil, 1981), p. 130.

11. M. MEEHAN, in The Catholic Register of April 19, 1980, p. 4.

12. J. JENSEN, "Human Sexuality in the Scriptures," in Human Sexuality and Personhood (St. Louis: Pope John Center, 1981), p. 18, argues here that concubinage with slave-girls should not be construed as adultery "for such unions tended to be stable." This may be so. However, this behaviour goes against the "monogamous norm." It is difficult to understand how big an improvement that represents for the present discussion.

13. J. JENSEN, "The Relevance of the Old Testament. A Different Methodological Approach," in D. DOHERTY (ed.), Dimensions of Human Sexuality (Garden City: Doubleday, 1979), p. 5. The

article of C. STUHLMULLER, "The Relevance of the Old Testament - Prophetic Ideals and Sexual Morality," ibid., pp. 8-20, calls for the same fundamental objection.

14. For a thorough criticism of this "house of authority" criteriology, see E. FARLEY, Ecclesial Reflection. An anatomy of Theological Method (Philadelphia: Fortress Press, 1982), pp. 1-168.

15. B. W. HARRISON, "Sexism and the Language of Christian Ethics. Some Basic Theses for Discussion" (Paper circulated by the Faith and Order Department of the National Council of Churches. October, 1976), p. 7.

16. See ST, II^a-II^{ae}, q. 104.

17. On this whole question of sexual repression and authority, see the interesting reflections in E. FROMM, Escape from Freedom (New York: Avon Books, 1965). See also J. DOMINIAN, Proposals for a New Sexual Ethic (London: Darton, Longman and Todd, 1977), p. 12.

18. J. PIAGET, The Moral Judgment of the Child (New York: The Free Press, 1965).

19. L. KOHLBERG et al.., Assessing Moral Stages. A Manual (Available at the Center for Moral Education, Harvard University, Cambridge).

20. See in DS, nn. 2021-2065.

21. D. SOLLE, Beyond Mere Obedience. Reflections on a Christian Ethic for the Future (Minneapolis: Augsburg, 1970), pp. 13-53. Recently, A. MILLER, For Your Own Good (New York: Farrar, Straus and Giroux, 1983), has told again the story of Hitler's disastrous compulsion to avenge the trauma of his "education through obedience" years after his childhood.

22. S. MILGRAM, "Behaviorial Study of Obedience," Journal of Abnormal and Social Psychology, 67 (1963), pp. 371-378. See also the small-scale study, by L. KOHLBERG, of subjects who did and did not yield in the Milgram situation. Kohlberg found that 75 percent level-3 subjects (those who have moved beyond the 4 stages of prescriptive morality) disobeyed, whereas only 13 percent from various other stages ever disobeyed: "Stages and Sequence. The Cognitive-Developmental Approach to Socialization," in D. A. GOSLIN (ed.), Handbook of Socialization. Theory and Research (Chicago: Rand McNally, 1968), pp. 347-380.

23. E.g., H. JONE and U. ADELMAN, Moral Theology (Westminster: The Newman Press, 1961), p. 154, no. 234. These two authors are quoted here and in the following footnotes as representative of a jurisprudential approach in sexual ethics.

24. Ibid., pp. 145-146, n. 222.

25. Ibid., p. 149, no. 228.

26. I. CASORIA, "Consummatio matrimonii," in P. PALAZZINI (ed.), Dictionarium morale et canonicum (Rome: Catholic Book Agency, 1962), Vol. I, p. 943.

27. S. MISURACA, "Alcune precisazioni sul 'verum semen'," Ephemerides Juris Canonici, 21 (1965), pp. 185-191. Some

canonists are also beginning to find such biologizing casuistry unbearable: see C. J. MURTAGH, "The Consortium Vitae and some Implications of the Jurisprudence of Verum Semen," Studia Canonica, 8 (1974), pp. 123-135.

28. See, e.g., the tone with which such research is referred to in H. V. SATTLER, "Lust - Greatest of Sins?," Homiletic and Pastoral Review, 83/6 (1983), pp. 27-31.

29. A. VERGOTE, "Christian Misreadings of the Human," Concilium, 155/5 (1982), p. 21, says that this is the actual case with the official teaching in the R. C. Church. See also J.-L. FLANDRIN, Le sexe..., p. 135, who calls the official teaching a "fuite dans l'irrationnel" (an escape into irrationality). From the opening paragraph of the statement he made at the 1980 Synod, it is obvious that Archbishop J. BERNARDIN also agrees with similar assessments. He bluntly affirms that, in matters of sexual ethics, the Church has lost its credibility in many parts of the world: see "Sexuality and Church Teaching," Origins, 10 (1980), p. 260.

30. See, e.g., J. PIAGET, Biology and Knowledge. An Essay on the Relations between Organic Regulations and Cognitive Processes (Chicago: The University of Chicago Press, 1971). More specifically linked with a present-day debate in sexual ethics, see W. WICKLER, The Sexual Code. The Social Behavior of Animals and Men (Garden City: Doubleday, 1972).

31. See, e.g., F. LAMBRUSCHINI, Problemi dell'Humanae Vitae (Brescia: Queriniana, 1968), p. 97; F. BAK, "Bernard Häring and 'Humanae Vitae'," Antonianum, 49 (1974), p. 222.

32. It is still a leading principle in PIUS XI's 1930 encyclical letter Casti connubii, AAS, 22 (1930), pp. 539-592. See D. O'HANLEY, "Rights Within the Family Structure," Église et Théologie, 12 (1981), pp. 169-170.

33. Reflected in the condemnations of ALEXANDER VII (1666), in DS, no. 2060. See other Roman sources quoted in M. ZALBA, Theologiae Moralis Summa (Madrid: Biblioteca de Autores Cristianos, 1957), Vol. II, pp. 135-136, no. 311.

34. Reflected in the condemnations of ALEXANDER VII, in DS, no. 2062; of INNOCENT XI (1679), in DS, no. 2142; of BENEDICT XIV (1745), in DS, no. 2546-2550. See J. T. NOONAN, Jr., The Scholastic Analysis of Usury (Cambridge: Harvard University Press, 1957); J. T. GILCHRIST, The Church and Economic Activity in the Middle Ages (London: Macmillan, 1969).

35. Reflected in the warnings against democracy by GREGORY XVI, in his encyclical letter Mirari vos (1832), in ASS, 4 (1895), pp. 336-346; by PIUS IX, in his encyclical letter Quanta cura (1864), in ASS, 3 (1895), pp. 160-167, and in his Syllabus (1864), proposition 60, ibid., p. 174; by PIUS X, in his condemnation of the Sillon (1910), in AAS, 2 (1910), pp. 607-633. See the study of P. HÉGY, L'autorité dans le catholicisme contemporain. Du Syllabus à Vatican II (Paris: Beauchesne, 1975), in particular pp. 33-101. - We cannot imagine Pope John Paul II calling today upon the absolut e and

immutable principle of obedience to established political authority as Pope Gregory XVI did in his encyclical letter Cum primum written to castigate the Polish peasants after the Russian repression of 1830. Yet Gregory's stand was thought to rest on "immutable moral principles."

36. Reflected still in the condemnation of conscientious objection to war by PIUS XII in his Christmas message of 1956, in AAS, 49 (1957), p. 19. See the short study of J. C. MURRAY, Morality and Modern War (New York: Council on Religion and International Affairs, 1959). Only nine years after Pius XII's refusal to recognize the validity of conscientious objection, Vatican II states that "it seems right that laws make humane provisions for the case of those who for reasons of conscience refuse to bear arms...": GS, par. 79 (p. 1103; tr. p. 292).

37. The misunderstanding of this point constitutes, in my opinion, the basic weakness in Lawrence Kohlberg's system of analysis of "moral judgments." See A. GUINDON, "Kohlberg's Postconventional Yogis," in Église et Théologie, 12 (1981), pp. 279-306.

38. See W. N. PITTENGER, Love and Control in Sexuality (Philadelphia: United Church Press, 1974), 1974), p. 119; X. THÉVENOT, "Christianity and Sexual Fulfilment," Concilium, 155/5 (1982), p. 52. I must take issue, here, with recent attemps by some moral theologians to uncover a ready-made, normative sexual anthropology in Christian sources: e.g., J.-M. AUBERT, "Pour une épistémologie de la morale chrétienne," Studia Moralia, 18 (1980), pp. 98-102; É. FUCHS, Sexual Desire and Love. Origins and History of the Christian Ethic of Sexuality and Marriage (New York: Seabury, 1983).

39. MAXIM THE CONFESSOR, Ambiguorum Liber, in Patrologia Graeca (Paris: Migne, 1863), Vol. 91, col. 1334.

40. M. BELLET, "Le voyage du théologien," in J. AUDINET et al., Le déplacement de la théologie (Paris: Beauchesne, 1977), p. 167.

41. J.-M. DOMENACH, "The Attack on Humanism in Contemporary Culture," Concilium, 6/9 (1974), pp. 17-28.

42. See, e.g., C. E. CURRAN, "The Role and Function of the Scriptures in Moral Theology," in Catholic Moral Theology in Dialogue (Notre Dame: University of Notre Dame Press, second ed., 1976), pp. 24-65.

43. See J. SHEA, Stories of God. An Unauthorized Biography (Chicago: The Thomas More Press, 1978), particularly, pp. 41-75, and Stories of Faith (Chicago: The Thomas More Press, 1980), particularly, pp. 76-125. See also R. A. McCORMICK, "Theology and Biomedical Ethics," Église et Théologie, 13 (1982), p. 311-331.

44. FC, par. 5 (p. 85; tr. p. 9).

45. A. VERGOTE, "Christian Misreadings...,", p. 16.

46. I perfectly agree on this point with B. W. HARRISON, "Sexism...," p. 1. G. ABBÀ, Lex et virtus. Studi sull'evoluzione della dottrina morale di san Tommaso d'Aquino (Rome: Libreria Ateneo Salesiano, 1983), shows convincingly

that this is fundamentally the mind of Thomas Aquinas in the ST.

47. See THOMAS AQUINAS, ST, II^a-II^{ae}, q. 1, a. 2, ad 2.

CHAPTER TWO

A THEORY OF SEXUAL ETHICS FOR CONCERNED CHRISTIANS

Four basic elements make up the theory of sexual ethics for concerned Christians propounded in this chapter. Each one of them examines a fundamental question which a coherent theory of sexual ethics must discuss. The first question deals with sexual anthropology: How is a virtuous sexual self structured? The second deals with sexual activity: How is virtuous sexual practice structured? The third deals with moral efficiency: How is a virtuous sexual deed begotten? The fourth deals with sexual historicity: How is a virtuous sexual deed experienced by social human beings? In other words, the theory must explain what a sexually successful person looks like; what kind of sexual activity is conducive to such a goal; what sort of moral power is needed for this activity to produce its fruits; under what conditions of responsibility do these moral fruits ripen. The first two questions address the issue of ontological structures, that of sexual selfhood and that of sexual activity. The third question attends to the very foundation of moral normativity. The fourth question raises the issue of contextuality and, therefore, of moral responsibility.

The following claims are made concerning the four components of the theory. First, each of those components manifests what has been called, in the Catholic tradition, its "natural law." The discussion of each component starts, therefore, with an analysis of sexual reality as human reason is able to perceive it. Secondly, each of the answers given to the four basic questions is influenced by and, in turn, influences the author's Christian Posture. In this sense, the theory is theological and speaks to the Christian project as such even though a non-Christian may very well (because of the first claim) find it acceptable on its own merits. The discussion of each component ends, therefore, with an examination of the Christian perspectives which the sexual experience is liable to open.[1] Thirdly, the responses form a fourfold criterion for moral decision-making concerning sexual dilemmas and for assessing the moral quality of our sexual life. This third claim will be examined in the fourth chapter after a criticism of dualistic interpretations of fecundity in chapter three.

A THEORY OF SEXUAL ETHICS

1. INTEGRATION OF SENSUALITY AND TENDERNESS

Before venturing any kind of ethical statement on human sexuality, one must have at least a vague notion of the essential or formal features of a successful sexual self. How is anyone going to decide which model of sexual behaviour is, in the long run, humanizing if one does not know how a humanized sexual person is structured?[2] The basic choice to be made in this regard is, as the history of sexual ethics clearly manifests, between a dualistic interpretation and a unitive or wholistic view of sexual selfhood.

The initial and most decisive option is linked with the problematic of the structure of human "beinghood." Whatever vocabulary or philosophy is utilized to argue this point, there is widespread agreement to conceptualize human beinghood as "composed" of two elements: matter-form, body-soul, physical-cognitive, body-mind, organic-symbolic, and so forth. For the purpose of the present overview, the vocabulary of body and spirit will be retained.

The problematic raised by the dual nature of human beinghood lies less, it seems to me, with acknowledging the existence of this long-celebrated duality of sorts than with conceiving its mode of existence. There are various and quite opposite ways of doing so. At one end of the spectrum, dualistic currents of thought have the tendency to view two separate and separable subtances,[3] mysteriously glued together for the time of our earthly pilgrimage. Depending on one's life options and orientations, ascendancy is generally attributed to one of the two substances. The dominant substance becomes the essential self, the most valuable "part," that which, even at the expense of the expendable portion of the composite, we must care for and bring to its fulfillment. It is, perhaps, due to the fact that Descartes is so representative of this dualism of "body thing" and "acosmic spirit," that French contemporary philosophers have instituted an ongoing criticism of dualistic anthropology and have argued quite convincingly against a tandem model of the human self.[4]

At the other end of the spectrum, wholistic views explain, in one way or another, that corporality and spirituality designate only two complementary aspects of one human reality; that they never exist as human, one without the other; that they are mutually pervasive, forming one, indivisible, whole, human person. As long as we subsist, we are body as well as spirit. If, as Blaise Pascal claims, we do no better acting bestially than we do acting angelically, it is because a human spiritless body would be nothing more than a corpse while a human bodiless spirit would have no means of knowing and of doing anything in this world of ours.

A THEORY OF SEXUAL ETHICS

Few people stand at one or the other pole of the spectrum. Most of us are somewhere in between, with a penchant to indulge either in dualistic thinking or in unitive thinking. We may even have a tendency to shift from one pole to the other as we pass from one issue to the next. One should not be astonished to find, therefore, that many who theoretically stand for a wholistic view of the human person yield to dualistic thinking and language in the concrete realm of human sexual realities. Because moralists, until recently, identified sexuality with the genitals and their functions, sexuality is regarded by the majority of people as a mere bodily element, subject (though with difficulty) to the control of the "spiritual faculties."

Since we have finally recognized that the human self necessarily exists as male or female, is kneaded of chromosomal, hormonal, and gonadal ingredients which affect every particle of the self, develops wholesomely through a psycho-sexual process, maintains with the cosmos, with others, and with God relationships which are marked by sexuality, etc., the proof has been established beyond all possible doubt that whole persons, not bodies, are sexed and sexual.[5] This wholistic view is not an entirely new phenomenon caused by "Freudian pansexualism." As Philippe Ariès remarks, in Saint Theresa's mysticism, for instance, or, again, in baroque art, spirit and sexuality are never separated. The new phenomenon is that, today, we are conscious of it while they were not.[6]

In a wholistic view of selfhood, human sexuality necessarily comprises, like the being it qualifies, two aspects.[7] They have been called the affectionate and the sensual currents,[8] affection and desire, tenderness and eroticism,[9] the tender and the daimonic,[10] love and desire.[11] I intend to use the terms tenderness and sensuality. The sensual aspect is linked with this facet of the self called body. Body, here, is not meant as a mere organic system, as an object separated from personal activity. It refers to the body as flesh, as having an affective life, as the originator of erotic movements, of sensations, of desires, of pleasures, and so forth. The tender aspect is linked with this side of the self called spirit, creator of significance or of symbols and originator of movements from within such as love, attention, care, delight, amazement, and other meaningful sentiments.

Since sensuality and tenderness, like body and spirit, never exist separately in a human being,[12] they live in a tensional and dynamic unity. The moral task, on this level of being, consists essentially in sensualizing tenderness, as befits an em(=in)-bodied spirit. Thus, intentionality is incarnated and the word becomes flesh. Correspondingly, sensuality becomes tender, as is proper to an enspirited body. Corporeity expresses what is human. The flesh becomes a human word. As the sexual

23

virtue accomplishes its integrative work, sensuality and tenderness blend more and more into one another. They energize one another, forming integrated sexual selves whose spirits are enfleshed, perfectly at home in their sexual bodies, and whose bodies are spiritualized, expressive of their sexual selves' genuine identity. This sexual virtue was called "chastity" by the theological wholistic tradition led by Thomas Aquinas. Chastity is a properly moral category which evokes the idea of integrity. For contemporary ears, this virtue is probably best referred to as sexual integration.

In a wholistic perspective, sexual disintegration represents, then, a failure of tenderness and of sensuality to merge into an integrated human wholeness. This occurs in two basic ways which are well documented in the history of dualistic theories and practices. One consists in giving sensuality priority. Fun moralities, more technically called hedonistic ethics, are structured on this corporealist ideology. The other failure occurs when tenderness is favoured at the expense of sensuality. Shame moralities and, specifically in Christianity, "purity ethics," advocating will-power or prayer control, are built on this spiritualist interpretation.[13]

Both those ethical formulations, primarily the latter, have always lived and keep on living in the Christian Churches. "Sex is dirty, save it for someone you love" has often been the enigmatic message Christians have heard from sexually confused (or inhibited) Christian teachers. Yet, we must also acknowledge the fact that when, in the course of history, the dualistic premises of such ethical positions were clearly articulated in certain circles, mainstream Christianity took its distance from such systems and looked upon them as sects. Why? Surely not because all Christians would necessarily disagree on philosophical grounds as such. Christian faith is not a philosophy, but an assent and a commitment to the God of Jesus the Christ. If Christianity cannot accommodate itself to sexual ethics structured on a well-defined dualistic sexual anthropology, it is because it knows instinctively, with an instinct which is inspired by the Holy Spirit, that in such ethics the faith experience of God is distorted. The sensus fidelium, which in the course of history has constantly manifested the Christian instinct on this point, is correct. To regard either tenderness or sensuality as evil, or even as less good, and to construct a theory of sexual ethics which despises either aspect militates against Christian faith in a God whose parenthood is benevolent and from whom nothing despicable proceeds.[14]

Judeo-Christian faith experiences God as the loving, caring, and merciful Father, the giver and protector of human life.[15] He is not, as in juridically inspired ethics where God and the Law are mistaken one for the other, a deity whose demands are infinite and, therefore, never satisfied. The God of Jesus affirms the goodness of finite, incarnated human existence.[16] Has He not created sexual, mutually attracted persons, and seen that "it was very good" (Gn 1: 31)? Is it not true that the admirable and God-like nudity[17] of those who live in God's friendship is freed from all culpability (Gn 2: 25)? The paradisiac myth expresses the harmony of a well-integrated humanity, at peace with its own truth, a truth reflecting that of its Creator. The shameful fig leaf cover-up operation (Gn 3: 7-8 and 20-21), on the contrary, is clearly part and parcel of the broken-down world of sin, of a self-withdrawal syndrome. Because of who the Creator is, the sensuous flesh is linked with the condition of creature, not with that of sinner. The sinful condition is characterized, on the contrary, by a diminished and guilty sexuality.[18]

Sinless, Jesus, like the first Adam before the Fall, never manifests shame when confronted with sexual facts or gestures. Nor does he ever participate in the sexually insecure and culpabilizing censorship of sexual delinquents. Risen from the dead, he becomes in his glorified body the token of the resurrection of our own flesh endowed with incorruptibility and immortality (Rm 1: 4; 6: 4-5; 1 Co 15: 54; Ph 3: 21). With the promise of eternal life (Rm 8: 11), our own corporality must let itself be pervaded and transformed by the Spirit so as to become, in the risen Lord, a soma pneumaticon, a spiritualized body (1 Co 15: 44-49). If not, body and soul will perish. Nothing will remain but a disintegrated and broken-down self (Mt 10: 28). This integrative process is already at work in our earthly body which, having received the first-fruits of the Spirit (Rm 8: 23), is already the temple of the Spirit (1 Co 6: 19-20), the locus where the image of the first-born Son is gradually formed (Rm 8: 29). The children of God can live their corporality with thanksgiving (1 Tm 4: 1-5) since they are integrally redeemed (Rm 8: 23), a living host truly pleasing to God (Rm 12: 1).

Christian faith refuses the ambivalence of the deity confessed by Gnostic dualisms. The One revealed through the Jesus-event is not the God whom Maurice Bellet rightly calls perverse, a deity whose parenthood would be both the cruel principle of a damned sexual flesh and the benevolent generatrix of a pure, spiritual soul.[19] To experience human sexuality as shameful, following a body-negating ethics, is an obstacle to the existential knowledge of "God, the Father all-mighty, Creator of heaven and earth."

In his autobiographical novel, A Portrait of the Artist as a Young Man, James Joyce captures well the birth of the "perverse God" in the anxious sexual questioning of his sixteenth year. After a college retreat in which each sermon ends with morbid exposures of THE SIN, "impurity," Stephen Dedalus reflects on his sexual experience:

25

But does that part of the body understand or
what? The serpent, the most subtle beast of
the field. It must understand when it desires
in one instant and then prolongs its own desire
instant after instant, sinfully. It feels and
understands and desires. What a horrible thing!
Who made it to be like that, a bestial part of
the body able to understand bestially and
desire bestially?[20]

Yes, the sexual experience does raise the question of
God. Why would any healthy human being want to believe in a God
who created her or him with a bestial part?[21]

2. LANGUAGE OF INTIMACY

To state that the fully energized sexual self is one
in which sensuality and tenderness are harmoniously integrated is
to take a decisive stance for a wholistic view in sexual
anthropology. How this integration occurs, however, is still left
unexplained. In other words, an ethical model is still needed for
understanding sexual practice. How are we to conceive a sexual
activity which is formative and expressive of our fundamental way
of existing as both, and inseparably, sensuous and tender? Based
on certain cues which point in the direction of a close rapport
between sexual behaviour and a child's learning of his native
language,[22] I have proposed the use of a language model. The idea
is gaining ground in the ethical as well as in the sexological
literature.[23]

Human sexuality is irreducible to a mere physiological
or psychological or social capacity. Sex, as a consequence, is not
adequately understood merely in terms of orgasms or, for that
matter, of personal or social interactions. As the very condition
of our being-in-the-world as enfleshed spirits,[24] sexuality affects
our whole personality and is symbolic of it. Pope John Paul II
is right when he states that "sexuality [...] is by no means
something purely biological, but concerns the innermost being
(nucleum intimum) of the human person as such."[25] Sexuality is an
ontological reality, a word (logos) of being (onto).[26] Of itself,
it speaks of who we are. Philosopher Edmond Barbotin calls it "the
language of being itself."[27] How, indeed, will a carrier of an
enfleshed meaning express his or her unutterable experience of
personal uniqueness to others without the sensually tender
connotations of sexual expression? Any other form of language is
inadequate to express human selfhood.

When gestural language[28] is used to express ourselves

not about things, but about our intimate selves, about our experience of tender-sensuous existence, we are speaking the sexual language. Of itself, human sexual communication tends towards the establishment of a relationship based on the totality of who we are. This is what we call intimacy.[29] To experience and live human sexuality under the sign of usefulness (e.g., for producing babies) or of pleasurableness (e.g., for having fun) is a betrayal of its very nature. Of the order of being and not of having, sexuality's activities are gratuitous. Sexual activity finds in itself, in the truthful communication of intimate selves, its very meaning.

Like all other forms of human communication, the sexual language has a wide variety of expressions, tonalities, emotions and sentiments at its disposal. Do we seem to be talking exclusively about things? We seldom do so without letting out a few words about our selves. In fact, is it not when we are willing to surrender something of our selves to others that what we are saying about things is recognized by those who listen as "truly true?" True human words call on the other to share something with the one who speaks. Nor have human words reached their goal when they are merely spoken. They are yet in need of a receiver, that is to say of a person who listens carefully, who is trusting and consenting. The reception of the human word and the quality of this reception depend, to a great extent, on whether or not the receiver has been reached in his or her identity. This can never be realized so integrally as in the sexual language where words of intimate selfhood are spoken, words which convey the other in an intimate dialogue. Sexual modes of behaviour are subject to moral qualification insofar as they are "gestures," as they convey intimate meaning from one person to another.

Does the fact of granting that sexual acts are open to different personal meanings lead us into some whimsical "personalism" or "situationism" in which human actions would have no internal laws of their own independently of the agent's motivations? The very idea of sexuality as language should be enough to discard this fear of subjectivism voiced so readily against the emerging paradigm by code moralists. They themselves rely on legislation to secure a sacrosanct order which they take to be "objectivity." They do not seem to reflect that legislators are subjects, enunciating what they perceive or will to be the right thing to do. Their being "empowered" to enounce certain rules of social conduct does not give their own interpretation more "objectivity" than anyone else's interpretation. It merely confers upon this interpretation an authority which, given the conditions for its legitimate exercise, is functional for the common good. Properly speaking, "objectivity" can only be produced by the "object." The object, in the domain we are concerned about, is the sexual language, the language of intimacy which is being spoken by human persons.

This object, the sexual language, is, like any other human language, used by a subject. Considered in its relation to its user, it constitutes behaviour. This behaviour, as we have seen, is that of a subject who fills it with different emotions, who speaks it more or less fluently and gracefully, who adapts it to fit the situation, who invites others to share their own selves intimately, and so forth. However, if this language, more than any other language, is spoken with subjectivity, like all other languages it also has an objectivity of its own. Considered in its relation to the community of its users, it is a cultural reality with a structure of its own. Regardless of its user, it has a grammar, it represents an organized system. Not to comply with the objective rules of a language is to condemn oneself not to be understood or, at least, to be misunderstood. "Objects" which are not handled in accord with their internal law cannot be expected to produce what they are meant to produce.

If, therefore, an individual uses human sexuality in such a fashion that nothing significant is conveyed, one way or other, to someone else, then this person uses the sexual language in violation of its true relational nature. We could call this vice "sexual solipsism."[30] Instead of becoming a human gesture, namely the embodiment of one's intention to meet and learn to know someone else, the carnal word of one's desire to share something significant with this other person, sexual behaviour is degraded to the unhuman status of a raw sensuous pulsion, of a mere movement in one's body. Far from establishing a proximity between two persons, from being a mutual word of presence, from creating the openness of one person to another, the sexual caress becomes a way of appropriating another's body and of transforming the other into a mere object of desire. Men and women with their lovable uniqueness, their preferences and dislikes, their joys and sorrows, their daring creativity and their doubts, do not emerge from mere sexual games.

The call to share one's intimate life with others may, on the contrary, be totally repressed. Repressed persons may feel a longing for an absent someone, but they are unable to respond. By getting rid of sensuality, they have gotten rid of the only human vehicle of tenderness.

For Christians, a language model is not the only possible way of understanding human sexual practice. Montreal theologian Guy Durand, for instance, suggests an "encounter" model which proves most rewarding.[31] Whichever model is put forward, though, its theological plausibility should be established in the light of God's self-revealed personhood and intimate communication as these are grasped in the faith experience of the Christian community.

When Genesis 1: 27 speaks about human beings as the

image of God, it evokes their sexual make-up:

> God created man [adam: human being] in the image of
> himself,
> in the image of God he created him
> male [ish] and female [ishshah] he created them.[32]

In the ninth-century B.C. Yahwist narrative of creation, indications similar to those spelled out more theoretically in the later fifth-century B.C. Priestly source, quoted above, are already found. Woman is not presented, like other creatures, as man's property (Gn 2: 19-20). She is Adam's counterpart (2: 18, 20), the one who faces or confronts him, the one in whom man recognizes bone of his bones and flesh from his flesh (2: 23).[33] The sexual split (sexus) is that whereby the relational nature of human selfhood and interaction is symbolized.

Neither male nor female, human nature in each one of us is, in its very sexual structure, relational. Only by interpersonal communion are women and men humanized. This is the means by which they carve in themselves the image of God. Guy Durand remarks appropriately that "a human being is relational, he is 'for the other' as he is 'by the other.' In this, he is God's image: human selfhood in 'relation' as God himself is pure 'relationality'."[34] Relational sexuality reflects and teaches the relational personhood and activity of the Triune God, a God who generates the Word in Love and through the Word creates all things which have life in Him (Gn 1: "God said: ..."; Jn 1: 1-14). The profound truth of all creation is the Word (Col 1: 15-16). Those in whom the creative Word dwells are empowered to speak a sexual language whose life-serving function far surpasses their wildest human expectations. The speechless God once again becomes Word through the sexual stories of their own lives. Otherwise, God would remain the unreachable Other, characterized by a transcendence which would imply pure and insurmountable "strangeness."

The drama which is described in Genesis 3 and the following chapters is the story of the failure of the language of intimacy to express the truth of the human condition. Refusing to accept that the Word comes from God, the right relationship between Yahweh and his creature is distorted (Gn 3: 1-7). When God comes "walking in the garden in the cool of the day" for a moment of intimacy with his creatures, Adam and Eve hide among the trees (Gn 3: 8) Truthful relationships have broken down. This human alienation from God (Gn 3: 23-24) has repercussions on the whole of their relational life: Adam and Eve start accusing each other (Gn 3: 12-13); their relation to their world loses much of its former smoothness (Gn 3: 14-19); their children are at each others' throats (Gn 4); their descendants lose the social ability to communicate well with each other (Gn 11: 1-9). Like the Story of creation and redemption, the Story of sin also speaks, in a sad way, of intimate human communications.

Jesus lays claim to the creation narrative on relational humanity (Gn 1: 27 and 2: 24 in Mt 19: 4-5). The old perspectives are even interpreted by him in their widest sense, for Jesus makes it clear that "when people rise from the dead, they neither marry nor are given in marriage" (Mt 22: 30). While he assumes integrally the human condition - and therefore the sexual condition - Jesus himself does not seem to have been married during his earthly existence. Furthermore, he probably calls some "who can accept it" to a charismatic celibacy for the sake of the Kingdom (Mt 19: 3-12; Lk 18: 29-30). The sexual condition which no one is without and which makes of us relational beings does not aim essentially at the establishment of a conjugal bond. It calls for interpersonal communication.[35]

In Jesus, the full significance of the Covenant, celebrated throughout Biblical times in terms of a sexual bond, becomes manifest. We are gratified with a sexuality which is eternally linked with our quest of "blissful perfection"[36] because sex is that whereby we share our intimate life with others and, by the same token, learn to recognize the face of a God who is relational. To experience sexuality as "private property" and sexual virtue as a power of self-refusal and of uninvolvement in intimate relationships would be to mold in one's being an image of a God who is so transcendent that he is unrelated to us, the Totally Separated Other. Through their sexuality, Christians ought to live, on the contrary, the enlightening experience of a God whose Word became flesh so that the flesh might resume its dialogue with Him in the communion of all the saints. I leave it to the reader to judge whether or not the language model makes good Christian sense, whether or not it is in tune with his or her Christian instinct.

3. CREATIVE LOVE

As a generator of intimate interpersonal relationships, human sexuality opens up a space for personal freedom to enhance the personality of others through love and, indivisibly, to be created anew by love.[37] Well spoken, the sexual language does not aim exclusively at this or that quality of another person's body or mind. To be attracted to a person for her or his physical features, power-position, sharp wits, or cooking aptitudes is to like this person functionally, to like this person for my own pleasure or usefulness, to covet what he or she can bring me. Since the qualities a person has never express adequately who this person is, to be attracted by them is not to be attracted to a person for whom this person is. The ensuing interaction would not be the language of being itself.

This is not to say that interrelating with others in a merely "liking" fashion is necessarily evil. We meet some people exclusively on the tennis court or on the ski slopes because we enjoy playing tennis or skiing with them. We visit our dentist because of her skill at repairing our teeth. We follow a professor's lectures because he can teach us something. We watch a ballet company for the aesthetical enjoyment the dancers provide us. Nothing more may and need be involved in these and similar human transactions. But as long as they remain of this nature, the rapport between human beings is not properly sexual. They become humanly sexual when some degree of intimacy exists, when sharing is involved at the level of the person's whole being.

The love of friendship, the primary sense of love according to Aquinas,[38] effectively establishes this kind of wholistic bond since its object is the other's own good. Aristotle describes this "friendly feeling towards any one" as "wishing for him what you believe to be good things, not for your own sake but for his, and being inclined, so far as you can, to bring this thing about."[39] Awakened by the attraction of the good, by being as alluring, love is always stimulated by what, rightly or wrongly, it perceives the other's qualities to be. Since it cannot be really satis-fied (full-filled) with pretense and illusions, love aims, beyond appearances, at the whole reality of the other's being.

Mere infatuation, writes Thomas Tyrrell, "is disrespectful because it falsifies the existence of the beloved."[40] Real love, on the contrary, is, following Berverly Harrison's expression, "the power to act-each-other-into-well-being."[41] Because love of friendship avoids transforming reality into illusion, it reverently accepts the other in his or her weakness and vulnerability as well as in his or her strength. But real love, as Aristotle points out in the text quoted above, also seeks to create in the other what is still longing to be: the fullness of life.

Love is the utopia of the sexual encounter where the intimate well-being of each person is strengthened in the very act which offers to share it gratuitously with another. As Albert Donval remarks, love exerts over all other meanings given to human sexual transactions (organic relief, psychic relaxation, ecstatic pleasure, reproduction of the species, etc.) a critical function: none of them can make an absolute claim on sexuality at the expense of love.[42] Love is the afflatus which harmonizes the multiple sexual values, from pleasure to fertility, with the ever renewed modulations of the amorous poem of our lives.

It follows that, from an ethical point of view, sexual perversion cannot consist in specific modes of behaviour (such as incest, bestiality, or necrophilia) defined in their materiality. "To pervert" means to cause to turn from what is good to what is evil, to overturn, to distort, to corrupt. If the sexual language is meant, basically, to convey love in ways which are specifically human, to corrupt it is obviously to use it for suppurating hatred, the corrosion of love. An ethicist can only agree with Robert J. Stoller's title: <u>Perversion: the Erotic Form of Hatred</u>.[43] All forms of sexual exploitation, from violent outbursts, like rape, to disguised manifestations in attitudes of dominance and censorship are, morally speaking, sexual perversions.

Christian theology carries this analysis still further. Breaching the communion of love is that whereby a <u>sin</u> properly so called is distinguished from a moral fault, that is to say, a lack, by defect or excess, of "proper measure" in reference to the objective of the act.[44] To distort the language of loving intimacy into a spurious discourse, a discourse made with the intention of abusing someone, of using someone in ways which lead him or her astray from the paths of self-fulfilment, goes directly against man's Godlike reality.[45] Lacking the generosity of love, such a sexual language is an ugly corruption of the Father's language saying Love in his Word made flesh. This is, in point of fact, a perversion of the central Christian mystery.[46]

Here again, therefore, the stakes are high for Christians who cannot doubt that the radical meaning of human sexuality is to create loving bonds. As for every other human activity, love is ultimately normative for sexual practices.

> For God's Word – proclaims the second Vatican
> Council –, through whom all things were made,
> was Himself made flesh and dwelt on the earth
> of men. [...] He Himself revealed to us that
> "God is love" (<u>1 Jn</u> 4: 8). At the same time
> He taught us that the new command of love was
> the basic law of human perfection and hence
> of the world's transformation.[47]

Pregnant with love's generosity, human sexuality discloses, for those who have the experience of truly being cared for or of actively caring for another, the fecundity of a God who is love.[48] Saint Anselm of Canterbury drew our attention to the fact that the Holy Spirit is the <u>cry of love</u> uttered by the Father and the Son before the immensity of the infinite plenitude of God. It is this Love which also makes our God burst into the creation of women and men so that He may adopt them in his first-born Son as his children, children of light and of freedom.

32

Moved by the experience of a loving God, the author of the oldest narrative of creation represents sexuality as a function of loving reciprocity. Lived, on the contrary, as a closing in on oneself, sexuality manifests the broken-down world of sin. To mutual self-disclosure and admiring acceptance (Gn 2: 23-25) the Yahwist Tradition opposes self-refusal, symbolized by the attempt to hide in the shameful awareness of one's vulnerable nakedness (Gn 3: 8-11). The lack of generosity in sexual practice explains, thereafter, Onan's condemnation because his sexual services to Thamar are voluntarily short-circuited so that Judah's heritage will pass into his own lineage (Gn 38),[49] as well as the Biblical interdiction of incest inasmuch as the latter signifies the refusal of the gift of one's children to society (Lv 18: 10 and 17: see Gn 2: 24).

To object that, with the advent of Jesus of Nazareth, "real love," the one which builds Christian fellowship, is agape, a totally "spiritual" love, and not eros or sexual love, is to commit theology to dualistic thinking.[50] Moreover, this view is also totally out of character with Jesus of Nazareth's own life style. His celibacy never strikes one as being an asexual condition which would facilitate the expression of disembodied divine love. Towards adulterers, prostitutes, and all the others who are pronounced contagious and outcasts by the laws of purity, his attitude manifests a Son of God who lives the agape of the covenant in our carnal condition. Besides, how would authentic love be expressed between human beings without the carnal accents of eros?[51] In Jesus, divine love has taken this law of incarnation upon itself. More religious than true believers in a God who is Love, the righteous Jews in Jesus' surroundings are scandalized when the Father's Witness sits down with those who are poorly loved, drinks and eats with them, listens to them, understands them, accepts them for who they are.[52] In the intimacy of Jesus of Nazareth, those who are in need rediscover their full truth and learn anew to love themselves and to love others as themselves "for the love of God."

These sayings and gestures of Jesus set generous sexuality back on its right course, that of the Kingdom where eternal life is celebrated in a communion of love. There can be no doubt left in the minds of Christians that the ultimate intent of the sexual language is to say love. Its primary purpose is to promote love and the reciprocal giving and receiving which love implies. As Francis Mugavero, Bishop of Brooklyn, puts it: "Sexuality is that aspect of personhood which makes us capable of entering into loving relationships with others."[53]

4. HISTORICAL CONDITION

Because the sexual language is the instrument of creative love, views which would reduce sexual life to genital activities directed "by nature" toward the production of limited goals such as orgasmic pleasure, organic hygiene or reproduction are clearly unsatisfactory. The inadequacy of such narrowly functional views are further demonstrated today by the philosophically richer strand of sexual anthropology which sees sexuality as that whereby human persons have the capacity to adhere to various environments and to acquire adapted structures of interpersonal conduct. Sexuality is that which gives human beings an interpersonal and social history and that which makes them responsible for its development.[54]

By their sexuality, human beings are males or females. They must identify their core gender identity, learn certain socially prescribed gender roles (and later on unlearn some of them!), and cope successfully with the sameness and the differentness of human dimorphism. By their sexuality, human beings are also differentiated from one another and they interrelate among themselves following a complex developmental sequence. Social scientists of all brands are busy plotting the course of sexual development. By their sexuality, finally, human beings establish intimate, but socially significant covenants with each other following elaborate cultural norms. Thus, culture permeates their sexual self. Their sexual behaviour, in turn, permeates the whole fabric of their culture. Such is the sexual condition of embodied spirits, a highly personalized and socialized way of existing dynamically in time.[55]

The significance of the historical condition of sexuality is paramount for an ethical consideration. This condition implies, in point of fact, that the sexual language can never be true when it contradicts the historical consistency and thrust of the partners. To astract from one's historically conditioned self, to "have sex" with this or that individual and come back to "real life" as if nothing had happened is a sexual lie. Sexual language is true to the extent that one says one's intimate self to other intimate selves following one's own and the others' historical actuality and intentionality. In the presence of others, the sexually integrated person knows how to devise a sexual expression which is adapted to the global reality of a personal and a social situation lived in time.

To behave sexually without engaging one's historically conditioned identity is sexual exhibitionism. Sexual exhibitionism is characterized (not unlike artistic exhibitionism) by a representation of forms in which there is no real encounter, no commitment to historical realities.[56] In this sense, we could say that Platonician erotics, for instance, suffer from this sexual pathology. They regard the beloved as a mere springboard which provides one with the necessary momentum for a soaring erotico-mystical experience. Sexual partners serve merely as enfleshed mediums for what Plato calls the "divine frenzy."[57] A-historical sex also runs counter to the Judeo-Christian tradition because in this illusory experience of impersonal and uncommitted sex the very notion of God is once more at stake.

If the sexual institutions of Ancient Israel do not differ substantially from the institutions shared by the inhabitants of the Near East,[58] nonetheless, the very anthropological status of sexuality is profoundly altered by the monotheistic revolution.[59] The myths concerning divine sexual unions are overthrown. In their downfall, they drag down with them the orgiastic rites which are meant to actualize the myths so as to exorcize daimonic forces and to communicate with the divine mana. Freed from such sacral pseudo-finalities, human sexuality is restored by the Jewish faith to its human integrity. The sexual paradigm born out of Israel's experience of a Covenantal God is a human prototype, that of Adam and Eve, of worldly loves and fecundities. The original couple and their descendants are seen as responsible for sexual behaviour which is linked with human historical becoming. Sexuality is not a mysterious energy which enables human beings to communicate mystically with the gods. It is a human dynamism of interpersonal relationships and historical development.

We touch here upon a crucial point for a religiously inspired ethic. The originality of the faith in the God of the Covenant depends to a great extent on the rapport which it establishes between God's Design and Man's History. Contrary to what is found in other Canaanite religions, Israel does not deify cosmic powers. It rejects the idea of a sacral universe which imposes its blind Destiny on human beings.[60] Men and women are seen as being responsible for their world. It is their task as well as their duty to bring it to its completion. Judeo-Christian faith contends, therefore, with obscure gods for autonomy over the world of man and woman, the location of human decisions and endeavours. Faith in the God of the Covenant gives back to men and women what is theirs, this earth which has been entrusted to their care by the Creator. Only the true presence of men and women to the world is capable of unveiling to their own eyes God's presence, his creative and redemptive action, the ongoing gift of Himself to us. The only way to be in touch with the transcendence of God is in living the most ordinary realities of human existence. This is the reason why morality is the location where man meets God.

The favoured Witness of the Covenant, Jesus of Nazareth, illustrates perfectly, by his own sexual attitudes and behaviour, this understanding of responsible human stewardship and the way in which a sexual praxis reveals a liberating God. Confronted with "sexual sinners," he displays neither incantatory proclivities nor disguised erotic interests. On the contrary, those are the evangelical scenes in which he is shown to be exquisitely (or should we say divinely?) human. Contrary to those around him who judge others because of this or that act against the law, he is sensitive to the whole truth of the persons who need someone to listen to them and to confirm in their own eyes that their personal history is meaningful. For Jesus, persons are not faceless objects with no historical depth, sinful perpetrators to be exorcised, or interchangeable sexual mediums with whom to get high on God. Every single person has his or her own historical worth because God made a covenant of love with each one of us. By his responsible sexual attitudes towards others, Jesus opens us to the knowledge of this God, the covenantal God.

The Judeo-Christian experience of sexuality as a historical reality is not without dangers of its own. The sexual ethics we have sometimes elaborated bear that out. When the meaning of "history" is taken to be that of a species rather than that of a community of persons, sexuality is turned into a mere reproductive function; its pleasurable and playful dimensions are forsaken; its gratuitous aspects are ignored.[61] To acknowledge the historical nature of sexuality is not to deny its festive character. The issue is whether or not sexual pleasure itself creates humanity.

Notwithstanding excessive and sometimes erroneous expressions, the longstanding opposition of the Church to a contraceptive mentality[62] and to sexual pleasure sought for its own sake[63] follows the logic of faith in the God of the Covenant. The Christian experience of sexuality refuses to see any likeness between itself and a sexuality lived as the dreary repetition of orgasmic instants which would periodically draw us away from our existential truth in order to help us forget our daily chores and the insignificance of an existence without a History. The sexually integrated Christian lives in a world in which God seeks people who are accountable for themselves and for each other, people who speak an historically truthful sexual language. Such is the God of the Covenant revealed in the faith experience of those who seek Her.

The sexual ethic sketched out in this chapter and proposed as acceptable to Christians does not stand out as the one, universal, and irreformable model. The paradigm in which it is couched takes seriously both contemporary sexological findings and God's self-revelation. Of necessity, therefore, it is open to an ongoing revision. As the human sexual script is better understood and as the Christian experience of God's presence unfolds itself in historical communities through time, the implications for sexual ethics have to be continually discerned and reappraised.

The theory of sexual ethics suggested here radically transforms the fundamental question which should be addressed to our sexual conduct. This question cannot bear, as prescriptive moral theology understands it, on the "doings" and the "non-doings": "May I touch here or there, look at this or that, practice such or such a coital position, utilize this or that means of birth control?" It ought to seek the truthfulness of the "sayings" and the "non-sayings": "What am I saying about myself to this or that person in such or such circumstances when I behave in this or that fashion? Is it true to who we are in ourselves and for each other?" A sexually intimate self-saying which is integrative of sensuality and tenderness, relational, loving, and historically and socially responsible is truthful. Otherwise it is disintegrating, solipsistic, perverse, or illusory. This way of raising the question is likely to yield a formally moral response and to open Christians to the mystery of a God in whose image they are created and who seeks to reveal his truth in his Word made flesh.

NOTES

1. The theory presented in this chapter is more fully developed and its ethical ramifications are examined at length in The Sexual Language. However, the influence of a Christian Posture on the elaboration of a "Paradigm of Human Sexuality" (pp. 7-220) and the Christian implications of the theory were not clearly exposed in that work. Since then, two consecutive essays have helped me articulate this important aspect: "Le sens chrétien de la sexualité," Communauté Chrétienne, 17/101 (1978), pp. 444-452, and "Gestuelle sexuelle et révélation de Dieu," Église et Théologie, 11 (1980), pp. 371-398. Nonetheless, the approach used in these articles has been substantially modified in the present chapter.
2. F. CHIRPAZ, Difficile rencontre (Paris: Cerf, 1982), pp. 11-29.
3. "Substance," here, is understood in the Scholastic sense, expressing the basic characteristic of that which exists: a being which has the capacity to exist by and in itself and not merely as a modification of some other reality.
4. See, e.g., M. MERLEAU-PONTY, Phenomenology of Perception (London: Routledge and Kegan Paul, 1962); J. SARANO, The Meaning of the Body (Philadelphia: Westminster Press, 1966); E. BARBOTIN, The Humanity of Man (Maryknoll: Orbis, 1975).
5. See also X. THÉVENOT, "Christianity...," p. 53.
6. P. ARIES, "Réflexions sur l'histoire de l'homosexualité," in

Sexualités occidentales. Communications No. 35 (Paris: Seuil, 1982), p. 61.

7. S. FREUD, "On the Universal Tendency to Debasement in the Sphere of Love (1912)," in J. STRACHEY (ed.), The Standard Edition of the Complete Psychological Works of Sigmund Freud (London: The Hogarth Press and the Institute of Psycho-analysis, 1953-1966), Vol. XI, p. 180.
8. T. REIK, Sex in Men and Women. Its Emotional Variations (New York: Noonday Press, 1960).
9. P. RICOEUR, "Wonder, Eroticism, and Enigma," Cross Currents, 14 (1964), pp. 133-166.
10. R. MAY, Love and Will (New York: W. W. Norton, 1969).
11. É. FUCHS, Sexual Desire...; P. AUDOLLENT et. al., Sexualité...
12. This view is implied in Vatican II's statement to the effect that "the sexual characteristics of man and the human faculty of reproduction wonderfully exceed the dispositions of lower forms of life." See GS, par. 51 (p. 1072; tr., p. 256).
13. See the criticism of these philosophically poor traditions in A. PLÉ, Chastity and the Affective Live (New York: Herder and Herder, 1966).
14. P. S. KEANE, Sexual Morality. A Catholic Perspective (New York: Paulist Press, 1977), pp. 3-4, is right in founding his ethical reflection on the radical goodness of the sexual condition.
15. See, also, D. BAKAN, And They Took Themselves Wives. The Emergence of Patriarchy in Western Civilization (San Francisco: Harper and Row, 1979), pp. 12-22.
16. See É. FUCHS, "Loi et Évangile: de l'anthropologie à l'éthique," in Loi et Évangile. Héritages confessionnels et interpellations contemporaines (Geneva: Labor et Fides, 1981), p. 237.
17. G. VON RAD, Genesis. A Commentary (London: SCM Press, 1961), p. 56, shows how "the marvel of man's bodily appearance is not at all to be excepted from the realm of God's image."
18. D. LYS, La chair dans l'Ancien Testament: "bâsâr" (Paris: Editions universitaires, 1967), in particular the summary, pp. 135-139; S. SAPP, Sexuality, the Bible, and Science (Philadelphia: Fortress Press, 1977), pp. 1-21.
19. M. BELLET, Le Dieu pervers (Paris: Desclée de Brouwer, 1979), p. 117.
20. J. JOYCE, A Portrait of the Artist as a Young Man (New York: Penguin Books, 1977), pp. 139-140 (italics are mine).
21. J. B. NELSON, Embodiment. An Approach to Sexuality and Christian Theology (Minneapolis: Augsburg Publishing House, 1979), p. 44, is right: "Most basically, body alienation is alienation from God." Scores of biographies could be quoted to illustrate this statement. - This book by Nelson is, in my judgment, one of the best essays on sexual ethics written in the 1970s.
22. A child, e.g., begins to learn how to speak as he or she begins to establish his or her gender identity. See J. MONEY,

"Psychosexual Differentiation," in J. MONEY (ed.), Sex Research. New Developments (New York: Holt, Rinehart and Winston, 1965), pp. 3-23; A. McCUMBER, "Development of Sexual Identity in Children," in J.-M. SAMSON (ed.), Childhood and Sexuality (Montreal: Études Vivantes, 1980), p. 222. Children raised with animals and without human contact regularly show a double deficiency: an incapacity to speak and an inability to establish a significant sexual rapport with others. See the 36 cases studied by R. M. ZINGG, "Feral Man and Extreme Cases of Isolation," American Journal of Psychology, 530 (1940), pp. 487-517; and the 30 cases studied by L. MALSON, Wolf Children (London: NLB, 1972).

23. In sexology, see, e.g., J. MONEY, "Human Hermaphroditism," in F. A. BEACH (ed.), Human Sexuality in Four Perspectives (Baltimore: The Johns Hopkins University Press, 1976), pp. 77-79; W. H. DAVENPORT, "Sex in Cross-Cultural Perspective," ibid., pp. 120-121; B. SCHLESINGER, Sexual Behaviour in Canada. Patterns and Problems (Toronto: University of Toronto Press, 1977), pp. X-XI; E. J. HAEBERLE, The Sex Atlas (New York: Seabury, 1978), pp. 146, 150, 280. In ethics, see, e.g., J. DOMINIAN, Proposals..., pp. 61-63; J. B. NELSON, Embodiment..., pp. 25-30 and 105-106; B. HARING, Free and Faithful in Christ (New York: Seabury, 1979), vol. II, pp. 492-571; A. AUDOLLENT et al., Sexualité..., pp. 99-102.

24. J. LACROIX, Force et faiblesses de la famille (Paris: Seuil, 1948), p. 55; A. DONVAL, Un avenir pour l'amour. Une nouvelle éthique de la sexualité dans le changement social aujourd'hui (Paris: Centurion, 1976), p. 47. This is why sexual self-expression is akin to an artistic language: see R. MAY, The Courage to Create (New York: W. W. Norton, 1975), p. 85.

25. FC, par. 11 (p. 92; tr., p. 20).

26. P. RAMSEY, "A Christian Approach to the Question of Sexual Relations Outside of Marriage," The Journal of Religion, 45 (1965), pp. 102-103.

27. E. BARBOTIN, "La sexualité d'un point de vue anthropologique," Supplément, 27 (1974), pp. 445-457 (my translation).

28. For a good overall study of the human gestural language, see D. MORRIS, Manwatching. A Field Guide to Human Behavior (New York: H. N. Abrams, 1977).

29. The idea of intimacy will be developed in the fourth chapter.

30. "Solipsism" is the philosophical doctrine which holds that the individual conscious self is the whole of reality and that other selves have the status of mere imaginary constructions.

31. G. DURAND, Éthique de la rencontre sexuelle. Essai (Montreal: Fides, 1971). The model was subsequently used in a theological context in Sexualité et foi. Synthèse de théologie morale (Montreal: Fides, 1977).

32. See the remarkable comment of this text in GS, par. 12 (p. 1034; tr., p. 211).

33. For the history of this text's interpretation see M. DE MÉRODE, "Une aide qui lui corresponde: l'exégèse de Gn 2,

18-24 dans les écrits de l'Ancien Testament, du judaisme et du Nouveau Testament," Revue Théologique de Louvain, 8 (1977), pp. 329-352; also, W. VOGELS, "It is not Good that 'Mensch' Should Be Alone; I Will Make Him/Her a Helper Fit for Him/Her (Gen 2: 18)," Église et Théologie, 9 (1978), pp. 9-35.

34. G. DURAND, Sexualité..., pp. 114-115 (my translation). That it is the relational aspect rather than the idea of incompleteness and of complementarity which is signified in the male-female humanity in God's image is convincingly demonstrated in P. K. JEWETT, Man as Male and Female. A Study in Sexual Relationships from a Theological Point of View (Grand Rapids: W. B. Eerdman, 1975).

35. É. FUCHS, Sexual Desire..., gives, following the Calvinist tradition of ethics, a highly "conjugal" interpretation of human sexuality. This interpretation is not questioned sufficiently, in my opinion, by the works and the life of the celibate Jesus.

36. GS, par. 17 (p. 1037; tr., p. 214).

37. N. PITTENGER, Love and Control..., pp. 21-22; A. DONVAL, Un avenir..., p. 54.

38. THOMAS AQUINAS, ST, I^a-II^{ae}, q. 26, a. 4.

39. ARISTOTLE, Rhetoric, II, chap. 4 (1380b35 - 1381a1), in R. McKEON, The Basic Works of Aristotle (New York: Random House, 1941), p. 1386.

40. T. J. TYRRELL, Urgent Longings. Reflections on the Experience of Infatuation, Human Intimacy, and Contemplative Love (Whitinsville: Affirmation Books, 1980), p. 82.

41. B. W. HARRISON, "The Power of Anger in the Work of Love: Christian Ethics for Women and Other Strangers," Union Seminary Quarterly Review, 36, Supplementary Issue (1981), p. 47.

42. A. DONVAL, Un avenir..., p. 49.

43. (New York: Pantheon Books, 1975).

44. THOMAS AQUINAS, ST, I^a-II^{ae}, q. 72, a. 5; q. 88, a. 2. See a good introduction to the distinction between moral faults and sins in L. MONDEN, Sin, Liberty and Law (New York: Sheed and Ward, 1965).

45. FC, par. 11 (pp. 91-92; tr., p. 19).

46. See the excellent remarks of É. FUCHS, Sexual Desire..., p. 173, on the "dramatic of sexuality," this violence of desire in which Christianity has refused, by branding it a sin, to recognize a fatal power. On p. 197, he also designates the violent products of sexuality as "perverse behavior."

47. GS, par. 38 (p. 1055-1056; tr., pp. 235-236).

48. See B. W. HARRISON, "The Power...,", p. 51.

49. T. and D. THOMPSON, "Some Legal Problems in the Book of Ruth," Vetus Testamentum, 18 (1968), pp. 79-99, particularly pp. 93-94.

50. See the judicious remarks of J. B. NELSON, Embodiment..., pp. 109- 114.

51. This position is clearly that of the Second Vatican Council.

See, e.g., GS, par. 49 (pp. 1069–1070; tr., pp. 252–253).

52. J. POHIER, "Preaching on the Mountain or Dining with Whores?," Concilium, 110 (1977), pp. 62–70.
53. F. J. MUGAVERO, Pastoral Letter "Sexuality – God's Gift," (February 11, 1976), Origins, 5 (1976), p. 581.
54. M. MERLEAU-PONTY, Phenomenology..., p. 158, interprets Sigmund Freud's own thought in this sense.
55. Those three aspects of the sexual condition – gender, growth, and culture – are exposed in more detail in The Sexual Language..., pp. 113–162.
56. See J. W. MOHR, R. E. TURNER, and M. B. JERRY, Pedophilia and Exhibitionism (Toronto: University of Toronto Press, 1964), pp. 111–170, in particular, pp. 162–164.
57. PLATO, Phaedrus, 244a, in The Collected Dialogues of Plato, including the Letters (Princeton: Princeton University Press, 1961), p. 491. For Plato's mind on this, see F. BUFFIÈRE, Eros adolescent. La pédérastie dans la Grèce antique (Paris: Belles Lettres, 1980), pp. 409–422.
58. R. DE VAUX, Ancient Israel. Its Life and Institutions (London: Darton, Longman and Todd, 1962), pp. 19–55.
59. See W. G. COLE, Sex..., pp. 161–192; W. EICHRODT, Theologie des Alten Testaments (Leipzig: J. C. HINRICH, 1962), Vol. I, pp. 91–92 and 143; P. GRELOT, Le couple humain dans l'Écriture (Paris: Cerf, 1962), pp. 17–36; E. SCHILLEBEECKX, Marriage. Secular Reality and Saving Mystery (London: Sheed and Ward, 1965), Vol. I, pp. 33–51; G. VON RAD, Old Testament Theology (Edinburgh: Oliver and Boyd, 1967), Vol. I, pp. 27–28); J. BLENKINSOPP, Sexuality and the Christian Tradition (Dayton: Pflaum Press, 1969), pp. 16–41.
60. FC, par. 34 (p. 123; tr., p. 66).
61. See D. DE ROUGEMONT, The Myths of Love (London: Faber and Faber, 1963).
62. Is this not what stands out most clearly in the masterly study of J. T. NOONAN, Jr., Contraception. A History of its Treatment by the Catholic Theologians and Canonists (New York: The New American Library, 1967)?
63. See the insightful essay of J.-M. POHIER, Le chrétien, le plaisir et la sexualité (Paris: Le Cerf, 1974).

CHAPTER THREE

THE DUALISTIC TRADITION OF FERTILITY

If the old notion of fecundity-as-fertility is still functional, then no sensible person should invest intellectual energy in exploring a new notion of human sexual fecundity. Before a different notion is proposed, the case should be made, therefore, that the reproductive interpretation of human fecundity is a creature of dualistic thinking and, as such, does not work for human persons.

Dualistic thinking is too deeply rooted in our body-spirit experience to be eradicated by a mere act of the will. Therefore it should not surprise us that moralists failed to recognize the degree to which the corporealist interpretation of fecundity is a product of dualistic thinking until a spiritualist interpretation which opposed the dominant reproductive view was articulated in the forties and fifties. To allow the reader to experience this discovery, a brief analysis of fecundity-as-spiritual-power will be proposed after the notion of fecundity-as-fertility has been elaborated and criticized.

Until the dualistic nature of a reproductive interpretation was highlighted by the emergence of a spiritualist interpretation, moralists were satisfied with cosmetic changes that toned down the biologizing connotations of the reproductive view to make it presentable to contemporary Western society. Moral theologians have made repeated efforts to adorn this notion with affective attributes: reproductive fecundity should _also_ be, we were told, unitive, loving, caring ...[1]

The moral and canonical application of this dressed up notion to sex-related issues shows, however, that the reproductive element is much more than an _aspect_ of fecundity: it is still the essential element, the one which is ultimately normative for all sexual behaviour. A close examination of the argumentation of the 1975 Declaration on Certain Questions Concerning Sexual Ethics (_Persona humana_) issued by the Roman Congregation for the Doctrine of the Faith against three "abuses of the sexual faculty,"[2] namely sexual union before marriage, homosexual relations, and masturbation,[3] manifests that this is still the case. Its authors were so convinced that the test of their position was the "essential and indispensable finality"[4] of "procreation" that they made no serious effort to develop other arguments. They are absolutely right, of course, if human sexual fecundity is to be equated with fertility. If this is how things stand, the new qualifications of fecundity remain merely accidental.

The praiseworthy effort to salvage reproductive fecundity by adding the quality, "loving unity" to it is not radical enough, therefore, to redeem the notion of fecundity from its dualistic origins and defects. We need a more basic notion which will be ethically normative for all forms of human sexual fecundity, including reproduction itself. The claim of this chapter is that reproduction cannot be the norm of human fecundity, but merely a remarkable application of it. On the contrary, human fecundity is, as will be argued in the fourth chapter, the norm of reproduction itself.

1. CORPOREALIST INTERPRETATION

The Judeo-Christian corporealist interpretation of human sexual fecundity goes a long way back. Though it is absent from the older biblical accounts of sexual love, it does appear in the more recent narrative of creation which was composed, according to the currently admitted theory, by a witness to the Babylonian deportation in the fifth century. Here, the very concept of sexual generosity expounded in the older Yahwist narrative is interpreted as fertility. To the exiled Jews threatened with extinction, the Priestly author preaches a natalist policy: "Be fertile and multiply; fill the earth and subdue it" (Gn 1: 28). The Scriptural slogan for survival enlivens the march of God's holy people toward the promised land, specifically under the guise of blessings and invocations for a bountiful progeny.[5] Wisdom literature stands somewhat as an exception to the Priestly tradition's high regard for fertility. Mainly the product of an urban perspective, wisdom literature[6] praises woman for herself and not merely for her fertility. By and large, though, sterility as well as celibacy are regarded as maledictions in the Old Testament. The only famous celibate, Jeremiah, parades his sexual condition as a symbol of Israel's religious sterility.[7]

Catholic authors often turn to the Bible when they advocate a natalist ideology. They quote a few Old Testament verses, notably Gn 1: 28, as the universal law of a sexuality monopolized for the maximal production of children.[8] In an effort to show that, under the Christian regime too, offspring are "the normal fruit of marriage and a blessing of God," some authors refer their reader to Pauline texts: 1 Co 7: 14, Col 3: 20-21, Eph 6: 1ff., 1 Tm 3: 4 and 12, Tit 1: 6.[9] Yet, even if one agrees with this criteriology (and I do not), none of these quotes states or even implies that children are the normal fruit of marriage, that

it is better to have children than not to have them, or that
children are a divine blessing of sorts. The texts merely state
that children of Christian parents are holy, ought to be educated
in the faith, and should not be driven to resentment and
frustration by their parents.[10]

Finding it difficult to uncover an incisive text to
sell the reproductive arguments, other authors manage, somehow, to
create the impression that the New Testament establishes a link
between matrimonial love and fertility.[11] A careful scrutiny
shows, however, that the New Testament is silent on reproductive
fecundity.[12] While Jesus appropriates the other significant
elements of the creation narratives, he makes no allusion
whatsoever to fertility. Even when he has a good opportunity to do
so, as in his defense of the utopia of indissoluble marriage (Mt
19: 3-9), Jesus does not so much as hint at the presence and the
welfare of children.

The change of emphasis from fertility to celibacy made
such an impact in the Early Church that texts like Mt 22: 30, Mk
12: 35, and Lk 20: 34-36, foretelling the absence of marriage in
the resurrection, or again the text of Lk 21: 23, "The women who
are pregnant or nursing at the breast will fare badly in those
days," will often raise serious difficulties about reproduction.[13]
There are strong reasons to believe, as John Kevin Coyle has
shown, that Christianity later reintroduced the natalist vision of
sexuality for apologetic considerations which are foreign to New
Testament preoccupations.[14]

If, as the first generations of Christians clearly
perceived, Jesus displays no interest whatsoever in demographic
problems, he does not repudiate the primeval idea of the
generosity of sexual love. Unremittingly challenging the narrowly
nationalist interpretations of his contemporaries, he disconcerts
those pious Jews who lavish him with traditional blessing exalting
the fecundity of his parents: "Still happier," replies Jesus,
"those who hear the word of God and keep it!" (Lk 11: 27-28: see
Mt 12: 46-50, Mk 3: 31-35, Lk 8: 19-21). The perspectives are
focussed once again on ultimate concerns. Since he comes to
accomplish the Promise by gathering the community of believers in
love, the Son of Man identifies his kinship not by blood ties (Mk
3: 20-21), but by divine affiliation through faith (Mt 19: 29, 23:
9).[15] The limited human horizons in which nothing more could be
hoped for beyond reproducing the species and surviving through
progeny have definitively exploded when "in our own time, the last
days, God has spoken to us through his son" (He 1: 2).

Yet political ideologies based on random observations
of all species gradually led people to understand "sexual
behaviour" as "all actions and responses that make fertilization
possible."[16] Medieval systematized moral theology followed suit.

45

Sexual fecundity was interpreted as the faculty which human beings hold in common with all other animals to reproduce their species.[17] From the point of view of the species, the quality of specimens is appraised, to a great extent, by their fertility rate. Sexual fecundity will surreptitiously conjure up the idea of bountiful progeny. Popular Catholic writings in the first half of this century end up praising sexually fecund couples, namely those who produce numerous offspring.[18]

This reproductive interpretation of human sexual fecundity is irremediably marred by a corporealistic vice which leads to ethical and theological impasses. The assignation by this view of the service of the species to intimate human sexual relationships must be considered highly problematic. A devastating abstraction is made when one expatiates upon man "qua animal" and when, as a result, one assigns to individuals a generic goal, namely the superior good of the species and demands that, if need be, they sacrifice themselves to it.[19] Though human nature, like all other living natures, tends toward self reproduction and survival by adapting to its ever-changing environment, this inclinatio cannot ultimately finalize sexual activity. Persons are meant to fulfil and save themselves not in reproduction but in a communion of love and truth.[20]

To call beings into human existence solely in the name of the socio-biological salvation of the species goes against a basic belief in the human dignity of each person. The goals of persons and communities cannot be identified with the goals of individuals and species without denying the spiritual dimension of human beings. Is this not the reason why the natural law obligation to reproduce is, according to Thomas Aquinas, only an obligation on the human species to preserve itself, not an obligation on individual persons to breed limitlessly?[21]

To hold that our personal and common goal is to populate the earth with the maximum number of human beings which the ecosystem can tolerate is irrational. That our earth could theoretically support six or twenty billion human individuals is totally irrelevant for the determination of a human duty to reproduce. What counts is that human beings, whatever their number, achieve the highest possibilities of their nature and that they create a world in which this opportunity is open to all.[22] This is the human objective which should dictate our collective duty toward progeny as well as each person's sexual behaviour. Before using their sexual language to call a child into being, parents should be urged to consider their own welfare and that of their children, "those already born and those which may be foreseen," to "reckon with both the material and the spiritual conditions of the times as well as of their state in life," to "consult the interests of the family group, of temporal society, and of the Church herself." All of these are concerns raised by the second Vatican Council, acknowledging that there is more to human sexual fecundity than reproducing the species.[23]

How then is it possible, from a theological point of view, to defend the notion that sexual fecundity is ultimately ordained, in human beings, to reproducing the species? And, if it is not, why should propagation necessarily be the horizon of all sexual activity? Only a reflection slavishly ideological and falsely committed to a deficient sexual anthropology could have concealed the serious objections against a reproductive interpretation of human sexuality for such a long period of time.

Moralists have unmasked the way in which this systematization promotes biological laws to the rank of ethical norms. There is no doubt that, as James Gustafson puts it, "morality has to be developed with reference to the most accurate body of facts about that to which it pertains."[24] On this score alone the classical systematization already comes up against grave objections. Since its positions often rest on outmoded Aristotelian biology, it fears a dialogue with contemporary biology which would challenge many of the outdated conclusions. Yet, if one is to call upon biological laws, as Paul VI does repeatedly in Humanae vitae,[25] one is obliged to rationally discuss and ethically appraise all the relevant biological components of the issue. If the circumstances of the moral object are not adequately known, we can be certain that the ensuing moral judgment will not stand the test of time.

Contrary to the tenets of the older biology, modern scientific biological evidence indicates, among other things, that the seed of most living organisms is used more often for other purposes than for reproduction;[26] that animals themselves do not have sexual intercourse exclusively for the sake of reproduction;[27] that most acts of coitus in human beings cannot be biologically generative[28] and, therefore, that the biological infecundity of coitus is as "natural" as its fecundity;[29] that reproduction is not, properly, directly, and necessarily a function of coitus but rather the result of the penetration of an ovum by a spermatozoa which can be placed there with or without sexual intercourse;[30] that many corporeal organs, specifically the genitals, have many functions and purposes;[31] that we are artificially protecting our posterity whereas "nature" when left to itself eliminates nearly two thirds of it;[32] that the ecological equilibrium must be safeguarded if our posterity is to survive.[33] This new knowledge alone is enough to explode the notion that the biological law of human sexual fecundity is one of reproduction. Biologically, reproduction is one possibility of sexual intercourse, not its "law."

But morality is not blindly determined by biology. Not only, therefore, can objections be raised against Humanae vitae's methodology because of its lack of updated biological analysis of the issue, but also because of its direct passage from empirical fact to moral imperative, from is to ought. The fact that we have the knowledge to enable us to make thermonuclear weapons does not imply that we ought to produce some. The fact that hands can play a piano does not imply that they ought to do so. The fact that the mouth can eat does not imply that it ought to be used for so doing: the mouth can be used for speaking and other ways of feeding the body can be used. Why would the fact that sex can reproduce imply that it ought to be used for this purpose and for this purpose alone? The mere fact that it is a reproductive function does not imply that it ought to reproduce. The indictment of the naturalistic fallacy, a fault against ethical logic, has been rehearsed so much in the literature that it is useless to belabor the point once again.[34] Of more immediate concern to us here is the materialization of the moral object which is implied in this form of argumentation.

To have an act which, of itself, aims at reproducing human life ("that EACH AND EVERY MARRIAGE ACT must remain open to the transmission of life")[35] two heterosexual partners are needed. To choose intentionally infertile periods for sexual intercourse is to posit an act which does not of itself aim at reproducing human life since one of the two partners is in fact sterile and is known (through different methods) to be sterile.[36] The only possible meaning that the encyclical's stand can have is, therefore, that, even though the whole structure of this act is clearly non-reproductive, the fact that one does not tamper materially with the biological process is ethically decisive. The material accomplishment of biological acts which could lead theoretically to reproduction would constitute a moral reality in itself. In point of fact, it would be more decisive for moral judgment than a couple's non-reproductive intention. It would transform their non-reproductive intention (which they clearly manifest by choosing so called "natural means" of contraception) into a reproductive intention. Consistent with this line of thinking, the Ontario Conference of Catholic Bishops can commend the openness "in mind and heart to the transmission of new life" of those who "choose to limit sexual expression of their love to infertile periods which occur in each fertility cycle."[37] To state that, by choosing infertile periods as a means for not producing a new life, one is, in this very act, open in mind and heart to the transmission of new life is to make an unintelligible statement.

The isolation of the biological factor from all other aspects of the sexual act and the attribution of a moral significance to this biological element go so far as to prevail over a man's intention to reproduce by having a vasectomy before getting married. In 1977, the Roman Congregation for the Doctrine of the Faith decreed that the marriage of a male who has had a vasectomy is canonically valid. The rationale behind the decision is that, though he is not capable of ejaculating, he cannot be considered as perpetually sterile.[38] Here, therefore, we have the case of someone who decides that he does not want to have children and undergoes a surgical intervention in order to become sterile. Yet, because his coital acts could theoretically be reproductive if the intervention were reversed (something which is only hypothetically possible in surgery today) his sexual language is, against his active will, open to the transmission of new life. It is difficult to go farther in a corporealist interpretation of human sexual fecundity: one would be open to the transmission of new life against one's effective will and physical capacity to transmit new life.

A product of dualism, this reflection, wrongly engaged from the beginning, leads one to think that biological nature and its deterministic laws impose themselves upon freedom and muzzle it.[39] Yet does the civilizing process in its entirety not consist in pulling humankind out of its "state of nature" through "artifice?" Teilhard de Chardin rightly defines "artifice" as "nature humanized."[40] Nevertheless, the corporealist trend has established and maintains a discourse which indicates that everything which is "natural" is good and everything which is "artificial" is diabolical.[41] When, in 1819, the city of Paris set up the first system of artificial lighting (gas) to illuminate its streets at night, a journalist wrote in a Cologne newspaper that, "from a theological viewpoint, streetlighting must be rejected as a perversion of the divine order. Following this order, night has been instituted for obscurity, and this may only be interrupted, at set times, by the light of the moon."[42] Such an attitude of suspicion towards artificial interventions is still very much alive today in some areas of ethics. Reproduction is one of them.[43] Here, strangely enough, Jean-Jacques Rousseau's "noble savage" philosophy has prevailed. While Catholic teaching has rejected Rousseau's claim that the artificiality of civilization represents a corruption of human nature, its recent position on the intrinsic evil of artificial means of birth control espouses Jean-Jacques' romantic view.

Today, this distinction between "natural" and "artificial" means has been criticized so much that John Paul II's Familiaris consortio itself has abandoned the terminology of Paul VI's Humanae vitae on this point.[44] The two expressions used by John Paul II to identify the distinction between the alleged kinds of contraceptive means are "obstacle to birth" (conceptuum impeditio) and "observance of rhythm" (observatio intervallorum temporis).[45] This is most perplexing. For a couple, the "observance of rhythm" is meant to be an "obstacle to birth" or "contraception" (that is, all deliberate human behaviour which aims at regulating fertility by diminishing or removing the chances of insemination). If "observance of rhythm" is not seen in this light, then it is not a method for controlling birth. Does

Familiaris consortio's new terminology mean that the official position has changed since Pius XII's acknowledgment that Catholic couples may legitimately control birth responsibly through the use of certain methods?[46] Such a change is highly unlikely.[47] Aside from the natural/artificial distinction (at best, a questionable distinction), what is the basis for contrasting "observance of rhythm" with "obstacle to birth?" Is this not a case of mere nominal distinction since nothing is left of the moral reality we are trying to identify? We must recognize, it seems to me, that this issue of birth control is more obscure in the present-day state of the "official teaching" than it was before Paul VI authorized the promulgation of Humanae vitae in 1968. I, for one, do not foresee it being clarified until Rome decides to modify its way of understanding human sexual fecundity.

A number of authors who have perceived the pointlessness of the distinction between "natural" and "artificial" in this matter of birth control have appealed to the risk factor of those techniques considered kosher by Roman Catholic ecclesiastical authorities. Since there is a risk involved, the "Catholic means" would leave open the possibility of the transmission of new life.[48] First, such an argument based on the risk factor contradicts the teaching of Humanae vitae as much as do those positions which clearly formulate their disagreement with this point of the encyclical.[49] Indeed, the moral implications are staggering. Such an interpretation is biological determinism pushed to an extreme. In this line of thinking, responsibility for as grave a decision as that of producing a human being would evade the parents (contrary to the teaching of Vatican II). Following this view, "the power to initiate human life," as James O'Reilly calls it, is exclusively in the hands of Nature.[50] God would rather impose his will through an impersonal nature than through parental reason and will.

In the history of moral theology this reproductive understanding of human sexual fecundity has led to systematic consequences which are so inadmissible that its persistence is baffling. Fifteenth century moral theologians began to draw the unavoidable conclusion that faults "against nature" (defined as those sexual activities which are not conducive to reproduction) are more serious than so-called "natural faults." Therefore, juvenile masturbation and contraception are more immoral than incest or adultery.[51]

In fact, if the logic of the corporealist tradition were followed as consistently as it was in earlier times, its supporters would be obliged to hold that the use of sexuality for any goal other than reproduction vitiates the act. This position implies that sexual abstention should be practiced during all those periods when conception is impossible or untimely, for instance, during pregnancy or menstruation periods. This stand logically leads Ambrose to suggest that a couple who have already given themselves descendants should practice permanent sexual abstention.[52] Though this theory was never observed in practice, it was still being taught during the Middle Ages.[53]

Moreover, since the least sexual pleasure is physically linked with the process leading men to orgasm and to a loss of semen, post-Tridentine moralists formulate the disconcerting rule that there is no "smallness of matter" in the realm of sexual faults.[54] They teach, in other words, that all misdeeds in sexual matters are always objectively gravely immoral. In the writings of the more rigorist theologians the dualism undergirding this bizarre view surfaces.[55] If the same moral conclusions are not drawn by contemporary moralists who claim allegiance to this tradition of reproductive fecundity, it is because they do not dare to be consistent with their basic premise.

In the Roman Catholic Church some credibility is still given to these premises. This routine-minded loyalty to an ideological historical monument hinders us – as is so manifest on the occasion of international conferences concerning population – from contributing positively to reasonable and humanizing solutions to the demographic quandary of our time.[56] Any unqualified encouragement to reproduce because we want to stand indiscriminately "for life" is totally irreconcilable with the very idea of responsible parenthood set forth by the Second Vatican Council[57] and maintained by Paul VI in two consecutive encyclical letters, Populorum progressio[58] and Humanae vitae.[59] It is equally at odds with John XXIII's strong case for the universal, inviolable, and inalienable rights of each human being.[60] It is also contrary to every child's human rights as specified by the United Nations 1959 Declaration of the Rights of the Child.[61] In effect, to call someone to life with the foreknowledge that his or her right to food, clothing, shelter, rest, medical care, basic education, work, property, social services, etc., cannot be effectively recognized and secured by his or her family-to-be, is a crime against this potential person's humanity, no matter how much the parents-to-be "stand for life." The notion of standing "for life" unconditionally and in an unqualified manner is ethically indefensible.

The uncritical "pro life" position argues that this planet is capable of feeding all of its inhabitants. Such a claim does not square with present reality. First, every new meeting of the World Food Council demonstrates how extremely complex this question is. Second, far from making progress in our efforts to feed the hungry, we are losing ground each year. The problems linked with uncontrolled demographic increase and the principle of exponential growth[62] are too real to eschew the issue with statements .about the theoretical possibilities of feeding twenty-one billion people (or more?) through a thorough exploitation of the arable soil of the earth. While we are theorizing, one hundred million children are in danger of dying because of malnutrition and 30 percent of the world's children have no possibility of going to school.[63] According to Robin Lloyd, in Bogota alone an estimated 10,000 children of all ages are in the business of prostitution in order to buy their daily bread and to find some kind of shelter at night.[64] How responsible and moral is it to sire a child with the foreknowledge that his or her only chance of survival is, as a matter of fact, through prostitution? Is such a decision "for life?"

An increase in population demands more than food; there is need for more space as well. To allow expanding numbers of people the living space they need, or they think they need, we are mindlessly destroying ecological systems upon which we are utterly dependent for a wide range of essential "public services." It is estimated that, already at this point in time, one species is being exterminated every day. Conceivably, one-half of all living species on earth may be driven to extinction within the next half-century or so.[65] And this is but one of the mind-boggling problems raised by the contemporary population explosion: pollution of water and air, disposal of toxic materials, depletion of fossil-fuel resources and other raw materials, unemployment, inadequate housing, shortage of schools, lack of adequate sanitation and of health facilities, and so on. I am well aware that other elements should be considered in this discussion and I do not wish to minimize their importance. I recognize that population growth is only one important factor of the infinitely complicated ecological, social, and economical equation;[66] that a "contraceptive mentality" exists which is egoistic and anti-life;[67] and that not few of the contraceptive campaigners are colonialists at heart.[68] The existence of these other elements which should be considered in the discussion is no excuse, however, for maintaining an uncritical pro-life-at-all-cost position in front of the mounting evidence. Is it fair to brand the objections to such a position as "a certain panic deriving from the studies of ecologists and futurologists on population growth, which sometimes exaggerate the danger of demographic increase to the quality of life?"[69] Are these and similar attitudes conducive to a serious assessment of our present-day situation and to responsible decision-making about this earth of ours where resources are finite and, for all practical purposes, irreplaceable?

As it stands, the corporealist position is unable to grapple with these extensive and complex problems and some moralists, therefore, have introduced correctives to the idea of fecundity-fertility.[70] Interesting as they might be, such attempts to rescue human fecundity from ethical meaninglessness still remain enclosed in a dualistic formulation of the problematic.

This fact was probably not that obvious before the birth of a spiritualist interpretation. The articulation of this other pole helps to bring forth the logic of the dualistic view.

2. SPIRITUALIST INTERPRETATION

In the movement of "conjugal spirituality" launched by the 1931 encyclical Casti connubii of Pius XI,[71] a new way of thinking about fecundity surfaces. Not surprisingly, one of the most unequivocal cases for this new thinking is found in a journal stemming from this movement in France, the country where René Descartes' dualistic anthropology has left the deepest and most enduring influence. A survey of the readers' contributions and the articles of L'Anneau d'Or (the Gold Ring), published between 1945 and 1967, enables us to follow one interesting instance of the gradual emergence of a spiritualist notion of fecundity.[72]

In L'Anneau d'Or, one notices the appearance of a notion of fecundity which tends to be completely detached from any kind of sexual realities. This fecundity consists in the support given by the wife to her husband for the sacrifices he makes for his family (sic);[73] in the spiritual love of the couple, a love which will reflect the inward quality of familial interaction;[74] in the spiritual fruitfulness of parents toward their children's interior life and intellectual life;[75] in the love of the couple which "opens largely on the universality of charity."[76] In sum, this fecundity is a spiritual dynamism which has little to do with human sexuality.

The attention given to the "mystery of sterility," however, is the factor which contributes most to the definition of this spiritualist notion. A contributor to the journal severely condemns deliberately barren couples, couples who, he says, "through an anti-natural refusal of the child," are egotistical and turned inward on themselves.[77] Even unintended barrenness is experienced, by couples who write to L'Anneau d'Or, as a cross to be carried in atonement for sins committed in the world against reproductive love and fecundity.[78] Couples who lament their disability[79] are urged by other couples to lend their support, by their prayer and other kinds of assistance, to reproductive families.[80] Obviously, adoption is advocated by some as a solution to the moral and spiritual crisis brought about by their very condition.[81] Nevertheless, if some of the periodical's collaborators seem to understand fecundity exclusively in terms of one's own or others' children,[82] others, on the contrary, clearly voice the idea of a "fecundity of marriage, outside child-birth (l'enfantement charnel), ... a vocation to fecundity in spirit."[83] This other form of fecundity is "a call for a more available and apostolic giving of oneself, for a deeper form of conjugal intimacy;" "It also expresses God's will for intensified prayer on the part of those who are struck" by sterility.[84] By and large this literature does not seem, therefore, to go much beyond the idea of an unreproductive and asexual fecundity which, in married couples as well as in celibates, widows and widowers, remains "totally spiritual."[85]

This current of thought is akin to the themes of a certain "spiritual literature" for the benefit of vowed celibates (religious or clerical) and, more recently, for Christian homosexual persons. For the first group, this literature promotes the idea of mystical, spiritual, apostolic, or missionary fatherhood and motherhood.[86] This theme is traditional and is often found, for instance, in the Roman Catholic magisterial documents concerning clergy and religious men and women.[87] The only problem with this notion is that it refers to a totally "spiritual" reality. For one thing, this one-sided insistence on vowed celibacy as an "angelic condition" for generating mere spiritual effects exposes these realities to distortions similar to those of ancient Christian gnosis.[88] But over and above such possible distortions, this discourse on the "spiritual fruitfulness" of vowed celibacy avoids dealing positively with the sensual life of celibates and with their sexual fecundity. As regards homosexual persons, this literature advocates, as is to be expected, Platonic friendships and "works of charity."[89] This literature does not even raise the inescapable question of the sexual fecundity of gays and lesbians.

By its lack of realism, this spiritualist interpretation keeps piously alive the aspirations of couples and of celibates without ever enlightening them about the nature of a sexual fecundity which, reproductive or not, would be integrally human. We seem to have to choose between a sexual fecundity which is essentially a baby-producing ability and an asexual fecundity which is essentially a spirit-producing ability. Does this alternative not fall under Blaise Pascal's classic indictment against choosing between acting as a beast and acting as an angel?

Because it shows no respect for the structures of sexual reality, the spiritualist interpretation of fecundity runs the risk of giving in to the worst faults of the corporealist interpretation. Nor will those faults be less perverse for being more subtle. By denying the sexual longings of fecundity a conscious life outside the exercise of fertility, their erotic objects are repressed in the subconscious. Inhibited, they become more intense and more urgent because the life they lead is secret. Denied, those longings for the enfleshed manifestations of sexual fecundity beyond the vague and pointless impulses of "universal charity" will be lived with anxiety and, sometimes, with terror.

Confronted by anything which threatens to unmask them, inhibited sensuous cravings will eventually lash out vindictively against anyone who personifies the coveted but forbidden fruit. Who has not known sexually frustrated individuals who have become, over the years, inquisitors, domineering fathers or husbands, persecutors of witches and gays, censors of the "degenerate younger generation?" In not a few champions of inhuman virtue, voyeurism, sadism or good old lust hide under the guise of morality and "tough love." Maurice Bellet aptly speaks about "the relief of the obscene in the trappings of rigour."[90] The harmful endeavor to "spiritualize" sexual fecundity cannot but result, for enfleshed beings, in a mere absence of fecundity, in a sort of frigidity which has no means of welcoming and saving the other in the superabundance of a very real, sensuously tender, human love.

If the longings of a sexual fecundity which is confined solely to "spiritual" expressions do not take the road toward aggression, they often assume the guise of a seemingly devout self-surrender. How ambiguous is the "spiritual behaviour" triggered by repressed erotic needs! Parental or religious authority, exercised as a constraint, functions psychologically like rape. Obedience, sustained as passivity or as blackmail, borrows the ways of masochism or of prostitution. Devotion, nourished by an ambiguous, sometimes sickening imagery ("holy cards" produced through the years by so-called "religious piety" offer a large sample of this,), strangely resembles orgasmic fantasy. Community, experienced as flight from the world and withdrawal into oneself, has all the characteristics of incest.[91] Fruits from the vintage of aggression or that of passivity produce a wine which tastes as sour as the wine produced by corporealist wine growers.

It seems evident that, while there are philosophically and theologically poorer and richer interpretations of human sexual fecundity, they have all been excogitated within a dualistic tradition of fertility. Pressured to spell out other aspects of human fecundity as such, the natural tendency has been to isolate the "spiritual" component and to fabricate with it "another kind" of fecundity from which all sensual elements are evacuated. Sex, therefore, remains on the side of fecundity-fertility. Since we do not know, in this dualistic tradition of fertility, what all other existing forms of sexual behaviour (those which are not directly oriented toward making babies) are supposed to produce, the great majority of sexual gestures are left normless. To contend today that reproduction is the norm of all sexual activities, including the sexual language of children, gays, widowers and widows or vowed celibates, is either ignorant (ignorant of the fact that no one is without a sexual life) or meaningless. For how could someone, married or single, who is not in a position to have a child, morally regulate his or her sexual conduct by the reproduction norm of sexual fecundity? Surely, we must seek elsewhere. We must propose a more fundamental notion of sexual fecundity, one which will be normative for the moral exercise of the entire sexual conduct of all human persons living in a given society.

NOTES

1. Even a summary look at the main texts of twentieth century R. C. magisterial teaching shows that important efforts have been made to qualify the reproductive interpretation of fecundity reflected in the 1918 Code of Canon Law. This effort has not been very successful. See J. GALLAGHER, "Magisterial Teaching from 1918 to the Present," in Human Sexuality and Personhood (St. Louis: Pope John Center, 1981), pp. 191-210.
2. Persona humana, par. 6, AAS, 68 (1976), p. 82.
3. Ibid., par. 7-9, pp. 82-87.
4. Ibid., par. 8, p. 85.
5. Gn 1: 28 itself is understood today by Biblical scholars as a blessing rather than as a commandment. See D. DAUBE, The Duty of Procreation (Edinburgh: Edinburgh University Press, 1977).
6. Besides the famous Song of Songs, see Ws 3: 13-14, 4: 1, Pr 5: 19, 12: 4, 18: 22, Si 16: 1-3, etc. The remark is from P. DELHAYE, "Fécondité et paternité responsable," Esprit et Vie, 85 (1975), p. 340.
7. L. LABERGE, "Celibacy in the Bible," Donum Dei, 16 (1971), pp. 12-16.
8. P. TRIBE, "Ancient Priests and Modern Polluters," Andover Newton Quarterly, 12 (1971), pp. 74-79, challenges the abusive use of Gn 1: 18 to reinforce a natalist policy on the basis of a sound hermeneutics of the Priestly creation narrative itself. Dominion over nature and responsibility toward nature and toward God are always held together.
9. See, e.g., J. L. LARRABE, in the well known Roman Catholic B.A.C. collection, El matrimonio cristiano y la familia (Madrid: Editorial Catolica, 1973), p. 64.
10. I fail to see what more can be drawn from the study of A. M. DUBARLE, Amour et fécondité dans la Bible (Toulouse: Privat, 1967), pp. 75-86.
11. See, e.g., F. LAMBRUSCHINI, Problemi..., p. 113; P.-E. CHARBONNEAU, Morale conjugale au XXe siècle (Paris: Éditions Ouvrières, 1969), p. 93; and even C. E. CURRAN, Contemporary Problems in Moral Theology (Notre Dame: Fides, 1970), p. 174, and Issues in Sexual and Medical Ethics (Notre Dame: University of Notre Dame Press, 1978), p. 47.
12. Even J. JENSEN has to grant that "there is little in the New Testament of the Old Testament desire for numerous progeny and the blessing of fertility." See "Human Sexuality...," p. 31. This is also acknowledged in the report on human sexuality

commissioned by the French Bishops. See P. AUDOLLENT et al., Sexualité..., p. 49.
13. J. T. NOONAN Jr., Contraception..., pp. 84-87.
14. J. K. COYLE, "Empire and Eschaton. The Early Church and the Question of Domestic Relationships," Église et Théologie, 12 (1980), pp. 35-94.
15. É. MORIN, "La famille: points de repère évangéliques," Lumière et Vie, 25/126 (1976), pp. 73-76; D. BAKAN, And They Took..., pp. 169-173.
16. E. J. HAEBERLE, The Sex Atlas..., pp. 127-128.
17. E.g., ST, I^a-II^{ae}, q. 94, a. 2.
18. E.g., T. W. BURKE, The Gold Ring. God's Pattern for Perfect Marriage (London: Darton, Longman & Tood, 1962), pp. 89-104; F. DANTEC, Love is Life. A Catholic Marriage Handbook (Notre Dame: University of Notre Dame Press, 1963), pp. 19-28. Recent research in demographic history clearly establishes that the idea of the "large Christian families" of the good old days is, with a few exceptions, a social myth. These results are found in publications like those of P. LASLETT, The World We Have Lost (London: Methuen, 1965); and J.-L. FLANDRIN, Familles. Parenté, maison, sexualité dans l'ancienne société (Paris: Hachette, 1976), and Le sexe..., pp. 151-216.
19. See also R. MEHL, Society and Love. Ethical Problems for Family Life (London: Hodder and Stoughton, 1965), p. 144.
20. See A. McNICHOLL, "Person, Sex, Marriage and Actual Trends of Thought," in Human Sexuality and Personhood (St. Louis: Pope John Center, 1981), p. 158.
21. See P. R. HUGHES, "Loi naturelle et contrôle des naissances. Une nouvelle recherche," Revue des Sciences Philosophiques et Théologiques, 58 (1974), pp. 58-66.
22. P. TEILHARD DE CHARDIN, Human Energy (New York: Harcourt Brace Jovanovich, 1969), p. 77. See section pp. 72-77.
23. GS, par. 50 (p. 1071; tr. p. 254). See also THOMAS AQUINAS, Scriptum super Sententiis Magistri Petri Lombardi, L. IV, d. 31, q. 2, a. 2, ad 1um, in Opera Omnia (Parma: P. Fiaccadori, 1858), Vol. VII/2, p. 957: to desire children merely for the sake of reproducing the species would be sinful.
24. J. M. GUSTAFSON, Ethics..., p. 124.
25. See HV, par. 10 (p. 487; tr., p. 335), 11 (p. 488; tr., p. 336), 13 (p. 489; tr., p. 337); 16 (p. 492; tr. p. 339); 17 (pp. 493-494; tr., p. 340).
26. W. R. ALBURY and R. J. CONNELL, "Discussion: Humanae Vitae and the Ecological Argument," Laval Théologique et Philosophique, 27 (1971), pp. 135-151.
27. Traditionally, theologians have assumed the contrary. See, e.g., THOMAS AQUINAS, quoting ARISTOTLE, in Expositio super Isaiam ad litteram, in Opera Omnia (Rome: Editori di San Tommaso, 1974), T. XXVIII, cap. IV, 1 (p. 33, lines 28ff.) and in Scriptum..., L. IV, d. 33, q. 1, a. 1 (p. 967). See contemporary evidence to the contrary in W. WICKLER, "Das Missverständnis der Natur des ehelichen Aktes in der

Moraltheologie," Stimmen der Zeit, 182 (1968), pp. 289–303; A. LANGANEY, Le sexe et l'innovation (Paris: Seuil, 1979), particularly pp. 39–91. See my remarks on this topic in The Sexual Language..., pp. 204–211.

28. See T. L. HAYES, "The Biology of the Reproductive Act," Insight, 6 (1967), pp. 12–19.

29. L. BEINAERT, "Régulation des naissances et sexualité humaine," Études, 324 (1966), pp. 23–24; H. and L. BUELENS–GIJSEN and J. GROOTAERS, Mariage catholique et contraception (Paris: Épi, 1968), pp. 81–82.

30. A. MOLINARO, "Contraccezione e ricorso ai periodi infecondi," in A. FESTORAZZI et al., Nuove prospettive di morale coniugale (Brescia: Queriniana, 1969), pp. 104–106; J. DUSS–VON WERDT, "La polyvalence de la sexualité," Concilium, 10/100 (1974), pp. 111–120 (this article has not been translated in the English edition of Concilium). Coitus is essentially a relational act. Only accidentally is it reproductive. The reproductive result can even be achieved without it, e.g., through artificial insemination.

31. E. A. DAUGHERTY, "The Lessons of Zoology," in T. D. ROBERTS et al., Contraception and Holiness (New York: Herder, 1964), pp. 109–130; J. PLEASANTS, "The Lessons of Biology," ibid., pp. 92–108; F. SIMONS, "The Catholic Church and the New Morality," Cross Currents, 16 (1966), pp. 434–435; C. COHEN, "Sex, Birth Control, and Human Life," Ethics, 79 (1969), pp. 254–256; A. M. BARCLAY, "Bio-psychological Perspectives on Sexual Behavior," in D. L. GRUMMON, A. M. BARCLAY, and N. K. HAMMOND (eds.), Sexuality: A Search for Perspective (New York: D. Van Nostrand, 1971), pp. 54–66. E. J. HAEBERLE, The Sex Atlas..., p. 315, concludes that it makes no more sense, today, to refer to the human sex organs as "genitals" (Latin: organs of generation) or as "the reproductive system" than to describe "the mouth, teeth, tongue, and throat collectively as 'nutritionals' or 'the feeding system' and then forbid people to speak, sing, whistle, or kiss."

32. See the 1979 Report of Ethics Advisory Board of the U. S. Department of Health, Education, and Welfare, published as an appendix in C. GROBSTEIN, From Chance to Purpose. An Appraisal of External Human Fertilization (Reading, Mass.: Addison–Wesley, 1981), pp. 161–162: "According to the best available evidence, for the average couple the performance of the human reproductive system is only partially "efficient." That is, not every meeting of sperm and ovum results in the production of a viable embryo. [...] only 37% of human zygotes survive to be delivered subsequently as live infants." Other authors give even lower rates of success. The probability of live birth is estimated at 31% by J. D. BIGGERS, "In Vitro Fertilization and Embryo Transfer in Human Beings," The New England Journal of Medicine, 304 (1981), p. 339; at 30% by I. JOHNSTON et al., "In Vitro Fertilization. The Challenge of the Eighties," Fertility and Sterility, 36 (1981), p. 705; at only

25% by I. CROFT, "In Vitro Fertilization - a Fast Changing Technique: a Discussion Paper," The Journal of the Royal Society of Medicine, 75 (1982), p. 255.

33. D. C. MAGUIRE, "On Sex...," pp. 125-148; J. GROOTAERS and J. A. SELLING, The 1980 Synod of Bishops "On the Role of the Family." An Exposition of the Event and an Analysis of its Texts (Louvain: Leuven University Press, 1983), pp. 194-196.

34. On this precise point, see, among others: F. SIMONS, "The Catholic Church...," pp. 433-434; R. A. McCORMICK, "Notes on Moral Theology," Theological Studies, 29 (1968), pp. 729-730; C. E. CURRAN, "Natural Law and Contemporary Moral Theology," in C. E. CURRAN (ed.), Contraception. Authority and Dissent (New York: Herder, 1969), pp. 151-175; C. E. CURRAN, R. E. HUNT et al., Dissent In and For the Church. Theologians and Humanae Vitae (New York: Sheed and Ward, 1969), pp. 156-165; J. L. RUSSELL, "Contraception and the Natural Law," Heythrop Journal, 10 (1969), pp. 121-134; F. BOCKLE, "The Church and Sexuality," Concilium, 9/10 (1974), pp. 146-148; A. GUINDON, The Sexual Language..., pp. 212-213; L. JANSSENS, "Norms and Priorities in a Love Ethics," Louvain Studies, 6 (1977), pp. 233-238. - The most recent reiteration of the position in John Paul II's FC, par. 32 (pp. 118-120; tr., pp. 59-62) again merely assumes that the reproductive aspect is a necessary aspect of sexual intercourse. The 1981 exhortation does not explain how such a statement is arrived at without attributing a normative character to a biological process.

35. HV, par. 11 (p. 488; tr., p. 336): "ut QUILIBET MATRIMONII USUS ad vitam humanam procreandam per se destinatus permaneat."

36. A. DONDEYNE, "Réflexions philosophiques," in H. and L. BUELENS-GIJSEN and J. GROOTAERS, Mariage catholique et contraception (Paris: Epi, 1968), p. 20, had already made this point very clearly before the publication of Humanae vitae.

37. ONTARIO CONFERENCE OF CATHOLIC BISHOPS, Guidelines for Family Life Education (Toronto: Ontario Conference of Catholic Bishops, 1977), p. 5.

38. CONGREGATION FOR THE DOCTRINE OF THE FAITH, "Decretum. Circa impotentiam quae matrimonium dirimit," AAS, 69 (1977), p. 426.

39. We are far from the positions of a THOMAS AQUINAS, ST, I^a-II^{ae}, q. 82, a. 3, ad 1um (Vol. XXVI, p. 39): "Man's nature requires that the concupiscible appetite be ruled by reason. Its activity, then, is natural to the extent that it observes the order of reason. When concupiscence exceeds the bounds of reason, it is in man against nature."

40. P. TEILHARD DE CHARDIN, The Vision of the Past (London: Collins, 1966), p. 59.

41. M. LEGRAIN, Le corps humain. Du soupçon à l'évangélisation (Paris: Le Centurion, 1978), p. 78.

42. Reported by O. NEISINGER at the Katholikentag of August 23, 1962 (quoted in Evangéliser, 17 [1963], p. 523 - my translation).

43. A typical example of this is found in G. BONOMI, "La differenza essenziale tra metodi artificiali e metodi naturali," Lateranum, 44 (1978), pp. 146-168.
44. In HV, the "artificiality" of the means is clearly the issue: e.g., par. 7 (p. 485; tr. p. 334): "artificiosas vias;" par. 16 (p. 491; tr., p. 338): "prolis generationem artificiose temperare;" par. 17 (p. 493; tr., p. 339): "Ad natorum incrementa artificio coercenda adhibitas."
45. FC, par. 32 (p. 120; tr., pp. 61-62).
46. PIUS XII, "Allocutio iis quae interfuerunt Conventui Unionis Catholicae Italicae inter Obstetrices," AAS, 43 (1951), pp. 845-846. - I cannot see how else W. E. MAY's presentation of the papal doctrine (following its last developments in FC) can be interpreted. If May's argument is right, it implies that couples should not even follow the "observance of rhythm" with the intention of controlling births. See "The Liberating Truth...,", pp. 21-28.
47. If I understand what W. E. MAY is saying in "The Liberating Truth...," the official position has changed since Humanae vitae. Now spouses who follow the "observance of rhythm" must desire to be parents during conjugal intercourse. Is this not saying that they should not wish to control birth responsibly (against Vatican II's teaching)? For if they do not desire to have a child here and now and this is the reason that they "observe rhythm," then they obviously do not want to become parents through intercourse.
48. E.g., J. M. FINNIS, "Natural Law...;" and J. O'REILLY, The Moral Problem... It is interesting to observe that, from the discourse of these authors, an old concept of sexuality-flesh emerges which renders any notion of sexual language impracticable.
49. In par. 24 (p. 498; tr., pp. 343-344), Paul VI, following the lead of Pius XII, encourages scientists to intensify their research so as to find a surer basis for birth control practices founded on the observance of the cycle. The Billings method, which claims a high rate of effectiveness, is advertized in Catholic circles as a result of this papal appeal to researchers.
50. J. O'REILLY, The Moral Problem..., p. 11.
51. D. DOHERTY, "Sexual Morality: Absolutist or Situational?," Continuum, 5 (1967), p. 243. See texts quoted in J.-L. FLANDRIN, Familles..., pp. 186-187; and T. N. TENTLER, Sin..., pp. 141-143.
52. See Expositio Evangelii secundum Lucam, I, 43-45, in Corpus Christianorum. Series Latina (Turnholt: Brepols, 1957), Vol. XIV, pp. 28-29.
53. J.-L. FLANDRIN, Un temps pour embrasser. Aux origines de la morale sexuelle occidentale VIe-XIe siècles (Paris: Seuil, 1983).
54. J. M. DÍAZ-MORENO, "La doctrina moral sobre la parvedad de materia "in re venerea" desde Cayetano hasta S. Alfonso.

Estudio antológico y ensayo de sintesis," Archivo Teologico Granadino, 23 (1960), pp. 5-138.

55. L. VEREECKE, "L'éthique sexuelle des moralistes post-tridentins," Studia Moralia, 13 (1975), pp. 186-195. – This dualism is manifest in those few theologians who still propose this unwholesome view: e.g., H. V. SATTLER, "Lust...,", pp. 27-31.

56. See M. J. WALSH, "The Holy See's Population Problem," The Month, 7 (1974), pp. 632-636.

57. GS, par. 50 (p. 1071; tr., p. 254).

58. Par. 37, AAS, 59 (1967), pp. 275-276.

59. Par. 10 (pp. 487-488; tr., pp. 335-336).

60. JOHN XXIII, Pacem in Terris, first part, AAS, 55 (1963), pp. 259-269.

61. UNITED NATIONS, General Assembly Resolution 1386 (XIV), November 20, 1959, published in the Official Records of the General Assembly, Fourteenth Session, Supplement No. 16, 1960, p. 19. See principles 2, 4, 5, 6, 7, 9.

62. See R. K. SHINN, "Our Technological Time of Troubles," Religion in Life, 41 (1972), pp. 450-461.

63. E. I. CHAZOV, "A Clear and present danger – East," in R. ADAMS and S. CULLEN (eds.), The Final Epidemic. Physicians and Scientists on Nuclear War (Chicago: Educational Foundation for Nuclear Science, 1981), p. 65.

64. R. LLOYD, For Money or Love. Boy Prostitution in America (New York: Ballantine Books, 1977), p. 67.

65. See, e.g., N. MYERS, The Sinking Ark. A New Look at the Problem of Disappearing Species (New York: Pergamon Press, 1979); P. R. EHRLICH, "Variety Is the Key to Life," Technology Review, March/April (1980), pp. 59-68; J. C. COOMER (ed.), Quest for a Sustainable Society (New York: Pergamon Press, 1981).

66. See also B. W. HARRISON, "When Fruitfulness and Blessedness Diverge," Religion in Life, 41 (1972), p. 488.

67. See The Sexual Language..., pp. 178-188.

68. This point was well made by Third World bishops in the 1980 Synod: see J. GROOTAERS and J. A. SELLING, The 1980 Synod..., pp. 92-96.

69. FC, par. 30 (p. 116; tr., p. 56).

70. E.g., H. and L. BUELENS-GIJSEN and J. GROOTAERS, Mariage..., pp. 78-79; J. DUSS-VON WERDT, "La polyvalence...," p. 113.

71. In AAS, 22 (1930), pp. 539-592. See P. DE LOCHT, "La spiritualité conjugale entre 1930-1960," Concilium, 10/100 (1974), pp. 33-34 (this article does not appear in the English edition).

72. I must acknowledge my indebtedness here to Kenneth Russell for his contribution in researching this point.

73. L'Anneau d'Or, 2-3-4 (1945), p. 25.

74. Ibid., pp. 46-53 and p. 119.

75. Ibid., 29 (1949), pp. 336-337.

76. Ibid., 2-3-4 (1945), p. 139.

77. Ibid., p. 92.
78. Ibid., pp. 105-106.
79. Ibid., 79 (1958), p. 62.
80. Ibid., 83 (1958), pp. 390-392. See already in 55 (1954), p. 28.
81. Ibid., 55 (1954), p. 23. It is interesting to note that the possibility of a celibate woman adopting a child is mentioned at this early date: ibid., pp. 26-27.
82. E.g., ibid., 14 (1947), pp. 15-18.
83. Ibid., 55 (1954), p. 22. A text from D. VON HILDEBRAND, Marriage (London: Longmans, Green, 1952), pp. 25-27, which propounds a similar idea, was already quoted in 2-3-4 (1945), p. 106.
84. Ibid., 15-16 (1947), p. 63.
85. Ibid., 29 (1949), p. 334; 69-70 (1956), pp. 343-344.
86. See, e.g., J.-M. PERRIN, Virginity (Westminster: Newman Press, 1956), pp. 35-48; J. GUITTON, Human Love (Chicago: Franciscan Herald Press, 1966), pp. 126-149; A. AUER, "The Meaning of Celibacy," Furrow, 18 (1967), pp. 299-321.
87. See the texts of Vatican II (quoted from W. M. ABBOTT [ed.], The Documents of Vatican II [London: G. Chapman, 1966]) concerning bishops: Christus Dominus, par. 13 (p. 405): they "should manifest the Church's maternal solicitude for all men," and par. 16 (pp. 407-408): "Let him [the bishop] be a true father who excels in the spirit of love and solicitude...;" "Let him [...] gather and mold the whole family of his flock...;" "He should regard his priests as sons...;" concerning priests: Presbyterorum ordinis, par. 16 (p. 565): their celibacy "is a special fountain of spiritual fruitfulness on earth," or, in Lumen gentium, par. 42 (p. 72): "a unique fountain of spiritual fertility in the world;" concerning religious men and women: Perfectae caritatis, par. 1 (p. 467), par. 6 (p. 471), par. 7 (p. 471), and par. 12 (p. 474): their chastity is a source of fecundity for their apostolate.
88. See J. BUGGE, Virginitas. An Essay in the History of a Medieval Ideal (The Hague: M. Nijhoff, 1975).
89. E.g., ONTARIO CONFERENCE OF CATHOLIC BISHOPS, Guidelines..., p. 14: "Regarding those persons whose homosexual tendency may be diagnosed to be incurable, we can only encourage them to live a life of chastity through prayer for God's help and their own works of charity."
90. M. BELLET, Le Dieu..., pp. 278-279. See similar remarks in J. B. NELSON, Embodiment..., p. 109.
91. M. BELLET, ibid., pp. 142-143 and 256-257.

CHAPTER FOUR

TOWARD A RENEWED NOTION OF SEXUAL FECUNDITY

In the second chapter, we saw that in a virtuous sexual subject tenderness and sensuality blend to form an integrated self; that this integration is achieved by means of the sexual behaviour of interrelating subjects; that love is the energy which enhances the quality of life of the sexual partners; and that the socio-historical condition of persons is the context in which the sexual language is spoken realistically. This theory of sexual ethics offers a framework for revamping the notion of sexual fecundity.

Admittedly, this renewed notion will lack the simplicity and, as a consequence, the juridical and casuistic applicability of the fecundity-fertility notion. It should also be granted from the onset that it may even generate new problems of its own. One such foreseeable problem is that, because it is moral instead of biological, it lends itself to a wide range of interpretations in real-life situations. Because it is a moral notion, however, it becomes normative not only for a restricted, materially specified number of modes of sexual behaviour but for all the conceivable expressions of the human sexual language. This chapter will seek to show, therefore, how its four components constitute decisive criteria for moral decision-making in the area of sexual conduct.

1. INTEGRATED FECUNDITY

A wholistic interpretation of sexual fecundity avoids the dualism of reproductive fertility or spiritual wizardry. The difficulty with the dualistic tradition is that, since human realities are all seen as part of either a corporeal or a spiritual substance, sexuality, because it has to do with sex and with its highly perceptible physical characteristics, is classified as corporeal and is summarily identified with the "reproductive" system and functions. In this scenario, "spirit" is lucky if it gets a walk-on part in any play staged by sexual actors. In any event, "spirit" is never a full-time member of the cast. When it is called upon to play a part, it comes forward as an outsider and figures exclusively in support roles.

If anything is clear in John Noonan's study of contraception in the history of Catholic theological and canonical thinking, it is the gradual appearance in the Middle Ages of this outsider on the sexual scene. Before the thirteenth century, canonists and theologians held theoretically that one must always positively will the corporeal product of this biological function which sex was made to be. In the thirteenth century, Albert the Great writes against the seriousness of sin in the case of non-reproductive conjugal intercourse during a wife's pregnancy. This conduct, he argues, helps avoid adulterous behaviour.[1] While this "liberalization" sustained conjugal fidelity and the stability of marriages, it introduced incoherent elements into the doctrine.[2] This blow to the pure reproductive view will prove fatal. As early as the second half of the fifteenth century, Martin Lemaistre and other theologians began to realize that one may call on extraneous "subjective motivations" as an excuse for engaging in sexual intercourse even when reproduction is not positively intended.[3]

Thus it is that the outsider ("subjective motivations") was invited on stage over and over again. Before the Second Vatican Council, few Roman Catholic theologians, with the well-known exception of Herbert Doms in 1935,[4] had noticed that the one who used to be an outsider had now become a regular member of the company. During the Conciliar debates it soon became clear, however, that Dom's perception had spread rapidly throughout the Church.[5] The great majority of Conciliar Fathers, in point of fact, could no longer accept the view that reproductive goals could be sought morally when intentions of a spiritual nature were not also present. In the discussion of the first draft of Schema XIII's chapter on marriage and the family, a number of Conciliar Fathers picked out the contradiction which existed in the text between a new emphasis on the value of conjugal love, on the one hand, and its being finalized primarily by reproduction, on the other hand. This anomaly was subsequently corrected in a later draft. Though a conservative minority and Holy Office representatives opposed the chapter on marriage of Schema XIII (which became the pastoral constitution on the Church in the modern world, Gaudium et spes), the idea that reproduction is the primary end of matrimony was very consciously dismissed by the Council.[6] Three years later, Paul VI plainly voiced this new insight when he spoke about the inseparable connection between the "two meanings" of coitus, namely, union of love and reproduction of life.[7]

We have come a long way in a short period of time. Yet the question remains: Has this new doctrine of the inseparable connection between a reproductive and a unitive intentionality superseded the dualistic tradition of fertility? I would suggest that the intent was clearly to do so. In reality, this new formulation of sexual fecundity has not been completely successful in this regard. As long as we maintain that the result intended must be a child, we are no longer talking about an aspect of a sexual source (fecundity) or of a sexual product. We are dealing wih substances: chromosomes (the source) producing a child (the effect). If this physical element is a substance, then love (or its fruit, union of love) as the other element is either another separate substance or merely a qualification of the substantial element which is reproduction. Love as a separate substance returns us to the notion of "spiritual fecundity" as opposed to that of "reproductive fecundity." Love as a qualification of reproduction returns us to a corporeal interpretation of fecundity as essentially and primarily a fertile capacity. This second alternative is more difficult to reconcile, in my opinion, with the text of Humanae vitae and with the section on the transmission of life in Familiaris consortio.[8] In either case, though, we are still enclosed within a problematic set up by dualistic thinking.

The official doctrine, however, has more to offer to help bridge the gap between tenderness and sensuality. Vatican II's pastoral constitution on the Church in the modern world indicates, it seems to me, a new path to be explored. No precise definitions are given. We could probably pick out, in the Constitution, statements which would support a reproductive interpretation of sexual fecundity. This should not surprise us. There is general agreement today that one finds, in the Council documents, texts which are the result of a compromise between what are sometimes theoretically irreconcilable positions. Paradigmatic shifts are always marked by the simultaneous presence of contradictory views. Yet, is it not a sign of hope and of grace that while traditional views are not dismissed lightly, new perceptions in the experience of the People of God are acknowledged and celebrated in a holy synod as signs of the Spirit's fruitfulness among us?

After an introductory paragraph on marriage and the family in the modern world,[9] Gaudium et spes speaks of their divine origin, of the sacramental nature of marriage, and of the mission of the Christian family to manifest Christ's mystery of salvation:

> This the family will do by the mutual love of
> the spouses, by their generous fruitfulness,
> their solidarity and faithfulness, and by the
> loving way in which all members of the family
> work together.[10]

Instead of passing (as the preparatory texts of Schema XIII had proposed) from this "Christian" understanding of marriage and the family to considerations of reproductive fecundity, the Conciliary text introduces a new paragraph characterized by a strong personalist tone. This is a novelty in solemn Church

documents. In this refreshingly new paragraph, the Council
describes an "eminently human" love, a love which merges "the
human with the divine;" which involves "expressions of body and
mind," specifically sexual intercourse; which leads to intimate
unions, "pervades the whole of their lives," and "promotes that
mutual self-giving by which spouses enrich each other with a
joyful and a thankful will." The end of the paragraph alludes to
the positive effects of this conjugal, loving vitality on the
children.[11]

The editors of the Conciliar text have subtitled
paragraph 49: conjugal love. Such a rubric is not unjustified.
Nevertheless, the description of this creative dynamism goes
beyond what we would normally ascribe to love. If love is of the
essence, as we will claim later on in this chapter, the sexual
nature of this dynamism is also clearly spoken of. Indeed, if "it
far excels mere erotic inclination [...] selfishly pursued," it is
a language of intimate union, of "tender affection," and it is
"uniquely expressed and perfected through the marital act."[12] It
is tender, affectionate, bodily, all-pervasive, total, joyful,
dignifying, and enriching.

This vital force represents a wider and a more
fundamental notion of fecundity than fertility. It is mentioned
before the duties of reproduction and education and these are
shown to flow from its creative powers. The child, this "most
excellent fruit of marriage," as well as "the whole meaning of
family life" itself are seen as results of this sexual fecundity
called amor conjugalis in the text. After dealing with the
conditions for the exercise of responsible parenthood, the
paragraph returns to this basic reality of sexual fecundity and
concludes by stating that

> marriage persists as a whole manner and communion of
> life, and maintains its value and indissolubility,
> even when offspring are lacking – despite, rather
> often, the very intense desire of the couple.[13]

This, it seems to me, is the line of thought which
should be bravely pursued if we wish to steer clear of the
dualistic rut. The issue to be discussed here is not that of
childless or of child-free marriages. Whether the human or the
divine institution of marriage is "ordained toward the begetting
and education of children," as the Council maintains,[14] is
irrelevant for the present consideration. The question is whether,
in all possible circumstances in which the sexual language is
spoken, the fruitfulness of sexual transactions ought to be
inseparably "corporeal" and "spiritual" in the sense of
"reproductive" and "unitive," or rather in the sense of "sensual"
and "tender?" It is this latter approach which is the more
comprehensive interpretation and the only one liable to shed light

on all the instances of sexual interaction. It is the only one which can be used when couples interact sexually not only for the purpose of begetting a child but for other purposes as well. When young children establish their gender identity and their sexual orientation through the sexual language, when adolescents and young adults have interactions of a sexual nature with their peers, when gays and lesbians manifest their affection and love to a partner, or when celibates cultivate warm friendships, it is meaningless to ask whether such transactions are fruitful in the sense of inseparably "reproductive" and "unitive." However, it does make sense in each and every one of these instances to inquire about their sensual/ tender structure. I suggest, then, that human sexual fecundity should be understood in these terms.

Each person is the bearer, in the sexual condition, of a unique meaning of human existence and seeks to communicate this meaning to others. In so doing, one gives the ultimate gift since what is given is really one's self, the intimate self, an unprecedented incarnation of being. Each sexual self is thus a vital power, a power which benefits the giver as well as the receiver. For as this power is activated so is the self revealed. In the life which it generates for the benefit of others, the self of the generator also comes into its own. When this is done freely – for human freedom is, as the Council recalls, the indispensable condition of all moral deeds[15] – the fruits of the self's womb are integrally human creations.

We could say, therefore, that, freely exercised, human sexual fecundity creates a surplus of human life, a newness in the human quality of life. If reproduction is necessary for the survival of the species, this free fecundity of a sexual self communicating its own human existence to others is necessary for the survival of the human community as specifically human. No human being may dispense him/herself from this specifically human task. The traditional expression, "transmission of life,"[16] may still be retained to define this aspect of human sexual fecundity as long as we understand it to be a new quality of human life which is communicated in and through an integrated sexual experience. Anthony Kosnik and his colleagues are right when they speak about "the overriding life-serving orientation of the sexual experience."[17] James Nelson specifies that, when we say that sexual love is life-serving, "always this means the transmission of the power of newness of life from one lover to the other; sometimes it also means the procreation of children."[18] If the production of children is not itself a "transmission of the power of newness of life from one lover to the other," it is not a life-serving operation and, therefore, it is an amoral or, in some cases, even an immoral deed.

Our first ethical criterion for appraising the achievements of sexual language is that it must foster human life, something which is inextricably sensuous and tender. It would be fundamentally immoral to freely choose a course of action which would seek, at least in the long run, to destroy sensuality and tenderness in us and in those with whom we relate intimately. To seek sexual disintegration by denying the flesh or the spirit in our relationships would go against the very nature of human sexuality since it is destructive of human life.

This is not to deny the fact that, in the course of one's existence, there will be periods where more investment in either the sensuous or the tender will be called for. The need to establish a clearly defined sexual identity may demand periods of mostly erotic apprenticeships or, on the contrary, periods of conscious and freely chosen continence. This, however, may never be but a temporary means. Neither erotic experimentation nor continence can ever be a goal in itself.[19] An integrally successful or fecund sexual behaviour is always one in which there is a right balance of sensuality and tenderness. It produces, therefore, a fruit of the same sort, namely, that certain quality of life which is neither angelical nor animal but wholly human.

2. RELATIONAL FECUNDITY

To insist on the necessary sensual and tender components of human sexual fecundity and of the fruits it brings forth is decisive for the ensuing ethical discourse. This is the yardstick which will be used to measure the structural integrity of all sexual end results. At this point, though, we have not yet considered what kind of activity is liable to bring forth such sexual products. In Roman Catholic theology, this question has been dealt with in a natural law perspective.

Because of the obvious shortcomings of this view, some authors today are tempted to play a "personalist approach" against a "natural law ethic approach."[20] This, it seems to me, is as futile as debating whether nature or nurture accounts for human development. Not unlike social scientists who, today, recast the nature versus nurture problematic in interactionist terms (the interaction of an organic structure with its environment), ethicians must learn to refine their analysis of a human nature which, because it is ennobled by personhood,[21] unfolds its human potential through interactions with others. It might help to recall to mind a few of the classical notions which often seem to be "forgotten" in this debate by those very theologians who claim to defend Roman Catholic theological orthodoxy.[22]

In the philosophy of being which undergirds Thomistic ethics and theology, the act of existing is the perfection of all perfections and the immanent principle in all things. As John Shea expresses it: "Being is the 'to be' of whatever is, the power which makes beings possible."[23] That which exists by and in itself, and not just as a qualification of something else, is expressed in Thomistic ontology by the concept of substance. A substance is that which is absolutely real since it has the capacity to be in itself, since, in other words, it enjoys independent existence. A being which is a substance has a "selfhood:" it retains its own identity as a being even while it undergoes changes.

When a substance is considered specifically as tending toward self-fulfilment, as the source of characteristic activities, it is called a nature. The way (or ways) in which a nature is inclined toward self-fulfilment is called "natural right" (jus naturale). The way right reason interprets this inclination or aspiration is called "natural law" (lex naturalis). All this seems quite clear and simple. Yet there is room for widely divergent ways of understanding such basic notions. The history of scholasticism shows that Thomas Aquinas' own views regarding both natural law and, more fundamentally, human nature, have been distorted by some of his followers.

Here is another place where the repercussions of dualistic thinking have been strongly felt. Dualistic fallouts have contaminated natural law theories. The "historical misgivings"[24] of natural law - to use Jean-Marie Aubert's expression - can be divided in two main currents. One of them is a strong physicalist/voluntaristic trend. Natural law is understood by reference to the origins, to a state of nature before organized society (and sin), to the myth of the Golden Age. In this context, human nature is understood to be a set of biological data. Hence, natural law is reduced to a collection of biological laws indicating nature's developmental patterns. The second pervasive trend results from a rationalistic bent. Human nature is understood as a totally actualized essence. This creature looks somewhat like a programmed computer. Natural law is therefore seen, in this line of thought, as a set of abstract concepts, given once and for all, from which courses of action can be derived.

Concerning our own issue of fecundity, the impact of these two widespread ways of understanding natural law is essentially the same. Sexual fecundity never transcends the quantitative order. It serves to reproduce either biological organisms (ideally, clones) following the laws of genetics, or copies of a conceptual model following the laws of logic. Not only, therefore, is the sexual end result never integrally human, it is also the product of an activity which leaves no trace in the agent himself. How, one wonders, is such sexual fecundity ever a moral activity? Where is the imprint of a free subject?

The distortion of the natural law concept by dualistic thinking is not the only cause of the inadequate analysis of human sexual fecundity. More radically, the understanding of "human nature" which is operative in the corporealist and in the spiritualist interpretations of natural law is flawed. Under both interpretations lies the image of a being who has nothing to expect from others in his endeavour to become who he ought to be. In fact, is there anything to expect in these interpretations from outside of each one of us? At the limit, redemption from one's own imperfection and failures can only come from Nature, not from an Other.

Scholastic moral philosophers and theologians seem to have been struck more by the idea that, as nature, a substance shares many traits in common with other individuals of its own species than by the idea that such traits are realized in a unique way by each one of the individual substances. Nature, human or otherwise, is real only in individuals and is different in each one of them. It is as true to say that human nature is different in each individual as it is to state that human nature is the same in all human beings. The focus was so much on sameness that the differentness, the uniqueness, the originality of each nature was completely neglected.

As <u>person</u>, furthermore, the human being is "that which is most perfect in the whole of nature."[25] Consequently, the subjectivity which defines personhood (and not the objectivity of things) ought to be paradigmatic for our understanding of being, of substance, and of nature. Personhood is defined by self-consciousness and, therefore, by the capacity to freely dispose of one's own actions. Contrary to other beings, the person is conscious of the dynamic tendencies of his or her individual nature and is free not only to follow them or not but, more characteristically, to invent appropriate ways of acting for fulfilling the self. By its subjectivity, the personal self perceives what is other than the self and relates to other subsisting selves.

A human being is a personal subject only through reciprocal relationship with another subject which enables him or her to act as a self-conscious person. Without a relation which distinguishes them and unites them reciprocally, human substances do not exist as persons. The person is real only as inter-subjectivity. Personhood is a product of care between human beings and of shared responsibility. In other words, personal fulfilment is attained only through self-giving, through life-serving fecundity.

From those few elementary notions, it should be clear that any "natural law approach" to human fecundity which postulates that nature works in human persons as it does in beings

70

lacking self-consciousness and freedom is totally inadequate. "Nature" and "natural law" are highly analogous notions. If human substances find in themselves connatural inclinations, for instance, the inclination to establish a tender and sensual rapport with other human beings, not one of those inclinations prescribes a unique scenario of execution. Without the call of some other, heard and heeded by each self-conscious person, nothing human is ever begotten.

As we have already shown in the second chapter, the "saying" which calls human beings to their integral relational truth is of a sexual nature. We are aware, today, that sexuality is highly determining for human beings: it differentiates them, it particularizes them, it individualizes them.[26] At the same time as sexuality limits an individual's potential, it urges her to narrate herself to others so as to open up to them, to let them in, and to fulfill her being. As French philosopher Jean Lacroix puts it: "It is this aspiration, emerging from the depths of sex, which makes a man a creative and fecund being."[27]

Sexual fecundity is, therefore, primarily a matter of personal saying and becoming, a matter of interpersonal intimacy. Contrary to what is sometimes stated in present-day debates, it is only secondarily concerned with singular acts. We readily agree that a tree can be known by its fruits. This does not alter the fact that, fundamentally and primarily, persons are moral or immoral. Examining the morality of this or that act of a person is of relative interest compared with the issue of the agent's own morality or human integrity. A study of the morality of acts in themselves, without any concern for personal development, would even amount to a perversion of the moral sense. One may wonder if this perversion has always been avoided in a manualist tradition elaborating a jurisprudence of sex.

When persons and not acts are made the central concern of morality, sexual fecundity is that whereby an interpersonal matrix for the communication of intimacy is established. Sexual fecundity can be seen, then, as "sexual energy," as a "passion for being" coming forth under the guise of a tenderly sensuous desire. If it is experienced as a manifestation of our own existential vitality (which it is), it is also a manifestation of the relational structure of our personal consistency with its existential shortcomings, its incompleteness, its finiteness, and, therefore, its need of the other. True, sexual fecundity is a passion for being, but also for being in touch with others. As Thomas Tyrrell writes of eros (that whereby fecundity is felt as urgent longing), it is "a call to be deeply, personally touched. It is a call to intimacy. It is a call to go beyond ourselves."[28]

If "intimacy might be defined as the willingness to give and receive expressions of deep personal warmth, affection, and tenderness,"[29] it is a typically human passion, more deeply instructive of who we are than is implied in the above definition. It is, as Kathleen Kelley puts it, "the need to know and to be known at the deepest level by another human being."[30] Particularized and individualized by sexuality, the human self aspires to confess its poverty and its expectations to another self. It is by mutual self-avowal and mutual recognition of who they are that human persons break out of their own limited interior world, recognize their own and each other's significance, and are saved from sheer insignificance and isolation. Thus, the sexual meaning of the human self originates and is articulated in its encounter with the genuine otherness of others, in the sensually tender dialogue with other human sexual selves who allow themselves to be known intimately.

The moral evaluation of our sexual language finds here a second criterion: interpersonal relatedness. Since they need others to become persons, human beings are inherently other-related. They must have a will-to-relate. To be moral, sexual fecundity must be relational. It ought to be instrumental in the establishment of intimacy, the matrix of reciprocal accomplishment in being. Because much more than material things or even erotic feelings are exchanged, the sexual language belongs, thereby, to the level of profound morality. It deals with the structuring of personal identities through intimate relationships.

3. LOVING FECUNDITY

If it is essential to determine the ontological status of properly human sexual deeds, namely interpersonal relationships, it is equally indispensable, for a moral analysis, to specify that whereby such interpersonal relationships will contribute to the persons' moral well-being. For it is not sufficient, in order to become moral, that persons interact with each other. In point of fact, interacting people could be mutually cooperating in self- or community-destructive activities. After all, people do enter interpersonal relationships which result in theft, murder, drug addiction, bondage, suicide, mutual abuse, and other such disruptive activities. By interacting, they are made not better but worse persons. Only by acting lovingly do persons grow in goodness since love is the inner principle whereby the good is willed and achieved. We are dealing here, therefore, with the very foundation of moral normativity.

Only when they speak a sexual language which is loving do human partners acknowledge who they truly are and, in this very acknowledgement, make each other be in truth. By the very fact that they are known and loved in the humble singularity which makes them be them, each one becomes conscious in a totally new fashion of his or her own self-worth. Thus, each partner gives to the other, as he receives from him or her, a new, valorizing, and challenging way of existing. The very quality of how one looks at another and touches another lovingly makes this other person glow: he or she beams with new life and finds new self-expression.[31]

To be a good sexual performer is, actually, to "turn people on," but in a sense which is much more decisive than what the expression generally conveys. The "turning on" which truthful love makes possible is that of new human "suns" which irradiate the world around them because a new quality of life has been kindled in them. Is this not how human beings bloom into full maturity and achieve their life-goal: to lead an existence which has found its meaning amongst others; to live it out with trust, sure of one's inner truth and worth; and, therefore, to be able to let others come into one's life and share it without fear of losing oneself? The full acceptance of a human being by another loving person, the unqualified approval of his human truth, the due respect without judgment (Mt 7: 1) of his singular project constitute the only non-coercive way to enable another human being to become a full-fledged person.

Though Christian moral theologians would unanimously grant that love is the very heart of the matter of interpersonal relationships, hence of sexual fecundity as understood here, they have not always been very articulate when it comes to spelling out the consequences which this central article of Christian faith should have on the style of our human interactions. Should the primacy of love in moral life not affect our selection of ways and means of being effective in the promotion of good and in the avoidance or consummation of evil? How, in other words, do loving persons seek to implement their convictions morally in the communities in which they live?

It is not sufficient to answer, as is so often repeated, that this should be done "with love." Morality is neither a mere disposition of the head (being able to recite the Commandments) nor of the heart (to purify one's intentions). We are moral when we seek to accomplish what head and heart have discerned to be true and good. We must learn how to be as loving in our behaviour as we are in our heads and hearts. If we have devised for Christians an ethic which has molded good heads and good hearts but which has left them handless, how will they handle reality? The moral problem, in point of fact, arises precisely in the interval between what an agent desires deep down and what he or she accomplishes in real life.

This problem of becoming lovingly and effectively engaged in constructive conversation with others is complicated by the fact that this is done in a world broken by sin where resistances both within ourselves and in those around us jeopardize our pursuit of happiness. Yet, if one seeks what moral intentionality may exclusively endorse, namely, the humanization of men and women, one may not have recourse to means of action which strike a blow at human dignity. Since the end is never achieved independently of the means which are capable of producing it, one is hard put to explain how violence, the breakdown of significant communications,[32] will ever lead to the establishment of the human communion intended by the whole moral enterprise.[33] Since as a moral deed, i.e., as a freely done act, human sexual fecundity must bring the other to a mutuality of trust and love, it operates exclusively in non-violence. Fecundity must heed the fundamental criterion of active non-violence, namely, the very presence of the other endowed with his or her human dignity.[34]

Sexual perversion will consist in transforming the life-giving power of loving fecundity into a manipulative power over the other in view of egoistic goals. In sexual relations which are abusive of the other's dignity, significant communications are broken through the necessary introduction of hostility and hatred. The non-will of the other's real good in the search of one's own interests and/or pleasure is, in actual fact, the very contradiction of love, of bene-volence (a will of good). Sexual fecundity proliferates solely through love, never through violence, proclaiming thereby the God whose Kingdom has no other reality than that of a blissful communion. The Mahâtma Gandhi has a better sense of what is at stake in violence than many of us Christians when he states that "as long as we will not have unrooted violence from our civilization, Christ is not yet born."[35] How, indeed, will the communion of saints germinate in our soil if we do not even know how to act with the kind of realistic faith that gives benevolent love a chance to sprout?

This, I suggest, is the third criterion for assessing the moral quality of our sexual language: a firm, loving quality which alone gives the power to produce fruits which have recognizable human attributes. Beyond adulation (where the firmness of an autonomous agent is lacking) and violence (where the will of the other's good is absent or defective), loving sexual fecundity produces valorized and humanly significant personalities.

4. RESPONSIBLE FECUNDITY

The loving, life-giving words of the sexual language are exchanged by people who belong to a community, normally to a number of communities. Each of these communities influences their sexual fecundity and, in return, is also affected by its quality and effectiveness. There is, as Beverly and James Harrison put it, "a fundamental dialectic between the presence of a liveable, humanizing community of persons and the quality of interpersonal intimacy and love which individuals can realize in their primary relationships."[36]

If this dialectic is fundamental, it is precisely because the human subject is a social construct. The self, as we have already seen, is a being which comes to self awareness in the presence of other selves and in dialogue with them. The human subject arises as subject solely in social interaction. The Second Vatican Council has reiterated the classical teaching of the Judeo-Christian tradition concerning the necessary interaction between person and society which follows from this understanding of the human subject as social:

> Man's social nature makes it evident that the
> progress of the human person and the advance
> of society itself hinge on each other. [...]
> Hence, through his dealings with others,
> through reciprocal duties, and through
> fraternal dialogue he develops all his gifts
> and is able to rise to his destiny.[37]

This view obviously calls for a rethinking of the multiple and complex rapport which exists between the sexual life of individuals and social life. For we must acknowledge that the social aspect of sexuality was seriously lacking in the thoroughly individualistic and confession-oriented textbook treatment of Roman Catholic sexual ethics.[38] While some of its basic sex-related positions did presuppose the social component of sexuality, its moral analysis of specific sexual behaviour generally failed to underline the social and historical meanings of sexuality. Can sexual fecundity ever be thoroughly assessed as a mere personal attribute or the fruits of sexuality viewed as private achievements when sexuality itself represents our way of being-in-the-word and of being-in-relationship with others?

The connection between sexual fecundity and society is much more stringent than the individualistic analysis of a certain brand of sexual ethics has set forth. Its indispensability comes from the very nature of moral inventiveness, notably in the domain of sex. The traditional notion of the influence of circumstances on the goodness or the evilness of acts[39] owes its existence to a richer insight than the shortsighted casuistic considerations of jurisprudential treatments of moral theology allow us to uncover. For in the latter tradition, circumstances are exteriorized. The vocabulary itself is telling. Instead of making use of words like "context," "situation," or "matrix," prescriptive moralists always employ the word "circumstances" which comes from the Latin circum stare, to stand around, to surround. Circumstances qualify, they bring a nuance, but they remain accidental and exterior to the agent and to his or her action. Much of casuistry's excitement consists precisely in foreseeing all the plausible circumstances which might "increase" or "diminish" the merit or demerit of diverse categories of deeds. Because they exteriorize circumstances, code moralists also marginalize them. Stripped of its flesh, the skeletal object always remains at the center of their moral analysis. This abstract way of viewing the object-surrounded-by-its-circumstances belongs to the same dualism which divests the subject of its body or empties tenderness of sensuality.

Yet, there is much more to "circumstances" in ethical analysis than this impoverished tradition suspects. The importance of this constitutive element of morality holds to the fact that, if the subject is to freely and, therefore, morally, create herself, she has no other choice than that of inventing the concrete form of her values straight from the circumstances in which she finds herself. Just how this inventing of values takes place must be carefully examined. However, one thing is certainly clear: the individual simply does not exist outside or apart from the circumstances. By her embodied sexual condition, she is incarnated in a vital milieu. She exists so thoroughly in symbiosis with it that it would be extremely difficult for her to communicate intelligibly with her fellow citizens through any language other than that of their common culture. Her surrounding world is the pattern of the significant interactions in which she expresses herself intimately and the design in which she participates with her sexual partners. No human creativity can escape this socio-cultural norm. This idea of the contextuality of moral creativity is not new. It is at least as old as Aristotle's notion of the mean (that is, the reasonable measure) which constitutes virtue: to elaborate an action "at the right times, with reference to the right objects, towards the right people, with the right motive, and in the right way."[40]

Not only is there a socio-cultural context to moral creativity, but also a historical one. Moral decision-making and temporality cannot be dissociated. Time, here, should not be conceived as chronos, chronological time, time which stands on its own, so to speak, and is measurable by a watch. The "right time" of moral decision-making is kairos, existential time, time considered as related to the becoming of a man and woman, to the history of their interpersonal and community relationships.[41] Situations and moments offer unequal opportunities for action. There exists a certain complicity of events, favorable occasions for the realization of a project. It would be a mistake to reduce temporal situations to some indifferent matter: the instants of time are not of equal value in reference to a given subject and the manifestation of meaning and of love are time-bound. Kairos is this favorable time for moral decision-making, a time which calls for an answer, a time which would remain empty if the subject did not jump at the unique opportunity which is offered.

As a consequence for sexual fecundity, the question raised by ethicists ought not to be: "How will the sexual language be taught to the citizens of a society, to children of a family, or to any other member of a given group?" The only pertinent question is the following: "How will a meaningful sexual language be begotten through time in this or that society, family, or group?" To conjure up an "ideal model" of sexual language which ought to be taught to others is a mirage. If sexual knowledge can be disseminated and sexual values can be discussed with a certain degree of objectivity, the modalities of a fecund sexual language cannot merely be imparted to others. We can only speak our own, individualized, culture-imbued, time-bound sexual language to other persons who will in turn, within their immediate socio-cultural environment, invent the form of their own sexual response. If there is such a thing, therefore, as a universality of sexual language, it cannot be one imposed from on high and, once learned, "applied" (as suggested in textbooks) to each individual situation. The universality of sexual expression can only be one we strive and hope for, one to be realized eschatologically when all the richness of cultural and individual diversities will have been brought forward in the plèrôma (Rm 11: 25, Ga 4: 4, Eph 1: 10 ...).

By serving life in a way which is properly human, namely, by enhancing the loving and meaningful characteristics of human existence, sexual intercourse unmistakably contributes to improve the quality of the fabric of society. A society held together through merely coercive, legal measures would not and could not really set forth the optimal conditions for individuals, families, and groups to achieve their own fulfilment.[42] The degree of humanization of social bonds depends upon the quality of the fellowship's interactions. Valorized and self-actualized by loving sexual relationships, individuals acquire an expanded capacity to commit themselves socially, to work creatively, to improve the texture of social rapports. Lived as a critical experience of history, one's own as well as that of one's society, sexual fecundity is as transformative of the social matrix as it is of the person's own selfhood.

We have here a fourth and last criterion for assessing the moral significance of sexual fecundity and of its exploits. Drawing upon Richard Niebuhr's notion of responsibility as a fittingness of response to the whole context, we may speak of responsible fecundity. The Niebuhrian "man-the-answerer, man engaged in dialogue, man acting in response to action upon him,"[43] is constitutively a socially and a historically inserted being. He perceives his own self as a composite of his personal and of his social past, present, and future. This time-full self acts in a way which is either fitting (in a responsible way) or unfitting (in an irresponsible way) in the whole social context and historical movement.[44] Seen in this perspective, <u>responsible fecundity means creatively fitting the sexual response to the socio-historical context which calls it forth.</u>

Where the emergence of highly personalized relationships in our culture have the tendency to become individualistic, one can question whether these have really enhanced the moral quality of sexual relationships. A fecundity which is not historically and socially inserted into the world so as to contribute to its ongoing revitalization, in other words, a fecundity which is not responsible, is illusory and cannot be regarded as integrally human.

CONCLUSION AND TRANSITION

We claim that we now have in hand a morally and theologically significant notion of human sexual fecundity that is more substantial than that which those who are dissatisfied with a mere fertility concept put forward.

Sensuous and tender, sexual fecundity produces a fruit of the same nature, an enhancement of human life kneaded of flesh and spirit. This fruit has the shape of a word which gradually awakens persons to their relational truth. In the mutual avowal which reveals them to one another and to their own eyes, these persons are saved in a certain way from anonymity and from insignificance. Because they have made sense to themselves, they become more adept at lovingly welcoming the singular human truth which seeks to be born and to express itself in others and in themselves. Thus, fecundity comes forth as that whereby women and men mold the human figure of their communion. It is a creative power of meaningful and loving relational life, the use of which must be regulated by the truth of the historical becoming of persons in the community to which they belong. In short, human sexuality is fecund when it promotes humanly <u>tender/sensuous life</u>, <u>self identity</u>, <u>personal worth</u>, and <u>community</u>.

A renewed moral notion such as this may not claim full recognition before it is shown to be operative in real-life situations. In the four remaining chapters, therefore, we will attempt to discern the modalities of human sexual fecundity in four different life styles: that of heterosexual couples, that of family members (parents and children), that of gay partners, and that of voluntary celibates. Though these obviously do not exhaust the categories of sexual life styles, they cover a broad enough basis for validly testing our notion and for checking whether the criteria we have offered are operative. With the help of the literature which bears on those diverse ways of experiencing sexual life we will examine the real-life features of human sexual fecundity.

Before proceeding any further, two important disclaimers should be made in order to avoid misinterpretations of what follows. First, I do not claim that the aspects of sexual fecundity which will be dealt with while examining one life style apply exclusively or even primarily to this life style. If I have chosen to treat these aspects here instead of there, it is because I feel that there are good reasons (which will be spelled out each time) to do so. I recognize from the start, however, that these reasons are never absolutely compelling: they represent nothing more than convenience. In other words, it is assumed that the moral journey in the sexual lives of spouses, parents, sons and daughters, lesbians and gays, or celibates does not differ substantially from one life style to another. Nonetheless, the following question can be raised: Given the unique cultural context in which each of these sexual life styles is experienced, is it not possible that each category of persons is graced with a special insight into the ways of human sexual fecundity? Moreover, if it is claimed that, for one reason or another, it appears to me that this or that trait of human sexual fecundity is characteristic today and in my society of a well-spoken parental or gay sexual language, for instance, this does not mean that this trait should not also qualify the sexual fecundity of spouses or of celibates. On the contrary. If, because of social circumstances or cultural idiosyncracies, this or that facet of sexual fecundity is liable to shine more on the sexual deeds of this or that group of people, the whole community is enlightened and warmed up by their special sexual glow. We may all learn something from those who, for some reason or other, are in a better position to develop certain sexual competences more thoroughly.

Second, I do not claim that the treatment of any of the aspects of sexual fecundity which will be examined here is exhaustive, particularly as regards their application to concrete, specific behaviour. If the four criteria described above ought to be applied by the individual moral agent to each of his or her sexual acts and if precise sexual conduct will indeed be considered in the second part of this book, the focus of the analysis is on attitudes, quality of life, values. I am much less interested, then, in assessing casuistically what physical acts are morally allowable between heterosexual couples, gay partners, a parent and his or her child, or celibate friends, than in appraising the creative power and the moral quality of the sexual language spoken in each of these relationships. The choice here is not for meaning over embodiment, but for being and becoming human persons over having and fabricating sex. This choice situates the moral analysis which follows in the tradition of a "virtue approach" of ethics such as one finds, for instance, in Aristotle's Nichomachean Ethics or in Aquinas' Secunda Secundae of the Summa Theologiae. Contemporary R. C. moral theologians have denounced in theory "act-morality" approaches.[45] Yet, when any concrete moral issue is raised, I see most of them engaged in a dispute concerning "right" and "wrong" acts (e.g., "homosexual acts," "contraceptive acts," "acts of just war") rather than in an ethical reflection on the moral disposition needed in an agent to do good well and to avoid its corruption by defect or excess (e.g., "gay fecundity," "responsible generativity," "active non-violent commitment.")

There are, therefore, at least two major biases in the analysis which follows. One is that in a given society and culture and historical time, each sexual life style offers specific assets and liabilities for human sexual fecundity: it is a bias in favour of prudential discernments and to the detriment of universal prescriptions. The other bias is that morality deals primarily with human beings, therefore with virtues and qualities, and only secondarily with things, therefore with performances and quantities.

To make explicit one's biases does not insure that intellectual gains will automatically ensue. But, at least, this constitutes less of an obstacle to intellectual progress than when the biases are hidden, unrecognized, and inaccessible to critical evaluation.

NOTES

1. J. T. NOONAN, Jr., Contraception..., p. 343, note 7.
2. J.-L. FLANDRIN, Le sexe..., p. 10.
3. J. T. NOONAN, Jr., Contraception..., pp. 368-372.
4. H. DOMS, The Meaning of Marriage (New York: Sheed and Ward, 1939). His teaching was cold-shouldered by the Holy Office in 1944 (see DS, n. 3838).
5. See L. JANSSENS, Mariage et fécondité. De Casti connubii à Gaudium et spes (Gembloux: J. Duculot, 1967).
6. See, e.g., P. DELHAYE, "Dignité du mariage et de la famille," in Y. CONGAR and M. PEUCHMARD (eds.), L'Église dans le monde de ce temps: Constitution pastorale "Gaudium et Spes" (Paris: Cerf, 1967), T. 2, pp. 387-420; J. GROOTAERS, "Histoire de deux commissions: éléments d'information, points de repère," in H. and L. BUELENS-GIJSEN and J. GROOTAERS, Mariage catholique et contraception (Paris: Epi, 1968), pp. 139-272; J. FUCHS, "The Theology of the Meaning of Marriage Today," in J. T. McHUGH (ed.), Marriage in the Light of Vatican II

(Washington, D.C.: Family Life Bureau, 1968), in particular, pp. 24-25; L. C. BERNAL R., "Genesis de la doctrina sobre el amor conyugal de la Constitución Gaudium et spes," Ephemerides Theologicae Lovanienses, 51 (1975), pp. 49-81, in particular, pp. 59-65 and 69-73. - J. P. HANIGAN, What Are They Saying about Sexual Morality? (New York: Paulist Press, 1982), p. 107, writes: "The one notable exception to this consensus [i.e., the "growing consensus that sexuality finds its primary significance in inter-personal love"] is, unfortunately, the Vatican Congregation for the Doctrine of Faith, which still insists that even Vatican II taught that procreation was the primary purpose."

7. HV, par. 12 (p. 488; tr., p. 336). See also par. 9 (pp. 486-487; tr., p. 335), par. 11 (p. 488; tr., p. 336), par. 13 (p. 489; tr., p. 337), and par. 24 (p. 498; tr., p. 344: in the quote from GS, par. 51).

8. FC, par. 28-35 (pp. 114-126; tr., pp. 53-70).

9. Par. 47 (p. 1067; tr., pp. 249-250).

10. Par. 48 (pp. 1067-1069; tr. pp. 250-252).

11. Par. 49 (pp. 1069-1070; tr., pp. 252-253).

12. Par. 49 (p. 1070; tr., p. 253).

13. Par. 50 (pp. 1070-1072; tr., pp. 253-255). See, also, FC, par. 41 (pp. 132-133; tr., pp. 80-81).

14. Par. 50 (p. 1070; tr., p. 253).

15. Par. 17 (p. 1037; tr., p. 214): "Only in freedom can man direct himself toward goodness" and come "to utter and blissful perfection."

16. E.g., in HV, par. 10 (p. 488; tr., p. 336): "in tradendae vitae munere."

17. A. KOSNIK et al., Human Sexuality. New Directions in American Catholic Thought (New York: Paulist Press, 1977), pp. 94-95. See also J. DOMINIAN, Proposals..., p. 60.

18. J. B. NELSON, Embodiment..., p. 118 (italics are mine).

19. See A. GUINDON, The Sexual Language..., pp. 160-162.

20. See, e.g., W. P. ZION's basic criticism of The Sexual Language, in Studies in Religion/ Sciences Religieuses, 11 (1982), pp. 95-96.

21. This had already been pointed out by H. R. NIEBUHR, The Responsible Self. An Essay in Christian Moral Philosophy (New York: Harper and Row, 1963), p. 57.

22. A. McNICHOLL, "Person...," makes a good presentation of those basic notions. See also his "A Chant in Praise of What Is," Angelicum, 57 (1980), pp. 172-196.

23. Stories of God..., p. 20.

24. J.-M. AUBERT, "Le droit naturel: ses avatars historiques et son avenir," Le Supplément, 20 (1967), pp. 282-322. See also: "Pour une herméneutique du droit naturel," Recherches de Science Religieuse, 59 (1971), pp. 449-492.

25. THOMAS AQUINAS, ST, I^a, q. 29, a. 3 (Vol. VI, p. 53). See the good development in SCG, L. III, c. 112 (Vol. III, pp. 170-172).·

26. H. VAN LIER, L'intention sexuelle (Tournai: Casterman, 1968), p. 162.
27. Force..., p. 55 (my translation).
28. T. J. TYRRELL, Urgent Longings..., p. 26.
29. M. NEUMAN, "Friendships Between Men and Women in Religious Life," Sisters Today, 46 (1974), pp. 82–83.
30. In a workshop for priests on human sexuality and the ordained priesthood given at Saint Michael's College, Winooski, Vermont, June 21-25, 1982. A similar idea is found in S. BRECKEL and N. M. MURPHY, "Psychosexual Development," Chicago Studies, 20 (1981), p. 56.
31. See also The Sexual Language..., p. 175. B. HÄRING, Free..., Vol. II, p. 516, has taken up similar formulas.
32. R. MAY, Power and Innocence. A Search for the Sources of Violence (New York: Norton, 1972). That violence introduces and symbolizes the reign of nonsense, indeed of absurdity, is a classic teaching: see THOMAS AQUINAS, ST, I^a-II^{ae}, q. 6, a. 5 and the parallel texts.
33. J. ELLUL, Violence. Reflections from a Christian Perspective (New York: Seabury Press, 1969) denounces the myth of a constructive violence.
34. A. GUINDON, "Du réalisme moral," Studia Moralia, 17 (1980), pp. 140-144; see, in a wider perspective, T. MERTON, Faith and Violence. Christian Teaching and Christian Practice (Notre Dame: University of Notre Dame Press, 1968).
35. Quoted by J.-M. MULLER, L'évangile de la non-violence (Paris: Fayard, 1969), p. 203.
36. B. W. HARRISON and J. HARRISON, "Some Problems for Normative Family Ethics," in M. STRACKHOUSE (ed.), American Society of Christian Ethics: 1977 Selected Papers (Missoula, Mont.: Scholars Press, 1977), p. 77.
37. GS, par. 25 (p. 1045; tr., p. 224).
38. I have already underlined the importance of this social aspect of sexuality in The Sexual Language..., pp. 132-145. See also A. KOSNIK et al., Human Sexuality..., pp. 93-94.
39. E.g., THOMAS AQUINAS, ST, I^a-II^{ae}, q. 18, a. 3.
40. ARISTOTLE, Nicomachean Ethics..., II, 6 (1106 b 20-22), p. 958.
41. In the remarkable rewriting of Robinson (Crusoe)'s tale by M. TOURNIER, Vendredi ou les limbes du Pacifique (Paris: Gallimard, 1972), Robinson passes from a régime of chronological time to one of existential time after his conversion to "Friday"'s presential life-rhythm. It is interesting to observe that it is through his sexual existence that Tournier's Robinson (contrary to Defoe's asexual Robinson) discovers the richness of time.
42. This is the traditional definition of society's common good: see, e.g., GS, par. 74 (p. 1096; tr., p. 284).
43. H. R. NIEBUHR, The Responsible Self..., p. 56.
44. Ibid., pp. 90-97.
45. E.g., C. E. CURRAN, Themes in Fundamental Moral Theology

(Notre Dame: University of Notre Dame Press, 1977), p. 209; "Method in Moral Theology: An Overview from an American Perspective," <u>Studia Moralia</u>, 18 (1980), p. 118.

PART II

MORAL EXPERIENCES

CHAPTER FIVE

CONJUGAL FECUNDITY or BEGETTING ADULTS

"Conjugal," from the Latin cum (with) and jugare (to join), means "conjoint." The term is used in relation to spouses and to couples. "Couples," however, is an equivocal term. Seeing a young girl and a young boy walking hand in hand, someone might exclaim: "Look at the lovely young couple!" Two gays or two lesbians living together may refer to themselves as a couple and even as spouses. An unmarried man and woman having an affair may also be identified as a couple. Some people, on the contrary, reserve the word "couple" and, a fortiori, the word "spouses" for a husband and a wife who are legally and religiously married. So it is that words, sometimes, have to be defined by their user.

The word couple - and the words which are generally associated with it, such as spouses, conjugal, wife and husband - will be used in this chapter to designate a publicly recognized moral relation involving the binding of a man and a woman, freely and in good faith, in the intention to share their existence, support each other, and grow together in the capacity for caring through their mutual life-time.[1] At least three other possible determinations which seem non-essential to an understanding of couple as a moral entity are left out of this definition. One is the form which public recognition will take. In North America, for instance, we would acknowledge that a man and a woman who have exchanged marital vows in front of an accredited official, but who live in a city where nobody knows that they are married, have received public recognition. In a tribal community this would not be the case.

In our society, this merely symbolic nature of public recognition is one of the anomalies which push many young people into new, more realistic ways of "phasing into" marriage. Some of these ways are not unlike the initiatory and ritual elements which are found in the customary marriages of folk-societies. An ever increasing number of young people join the group of POSSLQ - the Canadian Census Bureau's acronym[2] for Persons of the Opposite Sex Sharing Living Quarters. Undoubtedly, many such partners are merely moving in together for fun and/or commodity while others are "experimenting" (?) to see whether it will work or not. However, many think of themselves as "pre-ceremonial couples" and consider this stage as a normal way of successfully entering conjugal life. This is particularly the case where marriage is seen more as a journey than as an institution or a state of life.[3] Most contemporary legislatures acknowledge that this stage of pre-ceremonial cohabitation is, indeed, becoming a widespread way of initiating matrimony. In effect, they designate a good-faith POSSLQ, after a specific length of time, a common law marriage.[4] One could even argue that theologically, such a "marriage by phases" is not unthinkable.[5] For the purpose of this chapter, it is not useful to elaborate on this extremely complex issue. Since being-a-couple is a social reality and entails new social responsibilities, some form of public acknowledgment and institutionalization seems necessary. How this is done is a matter of custom and of positive law.

A second determination which is considered non-essential to the definition is the necessity of a religious or, a fortiori, a sacramental ritual. Though the Roman Catholic Church forbids its own members to marry outside of canonical forms, it has always recognized the validity of marriages between baptized Christians who are not Roman Catholic. Christian rituals of marriage, for that matter, represent a late development in the Church. It was not much before the thirteenth century that the sacramental nature of marriage was universally recognized in the Church, that the role of the priest became essential rather than merely occasional, and that what used to be a domestic and private ceremony became ecclesial and public. The entry of marriage[6] into the church was not completed before the seventeenth century. The more basic questions of knowing whether all conjugal unions have a specific religious meaning or not, and furthermore, whether every marital union between two baptized Christians is sacramental or not, can be considered within our definition. A positive answer to one or both of those questions would only enrich what is considered here to be the minimal conditions which are required for a heterosexual dyad to form a couple properly so called.

Thirdly, and more controversially, the intention to become family by having children through reproduction or adoption is, I suggest, to be disqualified from our present consideration. If this point needed to be discussed for its own sake, I would uphold a position which dissociates the notions of "marriage" and "conjugal union." I have come to believe that the profound mind of the Christian Tradition concerning the institution of marriage is that it is to be entered into by those who <u>wish</u> and <u>can</u> effectively establish a family, that is to say a <u>social cell</u> in which descendants secure the historical lineage. I recognize that the transformation of this opinion into a certitude would require more systematic research.[7] It seems clear to me, nevertheless, that, as historian Théodore Tarczylo puts it, "for the older society and for its Church, <u>marriage</u> is less the union of two beings than the <u>alliance</u> of two families. On this score,[8] the synonymy of those two terms is itself significant." Many arguments could be brought forth which suggest that, for the Tradition, the unit which can become, with God's sacramental grace, a "domestic Church" is not the couple as such but the family. The concept of "childless marriage" is nothing else, in my opinion, than an accident and a juridical accommodation. It would be more coherent with the sense of the Tradition, I would claim, to clearly distinguish, both theologically and ritually, between two realities. Those unions between a man and a woman which have fructified into family and are lived as a faith event would be seen as sacramental marriages and celebrated liturgically as such. A man and a woman who wish to be united to one another with the publicly manifested intention to share their existence, support each other (but not children), and grow together in the capacity for caring through their mutual life-time, are undertaking a morally, civilly, and religiously worthwhile enterprise. This enterprise is distinct, nevertheless, from what has been traditionally called "marriage." We could imagine that both a specific legal status and special ecclesial blessings could be conferred upon such a conjugal union.

For the purpose of analyzing conjugal sexual fecundity, this entire academic discussion on the Utopia (perhaps!) of Conjugal Units and Family Units can be and, for obvious reasons, will be bypassed. Phenomenologically, the conjugal reality, enriched or not by the presence of children, stands on its own. And the question we need to ponder is the following: Does the sexual language spoken by two spouses produce specific effects which verify the ethical criteria of human sexual fecundity?

1. SEXUAL WHOLENESS

If we must admit that the genital side of conjugality is oftentimes overestimated by youth, it would be a gross error to minimize its importance. Research has established over and over again that, in our society, satisfying coital relations and the ability to communicate coitally as whole persons characterizes happy conjugal unions. Unsatisfying or too sporadic coital relations, on the contrary, constitute a significant factor for the prediction of divorce.[9]

Granted that coitus represents but one of the sexual gestures available to couples, it is much more, for them, than just one among many. Coitus is their gesture. We are told by historian of sexuality, Jean-Louis Flandrin, that at the beginning of the seventeenth century, it was the custom in many regions of Catholic France to allow an unmarried boy and girl to "sleep" together in the same bed occasionally with the understanding that they could make love provided they stopped short of coitus.[10] It is no secret that today, in North America and in many European countries, "good Christian parents" are applying a similar rule of thumb to the courtship behaviour of their adolescent children.[11] In their minds accepting coition as a matter of policy (we are not talking about "accidents") would amount to the establishment of a premature conjugal union. The question which interests us, here, is less whether this is or is not a good idea or a wise practice. The task is rather to discern whether there is a valid insight in this widespread belief, expressed in diverse behavioural codes at different times and in different cultures, that coitus is not just one more step in the progressive apprenticeship of sexual activities (as, for instance, passing from holding hands to kissing) but a quantum leap of sorts.

If it is true that sexuality is a language which invites us to seek a diversity of expressions to speak our intimate selves truthfully, we must conclude that there ought to be a special sexual way of expressing a life-long commitment to the loving care of a spouse. If this mode of expression is not the coital gesture, what else can it be? And, indeed, the very words "coitus" and "copulate", born out of popular experience, carry this very connotation. Coitus, from the Latin coire, means to contract a covenant with someone. Similarly, copulare, to copulate, also signifies to unite and to tie. To use the coital language is to express "coupleness."

Because sexual language communicates intimacy, because its content is essentially "who we are" and not "what we do," its accredited purveyor is the sense of touch which is principally active in the sexual caress. No other mode of interpersonal communication is as direct as touching. In the same way as eating establishes the proof of the pudding, touching establishes the proof of the being (of the other as well as of oneself). Neither hearing, seeing, nor smelling could confirm the other's presence so immediately. By touching you, I may not know much about you. But I know in a unique way that you are, that you are in the flesh, that you are in my presence. Moreover, by letting me know you tactually, you give me permission to get closer to you than I would if you were to limit yourself to verbal, visual or olfactory disclosure. By the tactual sense, the embodied being penetrates the field of the other's consciousness in an unparalleled fashion. Also, it is not astonishing to find how important the phenomenon of restrictive taboos in the realm of touching is and how numerous are the phobiae linked with touching in neurotic persons.[12] Since touching awakens in us an acute awareness of the other's close presence, the threatening issues of intimacy and self-disclosure are automatically raised.

The form and intensity of touching in which two persons indulge should precisely correspond to the kind of intimacy which exists between them and to the degree of self-disclosure and discovery of the other which this demands. The sexual caress which prepares and culminates in coition establishes a maximum of mutual presence. It also structures the kind of exploration and disclosure which only couples, in my opinion, may truthfully allow in their relationship. A brief phenomenological description of its unfolding will enable us to detect some of its humanizing characteristics which account for my ethical assessment of its use. We cannot be content with the kind of raw physiological description and measurement of coitus for which William Masters and Virginia Johnson are rightfully famous.[13] Such research, I have no doubt, is extremely useful for a more exact understanding and a readjustment, where needed, of the physiological mechanics which are operative in sexual attraction. Nor should we deny the fact that sexual intimacy itself is rooted in a biological drive which pushes the partners toward the discharge of sexual tension. Yet, this physical need for release is intertwined, in human beings, with a whole gamut of psychological, social, and spiritual needs. Nothing that contributes to bring about this "release" is meaningless. Everything, from the escalated pulsating of the heart to the sweating and swelling of the body, has a properly human goal in line with the underlying coital intentionality.[14]

As man and woman engage humanly in the most intimate reciprocal disclosure and discovery, the highly stimulating activity which is thereby initiated calls on all sensory resources in order to create maximal wholeness and the highest quality of interpersonal presence. Breathing is altered and adopts a new beat which, contrary to its pattern in sleep, favours rapid, spasmodic expirations verging on moaning. Breast and abdomen soon become tense and the heart pulsates louder and faster, thus adding another throb in which life scans its presence with excitement. Simultaneously, body heat increases sharply, rendering the mutual proximity strong, obsessive, and diffuse. The warm and racy odour which emanates from the aroused bodies in turn transforms the olfactory faculty. This very primitive sense, so prominent in the pursuit of a fugitive object, opens the sexual caress to its final climax. The respiratory modifications also imperceptibly but efficaciously sexualize hearing. Words, if there were any at the onset, generally yield to the cadence of erotic modulations or complaints. The eyes, to the extent that they are still open, glimpse at the glistening and fluid forms. This visual effect adds to the general atmosphere of global presence. Even taste rides the wave of eroticism. An accelerated tempo of salivation is adopted which contributes to this mounting chorus of all living functions. This exploitation of all the senses by the coital intentionality and drive creates optimal conditions to further the goal of the sexual caress, namely, to establish an immediate presence between two highly concretized and singularized persons.

As the sexual caress gains momentum and becomes more and more overwhelming, the genital sensation gradually predominates. The other sensations which fostered its blossoming give way to its own unique characteristics. Unlike other sensations, in particular hearing and seeing, coital touching carries very little information. For all practical purposes, it does not discriminate between positions, bodily forms, or other such features. At the most, it is sensitive (but poorly so) to intensity. In this poverty of discriminatory power, though, lies its virtue. Confused and diffuse, the genital sensation subjugates all competing sensations. When it finally prevails and invades the whole human organism, all else is covered by its own indistinction. Emptied of self (at least of precise information about self) and isolated from all distractions, the subject is placed, without the mediation of computerized-like information, in the saturated presence of the other. In this, coition constitutes a prototype of the immediacy of touching.

This task of the genital sensation is also facilitated and further determined by its exceptional bodily situation: at the exact center of the body; in one of the rare human organs which does not come in pairs; in a mucuous opening, that is to say in a location where the interior life of the human organism emerges. And, as if these features were not sufficient to push the subject to the extreme edge of the self, this orifice terminates erectile tissues which, in both women and men, lift up a broad genital zone. When centrality, viscerality, and erectility become despotic, the coital experience culminates in orgasm, the most central, complete, and fulfilling instant of the sexual caress. This creates for the subject a peak sensation of both transcendence and immanence, of being wholly present "in oneself" and to the other.

Erection and, notably, orgasm are accompanied in women as well as in men by secretions, by a flow in each partner's genital passage. These are not mere "discharges," or, as Alfred Kinsey (such a good representative of mechanistic approaches) calls them, "sexual outlets."[15] Any observant subject knows that he or she experiences such genital emissions as a spilling of him/herself, as a liquefying of his or her own organs, as a melting sensation. There is always this same rhythm of being pulled out of oneself, of being projected to the extremity of oneself (transcendence) and yet, simultaneously, of remaining oneself and of being intensely present to oneself (immanence).

All things considered, the notion of ecstasis, of a projection of the subject outside of the self, is too hastily applied to the orgasmic experience.[16] This label is inexact for a humanly successful coition. In the latter the second general feature of the sense of touching is always verified: there is not only presence, but also distinction between the subject who touches and the object which is being touched. The same trait applies here. There is no confusion of partners in the coital sensation. Far from being abolished, the distinction is underscored in the sexual confrontation. The partners are fully present to each other. This brief analysis of the coital caress is reinforced in all its characteristics when the genital sensation is no longer considered (as was done here for the sake of facilitating the analysis) in terms of a subject touching an object, but is seen for what it is in reality, namely, a subject touching another acting subject. For the whole process is normally reciprocal. A woman touches while being touched by a man who is touched by and touching her. Over and above the heightening and fulfilling effects procured by this mutuality of sensations, the openness to the other, perceived in the coital experience of transcendence, is received by the acquiescence of the totally present partner. As each other's existence is confirmed by requited acknowledgement in the coital embrace, subjects are born to themselves as subjects. This is particularly the case in the frontal coition where man and woman fit together in so complete a way that it cannot be perfectly replicated in any other position or by same-sex partners. In heterosexual coitus a novel being is fabricated: being-in-couple. Is it astonishing that the wiseman enumerates coition as one of the wonders of this world?

> There are three things beyond my comprehension,
>   four, indeed, that I do not understand;
> the way of an eagle through the skies,
>   the way of a snake over a rock,
> the way of a ship in mid-ocean,
>   the way of a man with a woman (Pr 30: 18-19).

The reciprocal sexual generation of oneself as simultaneously both a being unto oneself and a being of presence is an indispensable condition for the successful generation and upbringing of human progeny. The art of generating humanly is learned first and foremost in the school of the spouses' own birth to one another[17] and to a new world which they have created together.[18] Once they are rid of a spirituality modeled on the monastic ascesis of fuga mundi (the avoidance of the sensitive world),[19] couples can acknowledge that sensually tender interactions form the word of fecund love between them.[20] Conjugal spirituality is then finally able to remark that coitus constitutes for the couple the privileged expression of the regeneration of their intimate self and the act which consummates their mutual self-avowal and acknowledgement throughout the process of developing of conjugal "we-ness."[21]

The instant of coital wholeness is not a privileged instant if it is the only instant of sexual presence, i.e., if it does not illuminate all other conjugal gestures during the day and make the couple glow so that everyone can read their joie de vivre in their faces. The urgent longing to be in the presence of the beloved is either manifest throughout the day or it does not exist at all. To be manifest, the desire of the other's presence has to be manifested. When it exists, it spontaneously finds a thousand and one ways of expressing itself. Being-in-couple provides an opportunity to develop an almost endless variety of tender and sensuous gestures which are uniquely meaningful for the spouses. These build up love's body. Couples who communicate this way on a daily basis are saying to each other: "I am in your presence as you are in mine. Our love is real because it lives in our bodies."[22]

Spouses who, in search of coupleness, play down either love's body or the body's love are seriously off base. They will never achieve the sexual wholeness which is so characteristic of conjugal fecundity. Some who, in a conjugal union, have visibly sought a sexual playmate rather than a spouse "to cherish and to love," fall prey to the corporealistic disintegration. Their sexual relationship (their coital relationship in particular), far from contributing to the other's well-being turns out to contradict the very finality of intimate interpersonal relationships. It becomes a utilisation of one's own spouse as a merely useful or pleasurable means.[23] To utilize one's life-enhancing sexual power as power over a spouse for self-enjoyment is to reduce the other to a thing. Like all sexual deviations, this represents just another version of a relief of passion which refuses the test of the other's meaningful and challenging presence.[24]

The most ugly and, alas, not so infrequent rendition of this corporealistic scenario is the rape of wives (14% of the 930 married women interviewed by Diana Russell) by husbands who subscribe to patriarchal attitudes. They believe that their wives are their property and that it is the duty of their wives to accommodate them sexually whenever they want. The coital attitude carries over into everyday life. Obedience and subservience to the husband become the guiding principles of all conjugal interactions. The story of wife abuse is the ongoing gloomy story of sexual disintegration.[25] Wives who are not in danger of being battered and who play similar games with their husbands easily indulge, especially if their husbands covet them, in what amounts to conjugal prostitution. They use their sex-appeal to blackmail their spouses into responding to all their fancies. The sexual caress serves as reward, refusal of coitus as punishment. For being less brutal, the results are not less unfruitful.

Other couples, on the contrary, seem to be leading sexless, dried up lives: no spontaneity, no warmth, no playfulness, no spice and joy. Sex for them is never what Sidney Jourard describes, namely, something "deeply enjoyed, freely given and taken, with deep, soul-shaking climaxes, the kind that make a well-married couple look at each other from time to time and wink or grin or become humble at the remembrance of joys past and expectant of those yet to be enjoyed."[26] What hard work must be involved in the antiseptic love-making of such couples! They have never overcome their childhood feelings of embarrassment about sex, never learned to speak its language, never let themselves go, never given their sexual body permission to humanize their tender feelings. Talk of foreplay, of being kissed by a spouse all over the body, of experimenting with new coital positions or new settings for the sexual caress is profoundly disgusting to them. Each one's body is off-limits to the other spouse because each one of them has never laid personal claim to his or her own body. Fundamentally, this spiritualistic disintegration is of the same brand as the corporealistic one. Instead of giving themselves to each other, such people try to give the impossible gift of only part of themselves: here, their souls.

In both the corporealistic and the spiritualistic disintegration lies an ideology in which what spouses <u>do</u> together or for each other (sexual or asexual services) is more important than what spouses <u>are</u>. Although doing things together is important for spouses, it can hardly hold them together for a lifetime and create them anew. As soon as establishing their career or raising children or whatever else they have been doing together finally gets done, doer-spouses find that they have never outgrown singleness. It is <u>being</u> together, sharing each other's worlds of activity as well as feelings, hopes, anxieties, and dreams that makes them become a couple. It is the being-together in the doing that, over the life span, provides the major vital resource. This is what conjugal chastity seeks to accomplish within the couple through sexual fecundity: the <u>integration</u> of male and female tender/sensuous resources and the <u>concentration</u> of the sexual sap of the couple for creating wholeness and quality of presence, not, as in hedonistic or purity approaches, the exclusion of persons and the elimination of life energies for the benefit of short-term, transient services.

In a sexually integrated couple there is a reality of mutual presence from which all other members of the community can learn. These spouses have coped with human divisions - their own interior divisions as well as those divisions implied in otherness - in a way which is accessible to few other people. Even religious celibates must humbly learn from them what it is to stand in truth in the presence of a real Other.

2. AUTONOMOUS MUTUALITY

The fifth proposition of the 1980 Roman Synod on the family comments on the "signs of the times." The first three mentioned are "a greater attention given to freedom and to personality, the quality of relationships in marriage, and the promotion of the dignity of woman."[27] The Synodal Fathers are right. These are new signs, signs of the times of postindustrial urban society. For, as ethnologist Luc Thoré has shown, this society of ours is different from all traditional societies inasmuch as it furthers the establishment of conjugal intimacy and affective verbal communication between spouses. Both matrilineal and patrilineal folk-societies proscribe spiritual and sentimental intimacy of the wife with her husband as stringently as they forbid sexual relationships with kin. Both those prohibitions are necessary, it is believed, for social cohesion. Conjugal sexuality is not a language.[28] It is instrumental in establishing alliances between families and clans and in passing on inheritances.[29]

By throwing each individual person into the arms of a "stranger" (and not, as formerly, into the arms of a member of a "known family") contemporary urban society strongly accentuates the rupture with the securing world of parental proximity. The conjugal adventure implies more interpersonal risks than in other societies. If the less demanding marriages of traditional societies could put up with a deficient capacity to relate effectively to a mate, today's conjugal unions cannot. This should incite us to examine the sexual fecundity of spouses under its specific relational aspect more closely and, thereby, unfold what is already implied in the notion of sexual conjugal integration. As Pierre Teilhard de Chardin suggested in Human Energy: "Man and woman for the child, still and for so long as life on earth has not reached maturity. But man and woman for one another increasingly and for ever."[30] This new moment of hominization which we are already entering, added Teilhard de Chardin, does not bring evolution to a stop. Another task lies ahead, "a more perfect concentration, linked with further differentiation, also obtained by union."[31] Differentiation obtained by union would be another way of expressing how relational fecundity operates in a conjugal union, namely, as autonomous mutuality.[32] And this, according to some observers, is the central problem in contemporary marriage.[33]

Conjugal sexuality, as we have seen, strengthens the bond between spouses and fashions in each one of them a new being-in-couple. However, this outcome cannot amount, without grave prejudice to the persons involved in the relationship, to a confusion in which the spouses lose their respective identity and autonomy. One is hard put to explain, at any rate, how a successful conjugality would alienate the spouses from their own humanity to the advantage of a mythical entity called "couple." "Couple," like "family," "club," or "society," does not exist outside the people who compose it. There is no such thing as the Smith family without the Smiths, a troop of boyscouts without boyscouts, Canada without Canadians. Not only do associations enjoy no existence of their own, but neither is their existence fully justified, as a general rule, if they do not provide a humanly enriching experience for their own members. A conjugal union is sexually fruitful to the extent that it liberates in each spouse his or her innovatory and creative resources.[34]

If the transition from adolescence to adulthood presents both sexes with the same dilemma - namely, how to resolve the conflict between integrity (autonomy) and care (mutuality) - this dilemma, argues Harvard psychologist Carol Gilligan, is approached by males and females from different perspectives. Boys conduct their lives following an imagery of hierarchy in which, by definition, one is alone at the top and fears that others will get too close. This triggers dynamics of separation, separation seen as defining and empowering the self. Such autonomy is further justified by an ethics of conviction and of rights predicated on equality. Girls' imagery of human relationships is typically that of a web in which one is at the center of connection and fears being too far out on the edge. This fosters dynamics of attachment, attachment which creates and sustains the human community. Such attachment is further justified by an ethics of responsibility and care relying on the recognition that different persons have different needs.[35]

To the extent that Gilligan's analysis is sound (which I believe it is) North American men, as a group, will experience less difficulty than their female spouses in coping with the problem of autonomy within a conjugal union. Wives must beware of falling prey to an ideology (which macho males will inevitably encourage) of pseudo-intimacy, a sort of "togetherness" which sacrifices healthy autonomy and self-care to the illusory security of continuing dependence. A certain brand of pious literature and talk on "love-fusion" covers up a moral aberration. Nor are the "bone from my bones, and flesh from my flesh" and the "one body" quotes (Gn 2: 23-24) valid proof texts. What such texts mean, essentially, is that when a man and a woman leave their parents and start living together they will find the same humanity in each other. Together they will face existence, sharing the same life conditions, running the same risks.[36]

At any rate, to dissolve oneself into a kind of two-in-one being would amount to a moral suicide. Nobody, neither spouse, nor child, nor parent, nor grand-parent, nor religious celibate, nor civil servant, nor soldier, nor anyone else may abdicate her or his personal selfhood ennobled by freedom. This abjuration would represent the ultimate immorality, the "unforgivable sin" of old, namely, terminal despair. Divested of free selfhood, nothing of worth would be left for the other to love. The very basis for human otherness would be lacking. The most that could be expected in such unions would be a form of parasitism. If, therefore, conjugal intimacy is the human experience of being mutually transparent, this transparency can never be such that personalities are obliterated or lost in the other.[37] Genuine intimacy thrives on personal originality. Here, the differences which distinguish each person's originality would be lacking.

Over and above their identity as separate, private individuals, spouses must gain a new sense of identity as a harmonious couple unit. After all, this is the goal of conjugality: a bond of creative, life-enhancing union. Just as personal identity is the foundation of genuine conjugal intimacy, conjugal identity and intimacy are the basis of conjugal fecundity. Nothing specific will result from the conjugal union as such where union does not even exist. Partners will merely produce more of the same of whatever they were already bringing forth into their world as singles. This output of celibate fecundity may be qualitatively high. But it will not bear the conjugal trademark which has been described, from the sexual point of view which is ours, as sexual wholeness.

If this conjugal union is to preserve and further serve the autonomy of the spouses, it cannot be conceived, as we have said, under the mode of fusion, as if by some uncanny melting of selfhoods and blending of unstructured and liquefied human organisms. The only way out of this autonomy/union dilemma is by the setting up of a mutuality of sensuous/tender language. What is needed is an interchange of intimate communication between the spouses which gradually makes them uniquely present to each other – to each other's bodies, minds, needs, feelings, hearts, desires, fears, hurts, joys, and dreams. From the new vantage point which this conjugal presence and sharing give them, spouses acquire an original insight into the nature and the fecundity of human affiliations.

Drawing on Carol Gilligan's study again, we can predict that, at least in North America today, women as a group are better equipped than men for mutuality. With a nonhierarchical vision of human connection, they are better disposed to spontaneously treat the other as one who is of equal worth, as one who cannot be left alone to hurt and heal by himself, as one to whom compassion and care should be given and from whom reciprocity of affection can be expected. Husbands, on the contrary, will readily resent such expectations as irrational and weak, as a breech of self-confidence and privacy, as a move against their independence and their legitimate individual effort to reach for the top. They will easily give in, sometimes in subtle ways, to the predominant patriarchal ideology for which it is below men's dignity to attend to the affective needs of others and to show concern in such affiliative matters. While they climb the ladder of social success and bear the torch of conviction and justice in the world-out-there, their wives, a mere extension of their own glorious selves, have the duty to comfort, support, and care for them. In ethics, the denial of the other's equal dignity belongs to the same category of radical evilness as the waiving of one's freedom.[38]

When husbands and wives trade autonomous mutuality for fusion and dependence, they automatically adopt a scenario in which sexual roles have been written before the actors arrive on the scene.[39] Their task is then understood as that of learning their assigned roles with as little interpretation and modification as possible. Assuming that he or she knows what the other spouse is really thinking, a spouse proceeds to perform a role based on that perception. In turn, the observed spouse oftentimes reacts to such inferential behaviour by playing the role assigned to him or her. Thus, a conjugal game is played which allows each player to pretend that everything is O.K. while dissatisfaction grows deep down. A vicious cycle of emotionally distressing responses sets in to compensate for the loss of genuine intimacy.[40]

For centuries, a duality of role expectations has prevailed on the conjugal scene. These role expectations, as Beverly Harrison says, "have subjugation as their principal characteristic."[41] The history of sexual ethics abundantly illustrates this point. The sixteenth-century Jesuit theologian, Tomas Sànchez, one of the greatest Christian moralists of marriage of all time, held, for instance, that the coital position in which the man lies on his back with the woman over him is against nature. Anti-reproductive features of this position were alleged by Sànchez. However, a socio-psychological reason strengthens his condemnation. This position, writes Sànchez, goes against the masculine and the feminine conditions: the latter is one of "acting" while the former is one of "suffering" (in the sense of pati, "being a patient," "being passive.")[42] The same message comes through in a commonly held view of older moralists regarding the question of who initiates conjugal intercourse. Though she shares with her husband the right to do so, a wife ought not to do so as bluntly as he does. Because of her "weakness," a woman ought to proceed indirectly, through sighing and cajoling.[43] A woman's sexuality, monopolized for childbirth, anchored her in passivity. Her's was a receptive stance, her husband's an active one. These role expectations are well captured by the traditional formula of the wedding ceremony: "I now pronounce you man and wife." He remains man. She does not remain woman. She becomes his wife. The sexual needs of the woman are either denied or sacrificed.

The debate that some feminists perpetuate on sex-roles runs the risk, however, of missing the fundamental issue. We are admonished to rewrite the roles: now men should do this and women that. The problem with sex-roles lies less with their content: man does the thinking, provides the goods, and performs on top during coitus; woman does the caring, provides household services, and "suffers" under during coitus. The problem with sex-roles lies mainly with their script being completely written by a third party instead of being a product of mutuality. That societal definitions, attitudes, priorities, etc., will influence some of the writing one way or another goes without saying. A society influences everything its citizens are, think, and do. But sexual functions, along with all other human behaviour and attitudes, must also be discerned and negotiated by the spouses themselves. To merely put on a mask and play an assigned role is to baffle both the other and oneself. As Roger Mehl comments, "perpetually playing a role leads to the point where finally the individual no longer knows who he is. He loses his own intimacy."[44] We should refuse any strategy which assumes that sexual fecundity is not the result of autonomous mutuality. Without this autonomous mutuality how could properly moral deeds result from conjugal fecundity?

Well established in the autonomy of their individual existence and freely engaged in a process of mutual discovery and care, couples who have a Christian commitment live a sexual fecundity which, under this precise aspect of autonomous mutuality, is also a word said to us all on the God in whom we believe. This God is One in the Trinity of his Persons and, as all the ancient symbols of faith proclaim, without any confusion of Persons. Again, it is one thing for us Christians to voice such articles of faith as we recite the Creed. It is another thing, a much more important one, to participate in this central divine Mystery because our life experience opens our hearts to its meaningful Manifestation.[45]

3. COVENANT LOVE

Autonomous mutuality sets the condition and provides the interpersonal matrix without which sexual wholeness will never be achieved in any significant way. The conjugal sexual strategy must reckon on autonomous spouses who strive for a privileged union through affective mutuality. The quality of this "affection" which is being reciprocated by the spouses is not immaterial, however, for the attainment of the expected result. Here, also, the human good which is sought for the other, and for both to share, calls for this very precise affection which is known in the theological tradition as love of benevolence. In the case of spouses, though, this love, which pursues the most intimate sexual communion of which a man and a woman are capable, is itself further characterized. I will use the word "covenant" to designate this conjugal trait of love.

The word covenant is more profoundly traditional and of a higher anthropological, ethical, and theological quality than a juridical term such as "contractual."[46] "Covenant," like "alliance," has historical connotations which are lacking in the notion of contract. Covenant (from the Latin convenire, to come together), like alliance (alligare, to join, to be allied), is evocative of a joint venture, a journey, an event with a life of its own. I shall consider the two terms synonymous. A contract (contrahere, to draw together, to strike a bargain), on the contrary, conjures up images of legal formalities cementing something already explicit or unfolded, namely, some commodity either possessed or to be possessed under well-defined and agreed upon conditions.

Applied to conjugal love, the notions of contract and covenant call forth totally diverging attitudes and expectations. In a conjugal union understood as marital contract, stability and eternity of love come to the fore. It is as if this very love which exists when the contract is signed - a love understood as a sentiment of eternity - is the commodity spouses agree upon and that they decide should last forever. Is this not an illusion? What is, exactly, this item which they both agree upon and promise each other that they will keep forever? Each party is probably ill-equipped, at this point in time, to ascertain with any accuracy the real nature of the love which thrives in each other's heart. Then, to the extent that what is found there is experienced or interpreted as a feeling of eternity, it expresses a refusal of historical time.[47] We are left only with chronos, this empty time in which the same ecstatic loving instants would be repeated over and over again. There is no place in this experience of love for kairos, the existential time during which human beings and their self-expressions change. The ecstatic and meta-historical notion of love is part of a mirage, that of Eternal Youth (love is the Fountain). If the conjugal union is to last during the earthly pilgrimage, such a sacralized notion of self, life, and love must be demythologized. Finally, is this eternal love upon which the parties make a matrimonial contract not necessarily stagnant? For, if the spouses do not grow together, they most likely grow apart. The conjugal community dies for not being renewed. If the spouses are growing together they become, for each other's caring love, an ever modified object. Love cannot remain unchanged. Alive, love moves and is transformed along with the spouses' own historical growth. Evelyn Eaton Whitehead and James Whitehead describe well this necessary transformation of love in marriage as a movement from romantic love (a largely passive experience of falling in love) to the love of mutual devotion (the experience of love as a chosen and cultivated commitment).[48] These are the reasons that "covenant," the coming together of persons for a life-long loving journey, is a more suitable qualifying adjective for conjugal love than the word "contract."

Theologian Roger Mehl states that "the conjugal community must, from the very first, admit that it is destined to live a history, that in this history many changes will be brought about."[49] Bride and bridegroom do not give each other the right to call on this existing thing between them called "love" and, when it pleases either one of them, to repeat its gestures, mainly its coital gesture. Both agree that this other will be the privileged witness of one's historical becoming who one is. Both agree that through an ongoing sexual dialogue they will unfold, under each other's loving eyes, the mystery of their own existence. We can speak properly of a self-commitment, "of committing one's being in a living-with."[50]

Of itself this major work of moral artistry, this carving in the flesh and heart of who one is, is a life-long venture, since no one has completed the masterpiece of one's own personality before one has uttered one's ultimate self-saying. If persons were immobile, sexual fidelity "until death do us part" would have no meaning. Conjugal relationships would be either instantaneously exhausted or fulfilled. Spouses are free historical beings. As such, they recognize and even constitute themselves as persons only in the very process of interrelating creatively with others, particularly with each other, in time. Since no person is totally present in an instant, the preferential project of conjugal love embraces the totality of the other's history. Love is, therefore, offered and received as a promise and lived as sexual fidelity. Fidelity is confident love's truth and temporality in interpersonal relationships. It guards each other's self from interior dispersion as well as from sclerotic habits which would hamper its necessary transformation. Throughout earthly life it celebrates the hope of enduring communion. We could define conjugal sexual fidelity as the conscious disposition to maintain a wholistic quality and intensity of loving presence between the spouses throughout their life-time.[51]

Contemporary commentators of conjugal life often call on divorce rates to argue their case for a crisis of conjugal fidelity. There is, in their demonstration, a statistical delusion. Not so long ago, around 1900, the expectation of life at birth for the average citizen of the world was probably somewhere around thirty years. An average marriage was, therefore, terminated within ten years after the wedding. By 1968, life expectation had escalated to fifty-three years.[52] If there is anything new, it is that marriages today hold firm for a much longer span of time than they ever did in human history. This is particularly the case in the technologically advanced societies where another twenty years must be added to the life expectation of the average citizen. Nor has this expansion of a person's life history reached its zenith. It has become common knowledge that the recent revolutionary progress of endocrinology promises further exploitation of the human body's dormant vital resources. We are told that we can still look forward to another jump ahead in life expectation. Increasingly, the art of conjugal love will coincide with the art of growing old gracefully and of dealing with time creatively in the evolution and structuration of the couple.[53] But as in all other ethical endeavours, this covenant love is subject to excess or to defect.

Its excess, it seems to me, consists in clinging to a conjugal form of life when the whole content has gradually leaked out of it so that nothing remains but memories and, possibly, legalities.[54] For we must recognize that between frail human creatures, a breakdown of interpersonal commitments is always an eventuality. In the theology of the last few centuries, marriage as institution has devoured marriage as interpersonal event. This was done to such an extent that theologians simply forgot to ask themselves how situations of shattered love could still be symbolic of God's loving covenant with us following the coordinates of the sacramental doctrine. Because sacraments express a symbolic understanding of essential realities of life, many contemporary R. C. theologians can no longer understand how an absence of covenant love can still be sacramental.[55]

Whether or not a sacramental marriage remains somehow forever (under some institutional form?) is quite irrelevant for an ethical assessment of the decision-making of the persons who are involved in a ruined conjugal union. How does a moralist justify the maintenance of common life where the conjugal bond is so profoundly affected that conjugal life has become unbearable and destructive? Any consideration brought forth to argue in favour of maintaining common life in such an instance would necessarily assume that spouses are for the couple, as in "people for the sabbath." In this interpretation, fidelity is given to a principle of indissolubility or to a social institutionalization of covenant love rather than to persons.[56] This represents a vice of covenant love by excess inasmuch as spouses who perpetuate such a destructive conjugal situation maintain its outer form long after it has died.

The opposite defect is, briefly stated, to give up on conjugal love as soon as serious and sometimes even not so serious conflicts arise. Living the kairos implies the recognition of the requirements of time and of space in our relationships with others. To wish for a world in which there would be no interval and no deferral between one's desire and its satisfaction is to succumb to an old satanic trick for thwarting humanizing projects.[57] Because it is the most intimate human relationship, a conjugal union holds the greatest potential over time for both personal growth and conflict. Like everything alive it will experience struggle. Some spouses are shocked and erroneously believe that love has faded away when they discover that the new bridegroom or bride has imperfections, does not smile on a twenty-four hour basis or has sudden changes of mood. Instead of giving up unrealistic expectations, they invest all their energy in trying to reform the other in their own idealized image. Since this cannot and will not work, they experience disenchantment and the couple is on its way to sexual dissolution.

From the very start, all spouses who wish covenant love to grow between them need two very basic dispositions of the mind and of the will. The first is the intellectual conviction that conflict is a law of growth and not, in itself, a block to sexual intimacy. The real enemy of intimacy is indifference, not conflict. Conflict shows that the relationship touches the spouses in areas where they are vitally concerned.[58] To accept that interaction can take place at this deeper level of our personal life stories is obviously to be ready to share more of ourselves than was possible before conflict arose. Intimacy cannot but deepen when conflict has been faced and worked through. A new degree, if not a new form, of closeness is thereby established between the spouses. The second essential disposition is a willingness to lower one's bridge and to reestablish smooth communication lines as soon as conflicts develop between spouses. As long as one remains self-centered in sexual relationships, one cannot meet the other in his uniqueness as a person. By not allowing him or her to be present on his or her own terms, one does not relate with a real "other."[59]

For these two dispositions to become operative, it is indispensable, furthermore, that spouses who lack the so called "natural" skills of interpersonal and sexual communication before entering a conjugal union acquire them later. Each year in North America, scores of books, courses, and workshops are offered to help couples develop such skills. They are, says John Shea, "a contemporary ascesis, a highly disciplined yet artful (non-mechanistic) shaping of the divine-human world."[60] In point of fact, their acquisition and utilization represent an ascesis which is in accord with the divine economy of covenant love. This makes more sense than most other ascetical practices which, out of a monastic Weltansicht, have been taught indiscriminately to married Christians.

A few months after my mother died, my grieving father was exchanging thoughts and feelings with an old friend of his on the condition of widowers. At one point I overheard him say: "You know, after my wife died, I realized that she was my best friend." For a man who, like most North American men of his generation (my father was born in 1900), is rather short on words when it comes to voicing intimate feelings, he could hardly have found a more eloquent expression of covenant love's goal. John Gottman's experimental study of marital interactions can be summarized by this very thought born out of my father's intimate experience: successful conjugal interaction exists where married partners have become "best friends," that is to say, mutually accepting, less dependent but more intimate.[61] So complete an elective friendship as that created by conjugal fecundity breeds a certain exclusivity of love which, in some aspects, cannot be shared with anyone else, not even with one's children.[62]

Where the spouses have become each other's best friends, the conjugal union is the school where sincerity of life and truth of love are learned. To live naked in front of the other either excludes hypocrisy or unmasks it ruthlessly. This might also be the experiential insight symbolized so realistically in Gn 2: 25: "Now both of them were naked, the man and his wife, but they felt no shame in front of each other." Shame is born out of the feeling that, threatened by the other's scrutiny, one should hide one's intimate sexual self. Shame is linked with a person's vulnerability, not with his or her true innocence.[63] To feel shame in front of a spouse for one's nakedness, to feel that one cannot appear before the other as he or she is, that one must play a role in front of a spouse, that the other spouse is no longer his or her best friend but a judging audience, are signs that conjugal fecundity is weak in love. Loving conjugal fecundity is a truth-making operation: it invites each partner to become lucid about himself and limpid in his conjugal conduct. It is that whereby the couple marches towards absolute transparence. When spouses pay heed to these exigencies of seeing, accepting, and mutually showing themselves as they are and in the totality of who they are, they have indeed set the scene for becoming profoundly liberated adults.[64]

Through this aspect of covenant love, conjugal fecundity becomes experientially instructive of Who God is. By a loving and faithful covenant with this mysterious "other" (i.e., this "who I am not": man for woman and woman for man), one acknowledges that one becomes who one is mainly through the other's redemptive care. This constitutes a privileged way of discovering the mystery of redemptive Transcendence. The Mystery of God's otherness combined with her loving concern for her creature is one which authentic witnesses of conjugal loving fecundity can help us all intuit. Obviously, no creature is as totally other and as completely caring for a fellow creature as the God of Jesus is for the Church. This constitutes for all Christians, including Christian couples themselves, a motivation of theologal hope.[65] "You have made us for yourself," muses Augustine, "and our heart is restless until it rests in you."[66]

4. DYADIC SOCIAL COMMITMENT

Everything which has been suggested to this point - how conjugal fecundity fosters and is characterized by sexual wholeness, autonomous mutuality, and covenant love - could be devastatingly misinterpreted if the fourth ethical criterion of sexual fecundity is not also applied to its conjugal modality. Sexual isolation of the couple from the community, withdrawal within their own sheltered coupleness, and exclusive dependence of the spouses on each other for affective support and growth-producing intimacy amount to conjugal narcissism, to a lack of sexual generosity. Where preoccupation with sexual and emotional well-being within the conjugal unity submerges the sense of social commitment and responsibility, the couple has become an unhealthy matrix for moral development. A spouse will never fully mature as a moral being if the area of sexual language shrinks to that of the couple.

Says the Prophet:

Give your hearts, but not into each other's keeping,[67]
For only the hand of Life can contain your hearts.

Kahlil Gilbran is right. Because of the spiritual nature of human beings, the constitution of a two-person universe is a dangerous illusion. Spouses cannot be satisfied with the identity which the couple situation alone enables them to realize. They must pursue the achievements that their growth requires beyond the couple because no single human partner can satisfy the urgent longings of a person's heart and mind. There are some aspects of one's intimate self which cannot be adequately challenged by one who "shares everything" and who necessarily loses the distance needed to appraise the situation impartially.

Added to this short-sightedness resulting from daily closeness, the finitude of each human person also sets limits to each spouse's sexual fecundity towards the other. Gender otherness itself is confining. A male spouse who cannot communicate intimately with another man or other men, and a female spouse with another woman or other women, are at a loss to express intimate aspects of who they are and, therefore, to explore and to expand these. Only with same-sex intimate friends can we share from the inside of ourselves gender-linked life experiences. Being biologically and culturally a woman, within a given society at a set time in history, molds reflexes, needs, feelings, and attitudes which men can learn from and, thereby, develop the femininity which lies in their own humanity. However, men cannot, out of their own experience, spontaneously and thoroughly identify with the feminine experience. The reverse is also true. Consider, for instance, two widely recognized developmental factors in the lives of North American women today: they do not peak sexually in their teens like boys do, but do so in their thirties; they generally live their youthful identity crisis as an affiliative task rather than as a struggle for independence and professional status. Can they empathize spontaneously, therefore, with some features of the Young/Old polarity which, according to Daniel

Levinson, characterizes the mid-life individuation process of males in North America?[68] The bibliographical account of John Barnes, biologist, exemplifies how a forty-one year old man, who is shifting from the position of young scientist-hero to that of mentor-to-younger-men, finds in "long and intimate talks with Dennis," "one of my very good friends [...] who is in almost precisely the same situation," the soul-brother whom he needs to come to grips with his mid-life identity crisis.[69] I am not sure that a woman would have provided the same intimate services, anymore than a man would have given his wife Ann the feminine intimate support she needed to help her come to terms with her own identity problems.[70]

Moreover there is no such thing, in my opinion, as "the Eternal Woman."[71] There are only women in time, each one a concrete, individual, and idiosyncratic woman. No one woman, therefore, may legitimately claim that she represents all womanhood for a spouse, that through her all the feminine virtualities are being unfolded for his eyes to behold. If we are talking about "real people," we must recognize that each woman is, indeed, a finite version of femininity as well as of femaleness. The same is equally true of each man. If there is some truth in the O'Neill's original case for an "open marriage,"[72] it is on this very point: not that marriage should be understood exclusively in terms of reciprocal growth-producing services nor that conjugal sexual fidelity be dismissed as irremediably linked with a "closed-marriage" model, but that relating intimately to others outside the primary unit of husband and wife is a necessary auxiliary avenue to growth.[73] If a spouse cannot recognize any ways in which self-worth is enhanced by his or her partner's affective involvement with others, then he or she needs to examine seriously why the other's sexual language is interpreted as a menace to the conjugal bond.

To ask couples to bear the burden of compensation for depersonalized and asexual relations elsewhere in society may seem a useful expedient. This is not, though, the most promising, long-term solution for the spouses' own well-being.[74] The restriction of intimacy to the couple creates a whole range of serious problems comparable to any other human situation where due social intercourse is lacking. Spouses become trapped in the conjugal relationship. They are stuck with an identity which no third party can validly challenge. They lose their freedom to choose to stay in the conjugal union. They live in fear of losing the only life-enhancing person with whom they can interact as tender and sensuous beings. Diminishing returns inevitably result from a sexual language which is spoken exclusively to one person.

If couples are endangered in their interpersonal development by a lack of sexual input from others, the contrary excess is not a better proposal for conjugal fecundity as such.

Admittedly, the empirical data do not warrant any solid conclusions on the effects of extraconjugal genital sex from the long-term point of view.[75] However, one is hard put to explain how any of the first three characteristics of conjugal fecundity will be realized where an "open marriage" means indiscriminate genital activity. Though Western societies have always regarded extramarital sex as leading to social chaos,[76] some unknown benefits may result in the future from non-conjugal forms of genital associations. Apart from representing as yet an enigmatic phenomenon, these sexual arrangements constitute, by definition, an undoing of the conjugal sexual bond. They must be generally considered, it seems to me, as counter-productive for conjugal fecundity.

The social aspect of conjugal fecundity is not covered adequately by considerations of the enrichment of the couple's own sexual well-being by its healthy opening out to the world. Society itself has everything to gain from fecund couples. The quality of social relations can only be improved by the fecundity of spouses whose sexual liberality surpasses the interests of the couple. The expanded ability to relate with a wholeness of presence and a covenant type of love should not be seen as a "private good." Community needs to be redefined by couples following insights and values which they are experiencing in their conjugal life. The fact that the universe of the female spouse has been reduced for so long to the domestic scene has manifestly deprived the human community of an essential source of its own humanization.[77]

As I ponder over the most urgent problems which our world faces today - ecological disaster, thermonuclear threat, increasing famine, worldwide violations of basic human rights, totalitarian civil and religious leadership, etc. - my conviction that we human beings will not make it to the year two thousand if women are not enabled to teach their male companions the art of caring for the earth grows stronger every day. Women as a group have mastered caring functions and men have not. The latter have been busy dominating and controlling for the sake of safeguarding what they identify as freedom, justice, or religion, while mutilating the environment for the sake of "technological breakthroughs." We men of the Western world have not developed a[78] sense for what the Hindus call "the maintenance of the world." If men - along with the few women who have made it to the top because they have outdone men in aggressive behaviour - keep the upper hand in politics, science, institutionalized religion, and other fields of social responsibility, humankind might just be running a disaster course. We seem to have forgotten what technology is good for. We know that it works, not how it takes care of our small, fragile earth and its inhabitants. The woman-man dyad must develop the total caring concern which is needed to hold back, and hopefully reverse, the suicidal forces which have been building against our precious little planet.

This also holds true of the community called Church. The conspicuous absence of equally responsible women at every level of government in the Roman Catholic Church, for instance, constitutes a major scandal of our times. The ecclesial society must also be shaped in its very institutional structures by the dyadic form of humanity. In the absence of an equally significant feminine input, not even the essential conditions for the Church's full revelation to itself and to the world are being met. How can the institutional Church be fully recognized as true Christian koinonia in a version[79] of fellowship which is still so overwhelmingly masculine? Have we not drifted away on this score from the primitive institution of Church in which the itinerant service of the Word[80] was accomplished, to a great extent, by Christian couples? The contemporary Church has yet to be rejuvenated by a conjugal fecundity filled with a Spirit of reconciliation.

The ultimate reconciliation of the sexes is, in point of fact, the typical prophecy of the Christian couple. The notion of couple refers us to the mystery of a differentiated sexuality reconciled in God through Jesus in the Spirit.[81] This mystery is not only for the couple to share and to cherish because, as Paul tells the Ephesians, "it applies to Christ and the Church" (5: 32). Unless we entertain a magical and totally unrealistic notion of the divine economy of salvation, the ecclesial reconciliation of humankind in Christ will not happen before conjugal fecundity pervades the whole community and transforms the very fabric of social relationships.

NOTES

1. This definition is substantially borrowed from B. W. HARRISON and J. HARRISON, "Some Problems...," p. 74. The only significant modification I have made is the addition of "public recognition."

2. In Canada, this increase is fourfold since 1970. In 1983, these couples constitute 3% of all the families. See "Death of the Family?," Newsweek, January 17, 1983, pp. 26-28. The U. S. Census Bureau reported a "doubling of unmarried couples living together from 1970 to 1978; and among those aged 25 and younger, the increase was eightfold." See G. F. KREYCHE, "The Family: Enduring Reality," Listening, 15/6 (1980), p. 7. In France, the number of unmarried couples has increased from 155,000 in 1975 to 400,000 in 1981. In Paris, one out of every five couples is unmarried. See S. CHALVON-DEMERSAY, Concubin, concubine (Paris: Seuil, 1983), p. 162.

3. E. E. WHITEHEAD and J. D. WHITEHEAD, Marrying Well. Stages on the Journey of Christian Marriage (Garden City: Image Books,

1983), p. 98, claim that marriage as an institution is dissolving, but that it is surviving as a journey.

4. Where this is not yet stated as a matter of principle, juridical provisions of all sorts - those, for instance, concerning social security benefits - increasingly liken POSSLQ's to legally married spouses after three, four, or five years of cohabitation. This is the case, for instance, in Quebec.

5. I have argued this point in "Case for a 'Consummated' Sexual Bond before a 'Ratified' Marriage," Église et Théologie, 8 (1977), pp. 137-181. The entire January issue of Église et Théologie dealt with this burning question of "Christian pre-ceremonial couples." This view has been strongly opposed, though, by the COMMISSION THÉOLOGIQUE INTERNATIONALE, Problèmes doctrinaux du mariage chrétien (Louvain-La-Neuve: Centre Cerfaux-Lefort, 1979).

6. For a summary account of this development, see E. SCHILLEBEECKX, Marriage..., Vol. II; B. I. MURSTEIN, Love, Sex and Marriage Through the Ages (New York: Springer, 1974), in particular pp. 86-203; G. DUBY, Medieval Marriage. Two Models from Twelfth Century France (Baltimore: Johns Hopkins University Press, 1978).

7. G. DUBY, ibid., provides historical data to support this opinion. Anthropological material would also back it up: see, e.g., ROYAL ANTHROPOLOGICAL INSTITUTE OF GREAT BRITAIN AND IRELAND, Notes and Queries (London: Routledge and Kegan Paul, 6th ed., 1951), where marriage is defined as a union between a man and a woman such that children born to the woman are recognized as legitimate offspring of both parents. An analysis of juridical material would also be instructive. See, e.g., L. E. ROZOVSKY and F. A. ROZOVSKY, Legal Sex (Toronto: Doubleday, 1982), pp. 117-119, who state that the legal reason for not recognizing "homosexual marriages" in Canada is not the sameness of gender of the partners but their incapacity to found a family.

8. T. TARCZYLO, Sexe et liberté au siècle des lumières (Paris: Presses de la Renaissance), p. 39.

9. E.g., E. H. MUDD, H. E. MITCHELL, and S. B. TAUBIN, Success in Family Living (New York: Association Press, 1965), p. 110; W. J. LEDERER and D. D. JACKSON, The Mirages of Marriage (New York: Norton, 1968), pp. 116-117; G. LEVINGER and O. C. MOLES, Divorce and Separation. Contexts, Causes and Consequences (New York: Basic Books, 1979); J. S. TURNER and D. B. HELMS, Contemporary Adulthood (Philadelphia: Saunders, 1979), p. 217; R. LANGELIER, "Sexualité et divorce. Analyse à partir d'une étude québécoise," Revue Québécoise de Sexologie, 1 (1980), pp. 252-258.

10. J.-L. FLANDRIN, Le Sexe..., pp. 285-291.

11. I am not astonished to find, therefore, that, among the students studied by L. J. SARREL and P. M. SARREL, 60% of the "virgin" females had had oral sex experience: see Sexual

Turning Points. The Seven Stages of Adult Sexuality (New York: Macmillan, 1984), p. 37.

12. S. FREUD, Totem and Taboo. Some Points of Agreement between the Mental Lives of Savages and Neurotics (1913), in J. STRACHEY (ed.), The Standard Edition (London: Hogarth Press and Institute of Psycho-analysis, 1964), Vol. XIII, pp. 33-34.

13. W. H. MASTERS and V. E. JOHNSON, Human Sexual Response (Boston: Little, Brown, 1966). Their latest major publication, however, situates their former contributions on sexuality in broader human perspectives: see W. H. MASTERS, V. E. JOHNSON, and R. C. KOLODNY, Human Sexuality (Boston: Little, Brown, 1982).

14. The following description is borrowed substantially, though in lesser detail and with a margin of liberty, from the superb analysis of H. VAN LIER, L'intention..., pp. 13-41.

15. A. C. KINSEY et al., Sexual Behavior in the Human Male (Philadelphia: Saunders, 1948) and Sexual Behavior in the Human Female (Philadelphia: Saunders, 1953).

16. C. OLIVIER, Les enfants de Jocaste. L'empreinte de la mère (Paris: Denoël/Gonthier, 1980), p. 29, also says that this does not correspond to the coital experience women describe when they speak freely about it.

17. M. ZUNDEL, La liberté de la foi (Paris: Plon, 1960), p. 112. L. MACARIO, "Ruoli maschili et femminili nella vita coniugale," in G. CAMPANINI (ed.), Sessualità e responsabilità oggi (Bologna: Dehoniane, 1976), p. 137.

18. See P. BERGER and H. KELLNER, "Le mariage et la construction de la réalité. Contribution à l'étude microsociologique du problème de la connaissance," Diogène, 46 (1964), pp. 3-32.

19. É. FUCHS, Sexual Desire..., pp. 149-157.

20. P.-E. CHARBONNEAU, Morale..., pp. 221-258; J. L. THOMAS, "Family, Sex and Marriage in a Contraceptive Culture," Theological Studies, 35 (1974), p. 152.

21. J. LACROIX, Force..., pp. 61-62; J. DOMINIAN, "Birth Control and Married Love," The Month, 234 (1973), p. 102.

22. See H. L. CLINEBELL Jr. and C. H. CLINEBELL, The Intimate Marriage (New York: Harper, 1970), p. 104. This I find to be a true-to-life, well-balanced, and useful book for couples. Many of the thoughts expressed in this chapter were triggered by this book.

23. THOMAS AQUINAS, SCG, Bk. III, c. 128 (Vol. III, p. 189, no. 3002). J. L. LARRABE, El Matrimonio..., p. 220, warns, here, against an assimilation of the institutional goals of marriage to the end of the persons.

24. In an exclusive interview with Elizabeth Hall, 81-year old Erik Erikson wisely observes that "some people today may fool themselves in their so-called recreational sexuality and actually feel quite isolated because they lack mutuality - real Intimacy. In extreme cases, you could have a highly active sex life and yet feel a terrible sense of isolation because you're never there as a person; you're never

perceiving your partner as a person." E. HALL, "A Conversation With Erik Erikson," Psychology Today, 17/6 (1983), p. 25.

25. See D. E. H. RUSSELL, Rape in Marriage (New York: Macmillan, 1982). Also: T. J. COTTLE, Like Fathers, Like Sons. Portraits of Intimacy and Strains (Norwood: Ablex, 1981); D. MARTIN, Battered Wives (San Francisco: Glide, 1976); R. E. DOBASH and R. DOBASH, Violence Against Wives. A Case Against the Patriarchy (New York: The Free Press, 1979); M. A. STRAUS and G. T. HOTALING (eds.), The Social Causes of Husband-Wife Violence (Minneapolis: University of Minnesota Press, 1980).

26. S. M. JOURARD, The Transparent Self (New York: Van Nostrand, Reinhold, rev. ed. 1971), p. 43.

27. SBF, prop. 5 (p. 141).

28. L. THORÉ, "Langage et sexualité," in Sexualité humaine: histoire, ethnologie, sociologie, psychanalyse, philosophie (Paris: Lethielleux, 1966), pp. 65-95.

29. J.-L. FLANDRIN, Le Sexe..., p. 9.

30. P. 73.

31. P. 74.

32. Since the specific aspect of femininity and masculinity will be treated along with the issue of androgyny in the last chapter, differentiation will be dealt here exclusively under the aspect of united but autonomous.

33. E.g., N. O'NEILL and G. O'NEILL, "Marriage: A Contemporary Model," in B. J. SADOCK, H. I. KAPLAN, and A. M. FREEDMAN (eds.), The Sexual Experience (Baltimore: Williams and Wilkins, 1976), p. 232.

34. G. CAMPANINI, "Sesso, cultura, matrimonio," in G. CAMPANINI (ed.), Sessualità e responsabilità oggi (Bologna: Dehoniane, 1976), p. 44. See also É. FUCHS, Sexual Desire..., pp. 181-184.

35. C. GILLIGAN, In a Different Voice. Psychological Theory and Women's Development (Cambridge: Harvard University Press, 1982).

36. J. ISAAC, Réévaluer les voeux. A vin nouveau, outres neuves (Paris: Cerf, 1973), p. 95.

37. K. CLARK, An Experience of Celibacy. A Creative Reflection on Intimacy, Loneliness, Sexuality and Commitment (Notre Dame: Ave Maria Press, 1982), p. 23.

38. JOHN PAUL II has recently recalled, as "above all important to underline," "the equal dignity and responsibility of women with men," in FC, par. 22 (p. 107; tr., p. 43). See also GS, par. 49 (p. 1070; tr., p. 253): "... the unity of marriage will radiate from the equal dignity of wife and husband, a dignity acknowledged by mutual and total love."

39. B. J. BOELEN, "Personal Maturity and the Christian Family," Listening, 15 (1980), p. 41.

40. D. M. REED, "Traditional Marriage," in B. J. SADOCK, H. I. KAPLAN, and A. M. FREEDMAN (eds.), The Sexual Experience (Baltimore: Williams and Wilkins, 1976), p. 225.

41. B. W. HARRISON, "Sexism...," p. 3.

42. T. SÀNCHEZ, De sancto matrimonii sacramento disputationum tomi tres (Nuremberg: J. C. Lockner, 1701. First edition in 1602), q. 1 (pp. 214-215).
43. T. TARCZYLO, Sexe..., pp. 35-36.
44. R. MEHL, Society..., p. 29.
45. See also J. ISAAC, Réévaluer..., p. 141; G. BONNET, Au nom de l'Église..., p. 66.
46. T. MACKIN, "Consummation: of Contract or of Covenant?," The Jurist, 32 (1972), pp. 330-348, shows that, in recent R. C. magisterial documents as far back as Pius XII, marriage is seldom called a contract anymore. It is referred to as a covenant. For the traditional prevalence and meaning of this notion see P. F. PALMER, "Christian Marriage: Contract or Convenant?," Theological Studies, 33 (1972), pp. 617-665.
47. J. LACROIX, L'Échec (Paris: Presses Universitaires de France, 1964), p. 36.
48. Marrying..., pp. 104-107.
49. R. MEHL, Society..., p. 44.
50. P. De LOCHT, The Risks of Fidelity (Denville: Dimension Books, 1974), pp. 6 and 10-11.
51. For this notion of conjugal sexual fidelity, see, e.g., J.-Y. JOLIF, "Le temps d'aimer," Lumière et Vie, 11/60 (1967), pp. 21-52; C. DUQUOC, "The Sacrament of Love," in G. CRESPY, P. EVDOKIMOV, and C. DUQUOC, Marriage and Christian Tradition (Techny: Divine Word, 1968), pp. 119-177; A. DUMAS, "Théologie biblique de la fidélité," in J. COLETTE et al., Engagement et fidélité (Paris: Cerf, 1970), pp. 9-23; J.-P. JOSSUA, "The Fidelity of Love and the Indissolubility of Christian Marriage," The Clergy Reiview, 56 (1971), pp. 172-181; P. De LOCHT, The Risks...
52. UNITED NATIONS, Department of Social Affairs, Population Branch, The World Population in 1970. Population Study No. 49 (New York: United Nations, 1971), p. 32.
53. A. GUINDON, "Le témoignage sexuel des personnes âgées," Église et Théologie, 16 (1985), pp. 107-133.
54. The problem of fidelity to children, if there is any, is structurally another problem and it is not considered in this chapter.
55. See, e.g., C. DUQUOC, "The Sacrament...," pp. 169-177; J.-P. JOSSUA, "The Fidelity...," pp. 175-181; P. De LOCHT, The Risks..., pp. 63-68. This concern was well expressed in the 1980 Synod on the family by Canadian Archbishop H. LÉGARÉ: see "Current Situations: Value, Risk, Suffering," Origins, 10 (1980), pp. 280-282.
56. See also R. GRIMM, Ce qu'aimer veut dire? Une réflexion théologique sur l'amour conjugal (Paris: Cerf, 1981), p. 147.
57. According to J. Le DU, La Tentation de Jésus ou l'économie du désir (Saint-Brieuc: SOFEC, 1977), p. 30, Jesus maintains a historical economy of salvation against Satan's plea for instantaneity in Mt 4: 1-11 and Lk 4: 1-13.
58. E. E. WHITEHEAD and J. D. WHITEHEAD, Marrying..., pp. 309-330,

particularly pp. 316-318. See also D. W. AUGSBURGER, Caring Enough to Confront (Scottdale: Herald Press, 1980).

59. J. THOMAS, "Le temps du vertige," Christus, 20 (1973), p. 95. See S. G. LUTHMAN, Intimacy. The Essence of Male and Female (Los Angeles: Nash, 1972), whose entire book addresses this issue from a therapeutical point of view.

60. J. SHEA, "A Theological Perspective on Human Relations Skills and Family Intimacy," Concilium, 121 (1979), p. 96.

61. J. M. GOTTMAN, Marital Interaction. Experimental Investigations (New York: Academic Press, 1979).

62. R. MEHL, Society..., p. 155.

63. This is clearly THOMAS AQUINAS's mind. See my study, "La 'crainte honteuse' selon Thomas d'Aquin," Revue Thomiste, 69 (1969), particularly pp. 611-619.

64. See the good analysis of J. ISAAC, Réévaluer..., pp. 100-105.

65. This last point is well taken in P. AUDOLLENT et al., Sexualité..., pp. 41-42.

66. AUGUSTINE, Confessions of St. Augustine, Bk. I, c. 1 (Garden City: Image Books, 1960), p. 43.

67. K. GILBRAN, The Prophet (New York: A. A. Knopf, 1969), p. 16. P. TEILHARD DE CHARDIN makes the same point less poetically in Human Energy..., p. 75.

68. D. J. LEVINSON et al., The Seasons of a Man's Life (New York: Ballantine, 1979), pp. 209-221.

69. Ibid., p. 268.

70. Ibid., p. 269.

71. G. F. Von LEFORT, The Eternal Woman. The Woman in Time and Timeless Woman (Milwaukee: Bruce, 1965). I have criticized this interpretation of femininity (and masculinity) in "L'être-femme: deux lectures," Église et Théologie, 9 (1978), pp. 111-141.

72. "Original case," because the O'Neills changed their views a few years later: see N. O'NEILL, The Marriage Premise (New York: Bantam, 1978).

73. N. O'NEILL and G. O'NEILL, Open Marriage. A New Life Style for Couples (New York: M. Evans, 1972); "Open Marriage. A Synergic Model," Family Coordinator, 21 (1972), pp. 403-409; "Open Marriage. Implications for Human Service Systems," Family Coordinator, 22 (1973), pp. 449-456; "Marriage...," pp. 231-237. For a view of "open marriage" which does not involve outside coital relationships, see also: J. J. KNAPP and R. N. WHITEHURST, "Sexually Open Marriage and Relationships: Issues and Prospects," in B. I. MURSTEIN (ed.), Exploring Intimate Life Styles (New York: Springer, 1978), pp. 35-51; E. E. WHITEHEAD and J. D. WHITEHEAD, Marrying..., pp. 331-339.

74. This problem is well identified by B. W. HARRISON and J. HARRISON, "Some Problems...," pp. 76-80.

75. See, e.g., C. ROGERS, Becoming Partners. Marriage and Its Alternatives (New York: Dell, 1972); I. B. PAULY, "Premarital and Extramarital Intercourse," in B. J. SADOCK, H. I. KAPLAN, and A. M. FREEDMAN (eds.), The Sexual Experience (Baltimore:

Williams and Wilkins, 1976), pp. 262-267; W. H. MASTERS, V. E. JOHNSON, and R. C. KOLODNY, Human Sexuality..., pp. 307-311 and 494-495; L. J. SARREL and P. M. SARREL, Sexual Turning Point..., pp. 159-169.

76. See R. J. UDRY, The Social Context of Marriage (Philadelphia: J. B. Lippincott, 1966); B. I. MURSTEIN, Love..., passim. Our own society is wavering in this belief. The result of an inquiry on whether the Québécois believed that extramarital coital relationships were always evil, researchers found that only 33.1% of them did compared with 60% of all Canadians and 72% of Americans: J. J. LÉVY and A. DUPRAS, "L'extramaritalité, facteur de rupture dans le couple québécois?," Revue Québécoise de Sexologie, 1 (1980), pp. 248-251.

77. As J. DONZELOT points out in The Policing of Families (New York: Pantheon, 1979), pp. 171-188, the Church has nothing to be proud of for having sided, for reasons which were often far from being disinterested, with the nineteenth- and twentieth-century parternalistic discourse on bourgeois society.

78. E. ERIKSON calls our attention to this in E. HALL, "A Conversation..," pp. 24 and 26.

79. See the courageous intervention in the 1980 Roman Synod by Canadian Bishop R. LEBEL, "Oppression of Women: Sinful Situation," Origins, 10 (1980), p. 302. Also the intervention submitted on the behalf of the U. S. National Conference of Catholic Bishops, "Changing roles of Women and Men," ibid., pp. 299-301. There are but faint echos of those pleas in FC, par. 23 (pp. 107-109; tr., pp. 44-46). See also the intervention of L.-A. VACHON, Archbishop of Quebec, in the 1983 Roman Synod on reconciliation: "La réconciliation hommes et femmes dans l'Église," L'Église Canadienne, 17 (1983), pp. 101-102.

80. J. P. AUDET, Structures of Christian Priesthood. Home, Marriage and Celibacy in the Pastoral Service of the Church. The Origin of a Tradition and its Meaning for Us Today (London: Sheed and Ward, 1967), pp. 53-76.

81. See P. RÉMY, "Le mariage, signe de l'union du Christ et de l'Église. Les ambiguïtés d'une référence symbolique," Revue des Sciences Philosophiques et Théologiques, 66 (1982), p. 407.

CHAPTER SIX

FAMILY FECUNDITY or CELEBRATING LIFE

If sexual fecundity plays a much greater part in human existence than fertility, the practice of sexual fecundity, since it is conditioned by spatial and temporal factors, remains limited in each one of us. We can be sexually fruitful solely toward persons who are present to us. Even then, our capacity to enhance human life is affected by all those factors of the human condition which restrain the expression of our boundless desires. We cannot bring the amount and quality of caring presence to all those people with whom we interact during the course of a lifetime.

The decision to share one's life or an important part of one's life with other human beings sets the scene for a privileged exercise of sexual fecundity. The family is the result of such a decision and represents a privileged setting for human fecundity. Even though "doomwatchers" of family life exist[1] and even though many families do breed destructive violence instead of caring love,[2] most people would acknowledge that prolonged face-to-face, nonmanipulative interactions are in short supply outside the family. In one of the best contributions to the contemporary R. C. magisterial discourse on the family, the Bishops of Quebec write: "The family appears to us as a privileged location where each one can feel at home, where each one can be loved and be recognized for what he or she is, where each one can make his or her own contribution."[3]

This chapter is nothing more than an attempt to explore some aspects of the sexual fecundity of the family. Most aspects of child-rearing - some of them very unromantic - will not be touched upon within our limited perspectives. The reader must keep in mind, therefore, that, though it examines a basic aspect of family interactions, this chapter does not tell the whole story.[4] Moreover, any treatment of the family faces formidable obstacles. The following remarks are intended to anticipate at least three such obstacles and, at the same time, to delimit somewhat the scope of this exposition.

To seek the expressions of sexual fecundity in family relationships presupposes a certain state of culture in which survival tasks are not so oppressive, because of the lack of elementary technology, that reproduction and the rearing of offspring polarize all familial energies and oblige one of the spouses to be sacrificed to the chore of providing, the other to that of nursing.[5] Sexual fecundity has greater opportunities to be creative when those conditions have been superseded and a unit meets the criteria of a "companionship" type of family. I believe that sociologist Ernest Burgess and his co-researchers are right when they claim that such a family unit fosters a much wider range of mutual self-expression than an "institutional" type of family linked with another state of culture.[6] In my opinion, moral practice gains little benefit, though, from knowing which of these categories of family relationships is "the best." Each one has its advantages and its disadvantages. There is no such thing as a pre-established hierarchy of moral goodness among facts. The most we can say is that, given this set of cultural facts, this type of fecundity is liable to make better sense of family relationships than another type. Family sexual fecundity will be described here according to a sexual paradigm which is marked by the bio-sociological and cultural realities which prevail in North America today. No opinion will be voiced regarding the sexual fecundity of Zambian, Brazilian, or Chinese families. Some of the ideas expressed in this chapter may apply to their own situation, but I do not know that they do.

Second, a treatment of sexual fecundity within the intimate family circle calls for precisions concerning the very nature of familial relationships. Here, the pitfall of univocal definitions of "family" must be avoided. Not so long ago, the family experience of a majority of North Americans was - to use Talcott Parsons's well-known terminology - that of a "nuclear family" constituted by a mother, a father, and their own socially recognized children, living together under the same roof.[7] We were told by sociologists that this kind of family experience was a very new thing. We learn today that this history of the nuclear family as characteristic of industrial societies is largely mythical, an invention of theoreticians in need of a family history which would suit their theories. The careful studies of the Cambridge Group for the History of Population and Social Structure, directed by Peter Laslett, have established beyond dispute that nuclear families already existed and were prevalent in North-Western Europe many centuries before the industrial revolution.[8] One thing is clear: the history of family structures and relationships is not a simple one and we should avoid sweeping statements.

Until Carol Stack redefined family as "the smallest organized, durable network of kin and non-kin who interact daily, providing the domestic needs of children and assuring their survival," she simply could not find "families" in the world of "The Flats."[9] Stack's discovery of another model of "family" in this black community called "The Flats" is also becoming, mutatis mutandis, everybody's discovery in North American society. From our everyday experience, we are learning that the nuclear family which our parents took for granted is not self-evident anymore, not even for ordinary people leading ordinary lives in their ordinary world.[10] According to the population census of Canada in 1976, one "family" out of ten is a lone-parent family (1,048,355 children were members of such families) and nearly one out of three families (31.1%) were childless.[11] In the United States, one child out of four is, or is about to become, a member of a family reconstituted by two divorced parties and their respective children.[12] To these statistics, others could be added concerning "families" or "households" constituted by members of three generations or where children live with their grandparents, families composed of many married or unmarried adults with or without children, gay couples living together with or without children, and so forth. The global result is that, both in Canada and in the United States, the majority of people live in primary social units which no longer verify the definition of a Parsonian family.

The adjective "family," which qualifies the fecundity studied in this chapter, will not refer, therefore, to this or that model, real or theoretical, of family. Instead, it designates qualified types of human relationships, mainly parental and filial ones. Only incidentally will the fecund relationships between parents themselves, between siblings, and between children and other kin, be touched upon. Since family fecundity has a constitutive social dimension, the sexual fecundity of a domestic family unit toward the larger community in which it exists will also be considered.

Finally, and this is my third preliminary caveat, family discourses generally assume some theoretical definition of family which purports to explain what constitutes familial solidarity. Some theories are primarily biological : blood relations and mating constitute their main focus. Others are clearly sociological: they are concerned with reproduction, socialization, patrimony, maintenance of the labor force, kinship, and so forth. Both those theories characterize the discourse held on family throughout the Middle Ages and the whole pre-industrial era. In the last two centuries, a third theory completed, and sometimes supplanted the two others. This, as Mary Durkin explains, is probably because "we no longer find the society needing monogamous marriage to assure the continuation of the society, the economic survival of the mother and child, or the continuation of family property."[13] As the family became less important as a reproductive and productive unit it gained in significance as a source of affection and of emotional support. This "surge of sentiments," analysed by historian, Edward Shorter, marked a change in family priorities.[14] As a consequence of this social shift, a psychological theory was added to the biological and the sociological theories. This latter explains family solidarity in terms of its psychological structure.

119

Ethicians cannot be satisfied with any one nor the sum total of these functionalist theories of family. As Bernard Boelen rightly observes, such theories do not tell us the whole story. They do not describe the basic family experience which is that of "a social group in which one is, in which one is involved with one's entire personality."[15] This remark brings us back to the fundamental question raised in the second chapter of this book concerning sexual anthropology. What is true of persons holds also of their community. Family relationships are essentially interpersonal relationships in which the members' very existence is shared. In this sense only can the family become, as Vatican II has it, a "school of deeper humanity."[16] In the absence of such an ontological view of family, can ethics become a discourse on ultimate concerns? It would have to be content, it seems to me, with pragmatic calculations of short-range benefits. Such a discourse has nothing to tell us about our humanity as family people. Because they are based on non-ontological definitions of family, most moral considerations are, as a matter of fact, ethically wanting and, in my judgment, ultimately inconsequential.

In this chapter, therefore, we will be looking at types of human relationship (mainly that of parent to child and of child to parent) rather than at this or that model of family. We will be thinking in terms of a culture where family relationships are generally experienced as a shared experience of the member's very existence and not merely as biologically, socially or psychologically useful rapports. And we will be asking ourselves: What are the characteristic features of fecundity in the sexual language spoken between parent and child?

The literature on the specifically sexual aspects of family relationships is (with the exception of the issue of sexual integration) wanting. Also, this chapter examines a number of family interactions with a view to uncovering and articulating their significance in terms of sexual integration, interpersonal communication, creative love, and social responsibility. Having sought to make sense of it all, I have come to the conclusion that family fecundity is the ongoing story of life's celebration.

1. EMBODIMENT OF TENDERNESS

If the Second Vatican Council clearly sets aside the old problematic concerning the goals of marriage and their hierarchical organization, it does not hesitate to state that "children are really the supreme gift of marriage."[17] The Council resists recipe seekers who crave for casuistic solutions to reproduction-related problems.[18] Instead, it urges couples to exercise responsible parenthood.[19] In so doing, the Council

120

removes reproductive considerations from the biologism into which they had sunk. In a filial relationship which is the result of a responsible parental decision the child finally appears as the word made flesh in the human community.

Not unlike the reproductive gesture itself, the whole parental language directed at enhancing the child's life is sexual. Already, the sexual quality of the conjugal relationship itself establishes the intimate and warm milieu which is needed for a child's healthy development.[20] Where the intimacy of conjugal life is broken off, warns Vatican II, the good of the child is imperiled.[21] What is to be feared most in collective educational experiments like that of Israeli kibbutzim is precisely the impoverishment of the sensual and tender atmosphere of the educative matrix.[22]

There is more to the sexual dimension of parenting than the quality of conjugal sexual language. The parent-child relationship itself cannot be de-sexualized without causing detriment to the human quality of the communication between the parent and his or her child. Only in gestures which give flesh to words of acceptance and trust will parent and child really acknowledge each other. Wherever their allegiance lies, sexologists and psychologists are unanimous in thinking that a child who has not been warmly caressed and hugged by a parent throughout his or her development will experience serious difficulties in recognizing that he or she is special and lovable. Such a child will have trouble acquiring enough trust in his or her world to feel at ease and move comfortably in it.[23] Physical contacts of the parent with the child mediate the loving language of the parent.[24] The joyous acceptation by the child of his or her own body and sex, of sexual otherness, and of the sensual modalities of human communication hinges, to a large extent, on the tenderly sensuous quality of parental fecundity.[25]

What is true of parents towards children also applies to siblings among themselves. Although sometimes quite subtly, affection is constantly being manifested in the playful bodily contacts of brothers and/or sisters, in shared secrets, in fights and reconciliations, in the protection given to the younger children by the older ones, in the confidence the younger ones place in the elder ones. This daily intimate intercourse with these very real beings, one's sisters and brothers, works towards the success of the processes of sexual identity, of objectal sexual choice, of sexual integration.

In his book on families in the old society, Jean-Louis Flandrin shows that, while we witness an emerging new sensitivity to the quality of family relationships at the beginning of the eighteenth century, warm and tender affections within the family circle remained a largely ignored phenomenon amongst Christian moralists.[26] In the sin ethics devised for confessors, the sexual celebration of family life found no place. The time has come to change our perspective and learn from contemporary experience which teaches that a family which enjoys being together establishes the proof of parental sexual fecundity. Families where parents are sexually fruitful are festive families.

If it is true, as Thomas Aquinas thought along with Aristotle, that pleasure signifies the success of human accomplishments,[27] families in which it "feels good" to live facilitate the strengthening of personalities, the blossoming of liberties, and the development of creativity. Family interactions which are generally morose and sensually frustrating cannot be considered virtuous unless one has a merely conventional and pejorative idea of virtue. Parents who sacrifice the quality of the sexual language to the regulation of conventional behaviour and of consumption destroy the very substance of this "good" which structures and nurtures the family bond.[28] Families where members have not learned to celebrate life with pleasure are schools of insecurity and anxiety and, oftentimes, of bitterness and violence.[29]

Like all other corruptions of virtue, the vice of sexual fecundity toward a born child can be found on the side of deficiency as much as on the side of excess. Even in our culture, where the rights of human sexuality have been vindicated, many parents are still extremely uncomfortable in their own flesh. This lack of sexual integration renders communication with their child arduous. This is a tragedy. For whether or not one agrees with the Parsonian theory of the American family, one can hardly deny the fact that contemporary forms of family have assumed the function of intimate support of the individual.[30] The Muria in central India have (or used to have) a youth dormitory, the Ghotul, where children and adolescents sleep together, learn bodily intimacy from each other, and receive mutual emotional support.[31] Similar social institutions for intimate support exist or have existed in other societies. But in Canada and in the United States today, the family is the locus where early sexual apprenticeship is expected to occur, where the body image will be formed in the child by the internalizations of skin sensations.[32] Yet, experimental findings indicate that white North American parents, especially fathers, refrain from touching their children, notably male children. The male child is socialized into non-touching. He is cut off from his own sensuality. The female child is touched more, but she is also taught that she cannot reciprocate. The message is clear: she is more a potential erotic object than a sensuous person.[33]

Parents who are badly established in their sexual identity will, on the contrary, blur, even completely erase, the distinction which exists between two kinds of sexual relationships, namely, conjugal and parental. Such parents do not seem to understand that the intentionality of these two family relationships differs radically. The conjugal sexual language seeks a unitive presence in a life-long covenant. This language is oriented towards consummation and wholeness of presence in coital togetherness. The parental caress, while it establishes the kind of warm, supportive, and caring presence which fosters peaceful trust and security, also intends the child's long-range independence and separation from the parent. A study has found that when parents are divorced, boys who live with their father and girls who live with their mother are generally more affable, less demanding, better integrated, more sociable, and more independent than children living with the other-sex parent. The authors of the study believe that the former arrangement avoids the sexual ambiguities which arise when the child becomes the emotional substitute for the absent spouse.[34] Divorced or not, a parent who is having his emotional needs met through his relationship with his child is unable to grant him or her the autonomy he or she needs to grow up healthy. This is not parenting, but smothering. This is as unhealthy for the parent as for the child.[35]

Parental sexual fecundity is obviously vitiated when the parent treats his child as an object of self-appropriation. If there is something we should have learned from Sigmund Freud, it is that in order to become a man or a woman a young person must initiate an operation of differentiation from his origin. As Xavier Thévenot remarks, language, here again, is instructive. Castus (chaste) and incastus (incestuous) are antinomic. To become chaste (or sexually integrated) the young man and woman must refuse parental almightiness and indifferentiation. A parenthood which utilizes the child to satiate sexual desire at the expense of the latter's liberation is one which is unchaste/incestuous.[36]

No one will be astonished to learn that experimentally verifiable negative outcomes of incest for children are generally associated with unloving, unsupportive, incommunicative, and forceful incestuous affairs.[37] In such cases, the profound meaning of incest is acted out overtly and naturally produces measurable trauma. Nor are such cases of violent incestuous incidents exceptional. The recent literature on the sexual abuse of children draws our attention to the fact that the family is where such abuse mostly occurs.[38] But neither should we disregard this other fact: of its very nature, incest is never oriented toward the child's liberation from parental bonds. Hence, even where the emotional context is at its best, we should not expect the child's long-range development to be enhanced by it. The extent of the incest phenomenon in our society, therefore, is rather dismaying.[39] Even in the absence of incestuous behaviour properly speaking, mores such as the display of conjugal coital relations in front of one's child raise serious questions concerning the dwindling of the sense of parenthood in some families. One is hard put to explain how conduct of this nature achieves anything positive in terms of humanization.

To acknowledge these facts is not the same as to swing over to the contrary vice. To dry out parental fecundity is neither more virtuous nor more meritorious than to lead it astray. "How then," ask parents, "should we act sexually with our child?" It is quite useless, in my opinion, to give quantitative prescriptions to parents who tend to overprotect themselves and their child against the risks inherent in sexual apprenticeship. Admittedly, some common-sense advice may help some parents to reassess their sexual behaviour.[40] There are serious reasons to suspect that warm parental affection has been replaced by non-parental responses when frequent genital arousal occurs while a parent is interacting with a child and the child starts to have unexplained problems of sleeping, eating, or other physical discomfort.[41]

As soon as such "clinical statements" are made, they need to be qualified. In caressing a daughter, for instance, even a young daughter, a father may find that he is sexually aroused. As Shirley Luthman remarks, there is a very simple reason for this: a human being cannot separate human warmth from his sexuality, and may I add, his sexuality from his genitality. If this father interprets his sexual emotions as manifestations of tenderness toward his daughter and as recognition of her nascent feminine difference, he can easily accept them and remain in charge of his conduct. If, on the contrary, he reacts to his own emotions with fear, he will lose control. Normally, this will lead him to take a distance from his daughter, either by avoiding all physical contact with her or by inhibiting his emotions, sometimes by becoming uselessly punitive. As we saw above, fear of homosexuality makes him commit the same errors in relation to his son. The child inevitably perceives the father's reservations towards her (or him) and, more often than not, decodes them as messages of self-depreciation.[42]

Intentionality is so much an essential part of morality - particularly in the case of virtues dealing with interior feelings like chastity[43] - that sexual casuistry is, to a great extent, an illusory game. It is extremely difficult to establish guidelines which distinguish touching which is allowed from touching which is forbidden, or bodily zones which are "decent" from those which are off-limits.[44] Those who worry so much about what "parts" of their child they may touch may have an inadequate experience of the sexual caress. Contrary to touching of a practical or a scientific sort, a human caress does not seek to make its object present by the adjunction of parts one with the other. In a caress, one "part" is touched in such an intense and diffuse way that the whole body somehow resonates in it. The part of the body which is caressed (the hair, for instance) becomes the whole. Not to have touched someone in this way is never to have caressed a person but, rather, to have merely touched a body-thing. Body-part oriented questions come from this impoverished experience of communication between body-individuals whose "detachable parts" seem to be of unequal value. I cannot relate to this latter experience and, therefore, neither can I consider ethical questions seeking quantitative answers which arise from this peculiar experience of "having" a body instead of "being" one.

It is not enough for parents to learn for themselve how to touch their child in ways which are tenderly sensuous and yet unambiguously parental. They should also recognize that the infant, the child, and the adolescent must consent to numerous sexual apprenticeships. Through a sequence of developmental stages beginning already in utero,[45] the child proceeds slowly to learn the sexual language. The child learns from birth to age 5 or 6, to establish orally, anally, and genitally a sensuous rapport with his or her world;[46] from age 2 to $6\frac{1}{2}$, to recognize herself or himself as girl or boy with stability and consistence;[47] from age 6 to 12, to develop a large part of his or her sexual potential particularly through dynamic fantasies;[48] then, starting with puberty, to undertake numerous and complex tasks of self-erotization, of definite objectal choice, and of sexual integration through the practice of a more conscious and explicit sexual language spoken to peers.[49] How naive an illusion it would be to imagine that such necessary sexual apprenticeships are successfully achieved in ignorance, in the verbal and gestural non-saying of oneself, and in shameful fear of every sexual manifestation of the intimate self![50] Falsely justified by the myth of a "latency period" during which the child needs to be protected from sexual realities and discussions, a conspiracy of silence is practiced in many families. Otherwise intelligent and sensible persons behave as if the classical axiom following which "practice makes perfect" would not apply in the realm of juvenile sexuality.[51]

Without confusing sexual apprenticeship and sexual obsession, parents should recognize that children have an inalienable right to sexual information and to a sexual life of their own since they are also sexual beings.[52] Parental dramas in reaction to a child's readings, conversations, inquisitiveness, or erotic activities (masturbation for instance) more often than not manifest a total misunderstanding of the exigencies of a healthy psychosexual development. Far from being disturbed by their child's sexual discoveries, integrated parents rejoice over them and lead their child into a correct appreciation and celebration of them. As Maurice Champagne-Gilbert writes in his perceptive book on the family, parents themselves are best situated to make the child familiar with the nude, for instance, while tactfully respecting the sense of decency which each child needs, according to his or her age and other given circumstances. Parents are better placed than anyone else, as a general rule, to tell a child about the beauty and the meaning of the nude, about the transparency, the fragility, the power, and the movement of the human body in its world.[53] The parents themselves should validate the sexual sensations which a normal child has already appreciated and legitimatize sexual pleasure in a way which is significant.[54] In other words, since most would admit that human sexuality is a good thing, and further agree that parents are the primary sexual educators of their children, it makes sense to affirm that parents should teach their children, mainly through their own parental sexual language, that sexuality is a normal, good, pleasurable, and creative reality to be developped, understood, and celebrated.

If so many parents are unable to handle this natural reality in a natural way, it might be an indication that sexual education is merely the tip of the iceberg. The iceberg is the whole sensitive life and its humanization. Sexual language uses all the senses to convey its intimate meanings. The ease with which tenderness and sensuality are integrated hinges not solely on the quality of the human values family members believe in and seek to implement in their lives, but also on the sophistication of their sensory equipment. How will parent and child touch each other caringly if touching a person has never been perceived as differing from handling a piece of furniture? How will they look if the contemplation of things of beauty is not part of their experience? How will they smell if natural odours have always been concealed from them? How will they taste if their palate is not refined? In this vast domain, parents have educative duties which are as essential as any other. Even though this will distract us from the main focus of this essay, a few examples are necessary in order to illustrate how sexual fecundity cannot be dealt with adequately as a narrowly understood "sexual problem." This, at least, is the claim of the ontological view which does not see family sexual fecundity as one, separate "sexual function," but as a capacity for festive, life-enhancing communication between family members.

A good place to start refining children's senses - and one which is not unrelated to sexuality - is the family meal. Boys and girls alike should be shown how to prepare and enjoy thoroughly homemade meals. This provides an opportunity to introduce the young to tastes, odours, colours, forms. To smell the rich variety of cooking aromas, to touch the texture of fresh fruits and vegetables, to discriminate by taste the subtle flavours of spices, to arrange dishes with an eye for colours and forms, to set an inviting table and to sit "peacefully" (well...peace is not irreconcilable with a tolerable level of childish pranks and adolescent squabbles!) and converse with others through a meal is one of the most humanizing collective activity families have at their disposal. The disappearance of this activity leaves one skeptical about the success of sexual education in those families where this is occurring. How does one educate without the basics?

Another area which needs to be considered seriously by North American families is ecology-sensitivity training. In the 1980 R. C. Synod of Bishops on the family, it is stated that "the family should cultivate the conservation of nature (the heritage of the human race) through a frugal and simple way of life."[55] If ecological considerations proceed from real awareness, they will not only influence parental fecundity during its first phase, namely, that of responsible decision-making concerning reproduction but will also affect the whole course of education. Sexual integration necessarily implies harmonizing tenderness with our greater body which is the earth. Supported by an ecology-conscious family atmosphere, children should be so much in touch with their embodiment in this endearing little world of ours, in this matrix of all human life, that the sight of ecological plundering should be as intolerable to them as the rape of their own body.[56] It is a far, far better thing parents do for the sexual development of their child when they contribute to the preservation of our natural environment and teach their child respectful appreciation and celebration of it, than when they worry unduly about the dramatic character of every instance of their child's genital behaviour.

The great parental endeavour to help a child embody tenderness affects the parent's own sexual integration. This aspect of a child's own sexual fecundity should not be excluded from the gift that parents "continually receive from their children."[57] The reciprocal nature of most interactions described above already connotes parental sharing of some of the sexual benefits. But the child's, especially the teen-aged child's sexual fecundity toward the parent, has something more specific to offer. Observers of the intimacy of family life have pointed out how parents tend to relive their unfulfilled lives through their children. Sometimes, a spouse must even protect a child from the other spouse's unfinished identity.[58] Just because Mr. Smith has never come to terms with the fact that he is not the athlete he once dreamt of becoming he does not have the right to push his son into athletics. Just because the Jones deplore their own Puritanical courting behaviour they should not prompt their prepubertal child into dating practices for which she is not yet ready. While they avoid such pedagogical errors, other parents, confronted by the vibrant and sexy youth of blossoming adolescent children, either start feeling like "has beens" or, on the contrary, begin competing sexually with their children.

Because similar mistakes by excess or by defect are often made it does not mean that parental sexual development has nothing to gain from the sexual maturing and the dating activities of a child. During the busy and exhausting years of parenting to the very young, parents sometimes place a moratorium on their own sexual development. All their affective energies seem to be drained by the task of being "good parents." A conjugal partner generally claims what little is left as his or hers. But surely a parent's sexual self is not fully expressed upon becoming a spouse or a parent. His or her own sexual self is still rich with unexplored dormant potential. To live in intimacy with young beings whose sexual quest recalls the parent's own yearnings of not so long ago is, for the parent, the occasion to reopen his or her own developmental files. This, the parent does partly through sexual fantasies.

Prior to expressed sexual language lies creative imagination, a vital milieu for the intimate self. The imaginative space between the subject and her adhesion to the tangible world establishes the distance the agent needs to guarantee her capacity to initiate, modify, withdraw, and to recommence so that she can construct an identity that makes sense to her.[59] Creative imagination is the locus where the possible is explored, where every sexual project is begotten, where the sexual innovation and renovation of the agent begins. Sexual fantasies should not be seen first and foremost as "impure thoughts" to be avoided. They are the necessary effects of the free play of creative imagination on our sexual perception and productivity. Without them, we would remain sexually stagnant. The mutilation of erotic imagination by a repressive continence is a deadly vice already denounced by the Ancients.[60]

Through the diverse phases of their own development, adults do not remain sexually fecund without constantly reinventing life, prompted by the great desires which, once upon a time, sustained their foundational options and which, today, feed[61] their assessment of the rich possibilities of their existence. The openness of parents to the sexual experience of the child is most beneficial for the parents' own development. This openness should remain respectful and discreet. Yet, parents should be disposed to receive with honesty and wonder what the child spontaneously reveals of her sexual intimacy. An adult, it is true, has made foundational choices. She has engaged her life on well-determined paths (this spouse, this profession, etc.) and thereby, has excluded many possibilities which, as an adolescent, she could still contemplate. Nevertheless, it remains functional for the adult self not to muzzle her adolescent yearnings and to maintain an active dialogue with them. The dreamless realism of some adults expresses nothing more that a hopelessness, a dryness, and a pragmatism which cannot reinvent life for today. To muster enough energy to pursue our sexual goals, the great desires which triggered our foundational options must be continually rekindled, verified, founded anew, revitalized.

The excess, here, is to deny one's history, to ignore the determinations of one's prior choices and the web of sexual fidelities one has spun. The defect is to negate one's potential, to refuse the fact that we are perfectible creatures, capable, through our God-given liberty, of more self-creativity and fulfilment than we dare imagine. To repudiate existential potency is as serious a crime against human nature as to disavow the actualization of our finite essence. For as long as we travel on this earth of ours, true selfhood will never be fully experienced until we are freed from the narrow definitions in which we enclose ourselves.

By their own sexual fecundity, teen-age children can be a primary source of parental sexual development through the fantasies and desires which they reawaken in their parents. Educators generally encourage children to share with their parents their own sexual questions so that parents may help them sort out their problems. Children should also be heartened in sharing some of their sexual dreams with parents who sometimes seem to have lost touch with their very own sexual reality. It is the duty of teen-age children, it seems to me, to contribute by their own fecundity to the sexual education of their parents and to sustain their parents' own efforts to embody their tenderness more thoroughly.

2. CONFIRMATION OF SELFHOOD

If so many parents experience difficulty in establishing a healthy, easy-going sexual dialogue with their child, it might very well be because the child's own autonomous selfhood has never been clearly affirmed and confirmed in the parents' eyes. The inability of some parents to acknowledge the separation which exists between their own child and their own self often goes back to the attitude which presided over the child's very conception. The rectitude of a child's insertion into a properly human world is dependent upon the rectitude of the dialogue of intimacy in which the parents have desired and conceived his very existence. "Even before being born," writes Louis Beinaert, "the child already exists in the word of the spouses, in the mutual desire they have of each other, in the destiny which is assigned to another by everything which is put in his evocation."[62]

The child ought to be the living expression of the couple's desire of mutual self-gift. This desire goes beyond itself in another being, one who is loved by the very love which enhances the spouses' own lives. Where such is not the case, the fetus is threatened by abortive parental intentions and the born child runs the risk of being haunted throughout his or her lifetime by defective parental desires.[63] To be pushed into reproduction for reasons other than those emerging from loving self-gift is to will the child as a means.[64] How many parents want a child for goals which are distinct from the child: for perpetuating the family name, for escaping other social responsibilities, for cementing a fragile conjugal bond, for establishing the proof of their fertility, and, perhaps most commonly, in order to gain immortality through a progeny?[65] In so doing, they already set the child up as a being who can be used or abused. While he is still being planned in the mind of his progenitors, he does not enjoy the status of a full-fledged person. He is not a person whose will-to-exist will be generously received and whose differentness and autonomy will become a source of mutual enrichment. Wrongly loved from his very conception, not willed for his own sake or willed different than he really is,[66] this child cannot be welcomed in the family community as a gift.

The realistic capacity and concern needed for establishing and for guiding the next generation characterizes, according to Erik Erikson, the penultimate stage in the process of human maturation leading to "ego integrity."[67] This stage, which he calls "generativity," marks for the parent the end of youth. Generativity also marks the beginning of a gradual expansion of the self's interests and of an authentic libidinal investment in the young beings who, by the very quality of parental fecundity, will be born to themselves.[68] Drawn from anonymity by a parent who, from the dawn of her conception, choses her daily as she is rather than willing her in conformity with the image of badly liquidated archaic desires, the child is in a position to achieve successfully her own sexual identity. Women and men who behave promiscuously are more often than not still looking for their identity in a desperate quest for a caring parent. The interior rage which drives them to belittle others by manipulating them in view of their own felt sexual needs has accumulated since their earliest years. Sexually unfruitful parents have not known how to liberate them, how to deliver them unto their own council.[69] Such parents have failed, therefore, to achieve the very goal of the "ministry" of parenthood which is defined by John Paul II as "a service aimed at helping them [their children] acquire a truly responsible freedom."[70]

No one disputes the fact that a child needs his parent and that the parent who has freely chosen to have a child has contracted child-rearing obligations. The infant is a dependent being. He depends on his parent for the satisfaction of nearly all of his basic needs. The psychological experience of family "hierarchy" is also linked to the experience of having one's needs met by a parent. The modalities of such hierarchy are not as pre-set as some have thought. But family disruptions and problem-children are often the result of not having a well-defined and acknowledged family hierarchy.[71] This situation represents a defect in the necessary recognition of the child's dependence upon a parent.

The opposite excess is the assertion of absolute parental power and authority. This vice characterized, for instance, the child-rearing practices of the early New England evangelical families studied by Philip Greven.[72] As Greven has shown, such a pedagogical doctrine and method formed suppressed selves, selves that were unreconciled with their human condition. Preoccupied with conforming absolutely and unquestioningly to the sovereign will of God, evangelicals were dominated by a persistent and virtually inescapable hostility to the self and to its manifestations. As Greven rightly observes, in eighteenth-century America, this childhood experience of paternalistic power and authority set up the very terms of the 1776 Revolution.[73] Similar conclusions can be drawn for the 1789 French Revolution from Raymond Deniel's study of the conservative Catholic doctrine under the Restoration. "Paternalism" best summarized the essence of their family experience, their political experience, and their religious experience.[74] Both Revolutions were, in Freudian terminology, the murder of the father. They initiated a transition from paternity to fraternity, from authoritarianism to companionship.

These historical experiences are instructive for and have an impact on contemporary parenting. Parents should reflect, first, that each and every time they force a child to do what they want him or her to do by using power alone, they deny that child a chance to learn self-responsibility. This does not mean that coercive methods are never justified. But it does mean that such methods should only be used where others have failed. Second, parents should consider that children, like adults, will normally fight back furiously when such denials begin to represent a threat to their basic freedom.

As the child grows, he or she is less and less dependent on the parent for need satisfaction. The child's developing autonomy is accompanied by a sense of himself as a separate person. It is significant that parents themselves manifest to the child (and do so in a sexual context) that they cannot continually meet his needs. Oral satisfaction is denied with weaning; anal satisfaction is denied with toilet training; parental attention is denied with the arrival of a new baby. Thus it is that the child moves away from the concrete familial embodiment of tenderness very gradually at first and then at an accelerated rate during adolescence and is helped to do so by loving parents.[75] The developing child must come to terms with the evidence that the world is not organized to gratify him or her alone.[76] The parent must learn from experience that too much closeness and caring is just as likely to produce rebellion and

131

break-ups as too much power and authority.[77] The Quebec Bishops appropriately write: "It is primarily through the conflicts, tensions, and tender moments that are part and parcel of the family's daily life that the child, serving an apprenticeship of real freedom which combines autonomy and solidarity with others, learns to live with others."[78]

The successful outcome of the parenting operations whereby a child will gradually make the transition from dependency to responsible autonomy hinges more on the very quality of sexual language spoken between parent and child than on how-to-do recipes. For, as the Rapoport and Strelitz study expresses it, "there are many ways of being a 'good parent': there is no single 'right' kind of parenting."[79] An intimate parental presence which makes the child secure in his or her own selfhood contributes to the transformation of the child's needs into self-service capacities. Is genuine security anything else, basically, than the capacity to take care of oneself, of one's life?[80]

This security-inducing parental fecundity implies a number of things. One is that each child must be allowed to go as far as possible in his personal identity, in his singularity, in his autonomy. Selfhood is not confirmed if each child's differentness is not upheld as a basic value of the sexual dialogue. A parent who tries to impose upon a child the personality traits of another child is inviting psychological disaster: "Look how smart your brother Michael is! See how he studies regularly! Don't you want to join the little league like your brother did when he was your age?" But Bobby is not Michael, should not wish to be Michael, and probably could not care less about acquiring most of Michael's idiosyncracies.

If Bobby should not be made to conform to some preconceived image of who he ought to be as an individual being, neither should he be pushed into a socially pre-determined male role. Roles, both "masculine" and "feminine" ones, should no longer be ascribed by virtue of sex. They are best achieved by virtue of competence and taste. However, since male and female role models will necessarily play an important part in the child's appropriation of sexual roles, the roles parents display in the family circle cannot but have a lasting imprint.[81] It is high time that families become aware of the injustice of perpetuating sexual roles which determine that some categories of persons are "better" than others: men better than women, consecrated celibates better than married people, mothers and fathers better than childless spouses, parents better than children, and so forth. Only with the disappearance of such biases will it become possible to acknowledge realistically the right of every child to develop her or his own individual potential independently of arbitrarily defined roles. Where parental fecundity is creative, the genuine personality of each child is recognized and household responsibilities can be negotiated equitably.

To allow a child to be different from an a priori image of the perfect child and of the male or the female child is already an important contribution of parental fecundity to the child's personality development. Permission to become oneself is not fully granted to the child, however, before he or she is allowed to differ (in the sense both of being unlike and of having an opposite opinion) from his or her parent. Though most parents would spontaneously say: "Of course, my child is different from me!," the behaviour of many of them often betrays a contrary attitude. In his popular books on Parent Effectiveness Training, Thomas Gordon repeatedly illustrates this point. Parents often behave as if they "owned" their children or, again, they do not let their children "own" their own problems and invent their own solutions like real persons do.[82]

Behind such attitudes is a view which holds that, in the family, adults are "mature" and children are not. This appraisal of family hierarchy is ambiguous and has harmful consequences. The message it holds for children is that anything they say or do can never be as perfect as what parents say or do. This is not so in reality. Depending on who they are and the degree of success with which they have mastered the skills which correspond to their stage of development, human persons are more or less competent to accomplish certain tasks. Children's competencies should, therefore, be recognized and allowed to become operative. How will children come of age if parents do not effectively grant them separate rights, ideas, competencies, problems, feelings, and values?

The reverse is also true. Here we touch again upon the child's own sexual fecundity. The fecund child too confirms his parent's selfhood both as an autonomous person and as a parent. The literature on parenting appears to assume, most of the time, that the child interacts with a fixed quantity labelled "an adult." Yet, not unlike the child, the parent is engaged in a developmental process. Filial relationships can deeply influence his or her own adult development. The reaction to an authoritarian parental régime which brought about a "children first, last, and always" philosophy is not a better deal. Child-centered family interactions are neither fairer nor healthier than parent-centered ones. A new resolution is needed which is based "on an appreciation of how parents' preoccupations, needs, and requirements can be reconciled with those of children."[83]

The whole process of helping a child make the passage from a state of utter dependency to one of responsible autonomy is of such an interrelational nature that it cannot but influence the parent's own evolution. The parent is forced to come out of his shell and to take upon himself new demanding responsibilities for someone else's well-being. As he confronts his own intimate existence with that of his child, the parent also learns about his own emotional reactions, limitations, prejudices, values, and so forth. When, notwithstanding unavoidable tensions and conflicts, the child (particularly the teenaged child) responds by a sensually tender recognition of his or her parent, the latter receives an inestimable confirmation of his or her own human significance. However, more specific tasks of infantile sexual fecundity can be described regarding either the female or the male parent.

Sexually fecund adolescents are perhaps more sensitive than those of former generations to the fact that, in our state of culture,[84] the mother is mother only transitorily and a woman forever. Never should these two aspects of her personhood be confused in such a way that, in the eyes of family members, she has no other existence than that of a Mom. The children will be the first ones to suffer from such an attitude. The mother who is made to trade her other womanly interests for the gratifications of motherhood is more likely to press her children into doing what she had to renounce and arouse their guilt at the sacrifices she has had to make for them.[85] Above and beyond such negative results for the family itself, the reduction of the mother's horizons to that of family interests amounts to denying that she ought to play a primordial role in the construction of a male/female society. Perhaps more than their fathers, many of today's teenagers acknowledge that family interactions alone cannot fulfil the life project of a woman whose humanity is no less social than that of a man. Their own intimate way of getting this message across to their mothers (and to their sisters) and of supporting their involvement outside the home is indeed a most precious gift to their mothers' (and sisters') womanhood. A filial attitude which allows a mother to really have and pursue a dream of her own (and not only a life lived vicariously) speaks highly of the quality of a daughter's or a son's own sexual language.

Towards their fathers, the greatest service which sexually fecund sons and daughters can render in North American families today is, on the contrary, to lure them into fathering. Yes, "a 'myth' has come into being in our culture that 'parenting means mothering'."[86] If it is so hard to turn our theoretical statements of the equality of men and women into practice, is it not partly because the notion of the joint parenting of mothers and fathers receives so little effective support?[87] If mothers and children stand to lose from the fathers' absenteeism the fathers themselves are the biggest losers. Findings indicate that they are more unhappy and dissatisfied than anybody else in this situation that they themselves create.[88] On the contrary, men who had the experience of fathering even young children have generally found out how rewarding parental fecundity can be.[89]

Robert Fein is right, it seems to me, when he describes three historical conceptualizations of fathering: a traditional one, a modern one, and an emergent one.[90] In the first perspective, the father is aloof and distant. From him, his child can expect to receive either a patrimony or the means and skills of production. As Bernard Boelen remarks, children of the post-industrial era cannot normally expect that from their fathers.[91] Now that the income of the mother and child often contributes to the family's financial resources,[92] the child buys this training from specialized agencies outside the family. Fathers who still detain the sort of family power which money can buy and who use it to blackmail their children into subservience can only expect disaster. Their children are bound to become either rebellious or venal. The fathers who get the rebellious children are the lucky ones. It is easier to live with a child who contests your tyrannical power than with the knowledge that you have corrupted your own child.

In the modern perspective, fathering means being involved in the child's education: in his or her sexual education, academic achievement, moral and spiritual development, and so forth. My guess would be that most conscientious fathers today conceptualize their parenting role in this fashion. They are out to prove to their children that they know more than their children do. After all, have they not much more "experience" than their children have? They are partly right, of course. Some elements of this conceptualization can be applied more generally and are more lasting than those of the traditional way of viewing fathering.

We should observe, however, that the teaching role which fathers are liable to exercise in what Margaret Mead calls "prefigurative cultures" is reduced. The speed of change is such in this prefigurative culture of ours, technological advancement is so rapid and so revolutionary in nature, the very experience of growing up in our radically transformed world is so utterly different for the children than it has been for their parents, that the generation gap is deep and unprecedented. One of the characteristics of the twentieth century is that each new generation of parents can draw less from its experience to teach its children than the previous generation. Conversely, each new generation of children have a newer experience of the world than children of the previous generation had in comparison with their own parents. In a prefigurative culture, therefore, parents need to learn perhaps as much from their children's experience as children need to learn from parental experience. Without a good amount of goodwill on both sides and an ongoing dialogue, the gap is unbridgeable.[93]

Admittedly, Mead's thesis can be partly challenged and, some fifteen years after she presented it, some pieces of the cultural puzzle are shaped differently. But as I listen closely to the young adults who attend my lectures or who participate in my seminars and as I observe the interactions between parents of my generation and their teen-age children, I surmise that, in general, Mead is right. Most fathers who think that they have a whole lot to teach their teen-agers about the world and who talk and act accordingly lose much of their influence over sons and daughters who sense that, on more than one count, their "old man" is "phased out."

In the emergent perspective of fathering, fathers are less preoccupied with being effective providers (of money, skills, education, etc.) than with being effective nurturers. If they have anything to prove to their children, it is the fact that they love them for who they are. Priority is therefore given to being (with) over doing (for). The ethicist who has an ontological theory of family and who holds that the basic good which structures family relationships and is shared by all is the members' very existence cannot but rejoice wholeheartedly in this newest development in family interactions.

From the prenatal development of the child to his or her leaving the home, today's fathers are included more and more in the child's intimacy. They no longer assume that this is the mother's privilege and prerogative.[94] A greater number of fathers realize that nothing more precious can be given the child (for a child's destiny finally eludes the parent) than a warm, supportive, caring matrix in which self-confirming and self-liberating relationships are possible. Out of their own past experience of the shortcomings of "father-teachers," more attentive perhaps to their child's attitudes, preoccupations, needs and requirements, fathers are discovering that the sexual language is the most adequate means of communication which they have at their disposal to reach their child creatively. Father-nurturers are the real sexual creators of their child. Children whose fathers hesitate to assume this fulfilling role have an obligation to help their fathers have a change of heart and to teach them how to share some of their intimacy. No one else is in a better position to work effectively at this conversion, this change of heart of non-fathering fathers, than their children.

Christian parents should also reflect that the kind of parenting which confirms their child's selfhood is the only effective way to transmit one's faith to a child.[95] A rapport based on authority may succeed in "imposing" and a rapport based on doctrine may succeed in "teaching" but neither rapport establishes faith communication. I give my faith exclusively to someone whom I perceive as deserving my trust. My own experiential knowledge of this person must be such that it arouses in me a loving confidence, that it triggers in me an intimate longing which impregnates my whole life. Only a nurturing rapport of intimacy has the power to awaken in the child a deeply set, loving trust in the parent and a mutuality of faith. Only in this context can a child also experience what is meant when his or her parent confesses that he or she believes in the God of Jesus.[96] I, for one, am rather sceptical about the existence of Christian faith in those who have never experienced faith in another human being. I suspect that what such persons identify as faith is, more often than not, nothing other than a form of fear resembling the one they had for a non-nurturing parent. Since they never had anyone to trust and to believe in, they have never acquired the "courage to be."[97] "Faith" is, therefore, the name they give to the great existential anxiety which presides over their life.

In a society where patriarchalism is still rampant, sexually fruitful children play an important role in supporting their female parent's sense of autonomy and their male parent's sense of affiliation. As for sexually fruitful parents, they establish with their children, from the very dawn of their conception to the time when they leave the nest, the kind of intimate interactions which allow the latter to come into their own with confidence and competence. By the quality of their mutual presence and intimate dialogue, parents and children confirm each others' selfhood.

3. CARING FOR LIFE

If there is a message which comes out clearly in John Paul II's 1980 exhortation on the family, it is that love constitutes the family's central reality. We are told that the family "is founded and given life by love;"[98] that the family essence and role are in the final analysis specified by love; that the family has "the mission to guard, reveal, and communicate love;"[99] that the first task of the family (that of developing an authentic community of persons) has love as its "inner principle, its permanent power, and its final goal;"[100] that "without love the family cannot live, grow, and perfect itself as a community of persons;"[101] that the family "finds in love the source and the impetus for welcoming, respecting and promoting each one of its members in his or her lofty dignity as a person;"[102] that the uniqueness of the loving relationship between parents and children grounds the parents' original and primary right to educate their children;[103] that parental love, as well as being the source of the parents' educational role, is also "the animating principle and therefore the norm inspiring and guiding all concrete educational activity, enriching it with the values of kindness, constancy, goodness, service, disinterestedness and self-sacrifice that are the most precious fruit of love."[104]

This insistence on the primacy of love in family relationships does not imply that the baby, the child or the adolescent should experience only happiness, peace, and other positive feelings. From the very onset of life outside the womb the child is part of a real world of pain and anxieties as well as of joys and satisfactions. Even though the child will see most of his needs met by a loving parental response, he still cannot avoid hurts and conflicts: from his aching body, but also from the angry words of a beloved parent who judges that enough whining or crying is enough, from annoyed or inconsiderate siblings, from the impatience of tired parents toward each others, and so forth. Overprotection of the child from negative parental emotions and conflicts is a mistake. A child who witnesses an honest argument between parents followed by a friendly resolution learns how strong and essential love is in human relationships. This is all part of those interpersonal family relations which, according to the Synod Fathers, "help ensure that attitudes of open dialogue and reverence for others will take root and grow."[105]

The positive outcome of family conflicts presupposes, nonetheless, that parents do not handle them like wars, but like negotiations. Wars always end with an arrogant winner and a humiliated loser (except thermonuclear wars where no one wins and everyone loses). Negotiations are settled with a solution which is acceptable to both parties. For a parent to manage conflictual situations with his or her child creatively, he or she must acknowledge that there is no such thing as a "best" or an already-made solution which a parent ought to know and to impose automatically on the child. One may only hope to find a "good" life-enhancing solution which is acceptable to this parent and to this child in this situation. Some parents seem to think that to negotiate an acceptable settlement instead of winning a war will make their child lose respect for them. This is like thinking that our respect for the Soviet and American leaders would decrease further if they agreed to sign a SALT III instead of building up their nuclear arsenals. What those parents really mean is that their child will lose his or her fear of them. Fear is induced by a threat resulting from an abusive exercise of power. Respect is won by understanding, reasoning, fairness, and benevolent love.

If caring and discerning love is to be fully operative between parent and child, an atmosphere of family intimacy must be fostered in the home. The quality of the family environment is not something incidental to the task of caring for life. Many factors contribute to the success of this family endeavour described by John Shea as "the transformation of physical proximity into intimate closeness."[106] One of them is, paradoxically enough, the setting up of private spaces and times allotted to silence. The intimate self, that which is being shared between persons through the sexual language, needs such living conditions in order to emerge from the realm of the subconscious. The difference which exists between conjugal intimacy and parent-child intimacy explains why privacy is particularly important in the case of the child. Intimacy between spouses is one which, if successful, grows deeper and pervades all of their lives as the years go by. Parent-child intimacy, on the contrary, gradually diminishes in intensity and in scope as the child gains his or her own autonomy over the years. Privacy is as necessary to the sexual life of youth as respiration is to life itself.[107]

The parent must, therefore, respect the private domain of the child, particularly of the adolescent: her room which the parent never enters without knocking and being admitted, his telephone conversations which other family members do not try to intercept on the extension, her mail, his secret drawer, her personal diary. These are but a few of the private items which a parent must scrupulously respect as the sanctuary where the child lives the mystery of his or her personal autonomy. A youth's need for privacy grows with age. A parent must make new adjustments and progressively negotiate with him or her new "house rules" meant to safeguard this privacy.

Silence is another commodity which, though essential to the quality of family intimacy, does not merely come along with the house. A family which does not plan for it and work at it will not find it. Families must learn how to silence, during certain periods of the day, the noises of the exterior world that run the risk of muffling their intimate voices. Those homes where people cannot eat together without a radio or a TV set playing in the same room, where a deafening music invades the whole field of conscious life all day long, where silence cannot be tolerated, are homes that do not provide the atmosphere in which people are mindful of each others' intimate lives. Parents often complain, and rightly so, of the noise produced by children. Yet, few of those parents are aware of the fact that much of their complaining about their children's music stems from the fact that it interferes with their own noise-producing TV addiction. Among the recommendations made by children to Quebec's legislative body during the 1979 Year of the Child, we read the following:

> We ask the Government to recommend to parents
> that TV be shut off one hour a week. Instead
> of watching "The Little House in the Prairie,"
> we could watch what is going on in our own
> living-room.[108]

According to the Synod Fathers, one way parents educate their children is "by personal dialogue with the children in an atmosphere of respect, trust and love where both parents and children listen and learn - without damaging parental authority."[109] When the child's right to privacy is effectively acknowledged and when enough silence is tolerated in the home for people to hear each other out, parents and children can really listen to each other and learn from each other. Listening "for real" is not always possible nor is it always advisable. There might not be enough time to hear out the child to the end or, again, the child may not wish to be heard on a given topic at a given time. Still, parents who wish to listen to a child should not expect him or her to write for an appointment. When 12-year-old Peter storms into the house and, against all the house-rules, slams the door, kicks the dog, throws his things around, pinches his sister, and makes some spiteful remark to his parent, he is obviously unhappy about something and he is probably asking to be heard. A caring parent picks up this body language, makes the child aware that he or she gets the message, and is ready to listen if the child wishes to talk.

Drawing on the responses of more than five hundred professionals who work with families, Dolores Curran has come up with fifteen qualities shared by families these experts call "healthy." At the top of everyone's list was "communication and listening."[110] "Real listening" is demanding. The listener must first manifest, by his or her whole bodily attitude, that the other has his or her undivided attention. Then the listener must be ready to be led by someone else into seeing things that are unfamiliar, or into seeing familiar things with someone else's eyes. This implies that the parent does listen, that is to say that he or she lets the child unwind, tell all the facts, react to them, and give his or her own interpretation and assessment. The attitude of a listening parent is such that even negative feelings are allowed to come out in the open. Negative emotions also serve human goals. Without fear, anger, sadness, hatred, etc., we would be ill-equipped to respond to threats, evils or obstacles. A parent who intervenes continually, warns, scolds, lectures, criticizes, advises, or blocks off negative feelings necessarily distorts the child's own experience or limits its scope. He or she imposes a view which does not correspond to the child's own understanding and cuts off communication.

The way some parents discuss with a child makes one wonder whether they are not trying to demonstrate their own alleged superior intellectual abilities rather than really trying to share something. They should reflect that no one likes to discuss real-life problems with someone who is more intent on scoring a point against you than on helping you out. This does not mean that a parent will not tell the child, when the latter has really been heard and understood, how he or she reacts or what he or she finds acceptable and unacceptable in the child's behaviour and why. When a parent pretends to react positively or to be accepting when his or her body language transmits the contrary, it shows and the child's confidence in the parent is badly eroded. Nothing is more unfair to a child than to say one respects his or her decision or, worse, approves of it and then use one's power to blackmail the child or to get back at him or her.

Some parents would do well to learn or improve their listening skills. But more decisive perhaps than skills is the human quality of their sexual language. The ability to "listen for real" is a typical fruit of sexual fecundity. As an aspect of sexual language, "real listening" does not concentrate so much on the objective content of what the other is communicating as on his or her feelings about this content. In such feelings lies and is expressed one's intimate experience of existing. If a child tells a parent about a good mark in mathematics, this child is less interested in transmitting this bit of information than in telling the parent how proud he or she is of this success. This feeling is what needs to be acknowledged by the listening parent.

Since real listening has a sexual component, the quality of intimacy which lies in the parent's experience is of the essence. A parent cannot effectively learn to listen to a proud child's account of her achievement without first listening to her own intimate voice to identify her personal feelings about such matters. Nor can a parent decide "real listening" is something to start doing here and now with a child who has never been allowed any real self-expression. A child who has always been expected to conform to the parent's unrealistic image of an "ideal child" will not easily tell about her real self. In other words, loss of contact with the intimate reality of the listener and/or of the talker makes real listening extremely difficult. To put oneself in a child's shoes, to live for a moment inside the child and to be able to convey to the child the awareness that the parent feels with her (to exercise what psychologists call "empathy") requires the sort of intimate-reality relatedness which the practice of a well-spoken sexual language alone develops.

Where such conditions prevail, a parent can have the valorizing and caring attitude towards the child which gradually draws him or her out of insignificance and conveys a lasting taste for life. A sexually fecund parent knows spontaneously how to tell a child: "You are a good child. You are like a shining sun which illuminates my life and warms my heart;" "You are smart, skillful, resourceful;" "You are my pride and joy, and I love you so." That our children take us to task, later on, for having been clumsy in certain matters or ignorant of others, for having believed too wholeheartedly in the ideas of our generation, or for having misunderstood some of their ideas or values is perhaps not very serious. Hopefully they will never have to tell us that we did not believe in them enough and that we failed to show them enough loving care. For this would amount to accusing us of infecundity, of having corrupted the very source of human parenthood.

Caring for the child's life opens up the parent's own life to the influence of the child's sexual fecundity. In the "real listening" made possible in a family environment which respects each person's privacy and where creative silence is practiced, the parent has much to learn about himself, about his ideas, behaviour, feelings, biases, options, experience, values, about everything which makes of his life a unique venture. The quality of a parent's life cannot be indifferent, for that matter, to a normal child. A family atmosphere where life is, in fact, the inner principle, the permanent power, and the final goal is one which also enables the child to care lovingly for the life of his parent.

4. REGENERATION OF SOCIETY

Historian Barbara Laslett has shown that, like the idea of childhood itself, the idea of the privacy of the family household is a genuinely modern conception. She quotes authors who insist on the good side of this revolution: it should increase the individual's freedom of choice, foster the development of a stronger moral conscience than previously, and contribute to a better brand of democracy. She also quotes studies showing that the heightened dependence of family members on one another in the intense intimate environment of the home contributes to the sense of loneliness and to confusion.[112] Studies conducted to compare the good and bad sides of the family as a private institution could be endlessly multiplied and yield other interesting results.[113] Because the notion of "privacy" is largely a matter of definition, the validity of such data depends on how private is private - how withdrawn it is from public view or company.

> Since the family is society's basic unit - state the Synodal Fathers - bound to it in a living and organic way, it must be open to other families and communities.[114]

Where a family does not have such openness, privacy stands for "family idolatry." The family and its interests are placed at the center of one's ultimate concern. Such privacy should be denounced by ethicists because it is a source of impoverishment for family members as well as for society at large.[115] Healthy families are characterized by an investment in wide circles of outside concern because they realize that an individual "needs the large society as well as the more intimate family group in order to satisfy the multiplicity of his nature."[116] Moreover, families should be conscious of the obligations which are theirs, as society's basic units, towards society as a whole. Without this social dimension, family fecundity does not pass the test of the fourth moral criterion.

If the idea of the privacy of the family is a modern conception, this is partly due to the advent and expansion of industrial society. As the complex social milieu in which the child lived became poorer, the family increasingly provided the much needed emotional security.[117] No one who is even remotely aware of the kinds of threats which our own society poses to the child will deny that the latter has a greater need than ever before of the emotional security which a family can offer. Think about only one of those new threats, the most ominous of them all, the haunting specter of global thermonuclear war. A nuclear holocaust, because of its unique combination of immensity and abruptness, is a menace without parallel in the known history of humankind. It represents the ultimate ecological peril since it would most probably render the biosphere unfit for human survival. No genocide in history (that of Amerindians, of Jews, of Armenians or of Cambodians) compares with the terror of an abrupt and final halt of all human life on earth, the extinction of the human race, the obliteration of the entire human future on our planet.

What is the impact of this one awesome contemporary threat on children and adolescents? Though little serious research has been conducted on this point, we can safely state that what Robert Lifton calls the "nuclear image"[118] is with them and that it cannot fail to affect their attitudes and behaviour.[119] From their own studies of this influence on children and adolescents of the Boston area, William Beardslee and John Mack observe how compromised is the formation of the psychic structures upon which the development of enduring values depends "in a setting in which the possibility of a future appears to have been destroyed by the adults to whom its preservation was ostensibly entrusted."[120] Similar conclusions are drawn by Sibylle Escalona from her own studies of the psychological effects of growing up with the treat of a nuclear holocaust. She contends that the adult response to the nuclear threat is, to children, the "ultimate test of the trustworthiness of adult society." No child will muster the will and the energy needed to develop long-lasting values and to deeply care for life if the message he or she receives from the adult world does not hold out as a reasonable promise for fulfilment.[121]

Many of the teen-agers' attitudes which diminish their own chances of leading fruitful sexual lives later on (for instance, their difficulty in delaying satisfactions, their distrust of enduring commitments, or their unwillingnes to plan for the future) are often attributed to faulty child-rearing practices. When one examines the literature on the thermonuclear threat, one is struck by the fact that many of the attitudes just mentioned can be attributed as well to the influence of the "nuclear image" and other contemporary global threats such as worldwide poverty, endemic unemployment, environmental pollution or overpopulation. There exists a widespread family mythology to the effect that social relationships are merely a prolongation of

interpersonal relationships learned and lived in the family.[122] We
must realize that family members are largely influenced by social
values as they are experienced in a given historical time and that
family members are also submitted to the rules of social
functioning. When society projects the image of a world without a
future, parenting is not an easy task.

This does not mean that parents have become helpless
in face of such gigantic threats. First, it is important that they
become conscious of the impact of such threats on their
children.[123] This enables them to understand what exactly it is
that they are "hearing" when they listen to their children.
Secondly, having heard correctly, they are in a better position to
educate their children to those realities "so that they [the
children] can be helped to overcome at least that aspect of fear
which derives from ignorance and which leaves them feeling so
powerless."[124] Thirdly, they can help alleviate their children's
insecurity by their own social attitudes and commitments. The
family is generally regarded as a natural and harmonious
association because, precisely, one "feels safe" there.[125] This
feeling can be improperly used by some families as an escape from
social realities and responsibilities. Of itself, though, this
feeling fosters the development of a much needed sense of trust
and of security in the child.[126] Confident and purposeful parents
provide the loving and committed model the child needs to believe
that others merit our trust, that significant and enduring
relationships are possible, and that the future may not be so
hopeless after all. Fourthly, where such a family atmosphere
exists, parents can successfully train their children in active
non-violent methods for dealing with issues of justice. This,
write the Bishops of the United States in their remarkable 1983
pastoral letter on war and peace, will "enable their children to
grow up as peacemakers."[127]

In these threatening times of ours, Christian children
have much to learn about Christian responsibility for the world
from confident and socially committed parents. A widespread strain
of Christian thinking - notably, though not exclusively, in the
Protestant tradition - has played God's sovereignty against human
liberty to such an extreme that the recent perspective of nuclear
obliteration of the human species poses, for Christians of this
school of thought, an unsolvable dilemma: either God wills this
unspeakable destruction as the ultimate purification and there is
nothing anyone can do about it; or God will not allow this
terminal holocaust and there is no need for us to worry about the
coming of Armageddon.[128] Why should we understand divine
providential care as opposed to the total human responsibility for
the future of humankind? Is not the God of Christian faith great
and secure enough in his own triune personality to respect
integrally a human freedom He creates?[129] Why should we wish to
mold Him in the image of our weaker self? What we make wrong -

notably this ultimate human evil which would be a nuclear
holocaust – God can neither make right nor be held responsible
for. To invoke divine will so as to let events follow their
course, let alone to be accessory to thermonuclear self-
destruction, is merely an evasion of our human responsibility for
our own history. The American Bishops address this issue with this
brief but concise formula: "The perfect world, we Christians
believe, is beyond the horizon in an endless eternity where God
will be all in all. But a better world is here for human hands and
hearts and minds to make."[130] Christian parents who put their
hands and hearts and minds to making a better world provide a
realistic basis for the strengthening of their child's trust and
hope.

A living Christian hope manifests itself by the
setting up on our earth of the loving conditions which reveal and
actualize God's real presence and redemptive action in our midst.
In the absence of active or missionary hope, prayer is pure
magical incantation. I see no other serious way of interpreting
the evangelical beatitudes in Matthew 5: 1-12.[131] What better
ground is there for the burgeoning of Christian hope in a child's
heart than the responsible commitment of a prayerful parent to the
future of humanity on earth? How else will a child acquire the
certitude that life is worth living because a life-giving God
dwells among us?

If, as I have suggested, parental sexual fecundity
creates a protective shield against overwhelming social threats
and establishes the security-producing atmosphere which children
need for healthy development, it must also be generous enough to
regenerate society through the gift of its children. If children
are protected, it is in the hope that they will grow strong and
become responsible citizens. A life which would be restricted to
family members would be unfaithful to its own truth. The Synod
Fathers warn that the family "should look out, not only for itself
but also for others so as to create a civilisation of love."[132] If
parental love focuses on the home, it is to better radiate and
warm the surroundings.

Without a relation to this "other," larger community,
the family sinks into incest just as an a-relational individual
sinks into narcissism. Is this not the basic reason why the incest
taboo – though highly dependent on concrete social customs which,
in each human group, govern the reciprocity of exchanges –
constitutes a most primitive phenomenon indicating the presence of
homo socialis?[133] Familial sexual fecundity is that whereby human
beings give rise to sociability itself, that is, to the very
principle of society.[134] The R. C. Church's oft repeated
statements to the effect that the family is the foundation of
society and the first and fundamental school of social living are,
indeed, well-grounded.[135] In point of fact, contemporary youth are

145

so impressed by this connection between family and society that they often adopt a practice of alliance which, following old and widespread customs, does not seek the institutionalization of their sexual union before they have taken a concrete decision to reproduce new life and become family. The family project alone is perceived by many of them as formally social.[136]

As in every other genuine sexual dialogue, the one which is established between family and society unfolds within a process of reciprocity.[137] In the family, the child lives his first socializing experience and learns the social knowledge and skills necessary to engage in associations outside the family sphere.[138] The family's primary task, in this respect, is to transmit to children the fundamental values of society.[139] John Paul II formulated the basic meaning of this duty well in the homily he pronounced during the liturgical celebration opening the Synod of Bishops on the family when he described it as "to guard and preserve humanity itself."[140] It would be a mistake to believe that this most essential task is not a matter of parental sexual fecundity. Following the data of the 1974 NORC survey of American Catholics, the strongest socializing influence drawing the young into a specific value heritage is neither the institutional Church nor the teachings or even the practices of their parents, but the quality of the relationship youth maintain with the significant adults in their lives.[141]

In a world where other institutions have assumed many tasks formerly assigned to the family, neither parents nor siblings may claim to fulfil all the needs of other family members.[142] Seeking new alliances outside the family circle, the child will not only begin to give to and receive from society, but he or she will contribute more than anyone else to opening the family to the greater community.[143] The child forces his or her primary group to avoid a characteristic temptation of nuclear families, that of monopolizing the whole affective life of its members. As I observe what is going on in the families I know, I am more and more convinced that, by their own sexual fecundity, teen-age children socialize their aging parents just as they themselves have earlier been begotten to sociability by their parents.

Christian families who, by their warm and generous hospitality, extend the benefit of their life-enhancing fecundity to other needy human beings[144] become what Michel Legrain calls "space of agape."[145] As efficacious signs of God's Covenant with his People, as the leaven in the ecclesial eucharistic body, they are, as John Paul II reminds us, a small Church (ecclesiola), a domestic church. They are constitutive of the Church in its fundamental dimension.[146] The Great Church, in effect, owes much of its existential reality to the fecundity of the sexual language spoken in the Christian families which are present in the daily existence of the world. Particularly in large urban conglomerations, numbers alone make it extremely difficult for social interactions to come even close to resembling genuine human relationships. The presence of a familial domus civitatis and of a familial domus ecclesiae, a household where a sense of social and ecclesial belonging can be experienced, is a precious gift to the community.

In gaining a new awareness of the family's ecclesial vocation,[147] the contemporary Church is merely rediscovering the primitive situation of an ekklesia (the Christian assembly itself) which sought in the domestic circle the warm natural framework it needed to unfold "all the wealth of its own life: the service of the word, the service of the eucharist, the service of brotherly communion."[148] Historical contingencies have pushed the Church into other institutional frameworks. However, it would be unwise to disregard the family's sexual potential to regenerate not only civil society but the ecclesial community as well.

NOTES

1. See D. G. COOPER, The Death of the Family (New York: Pantheon, 1970); J. R. MADDOX, The Doomsday Syndrome (New York: McGraw-Hill, 1972). In general, "conservative" theology and ethics also reflect a pessimistic and "doomsday" interpretation of contemporary family life.
2. M. A. STAUS, R. J. GELLES, and S. K. STEINMETZ, Behind Closed Doors. Violence in the American Family (Garden City: Anchor Bks., 1980).
3. ASSEMBLÉE DES ÉVÊQUES DU QUÉBEC, "Lettre de l'épiscopat du Québec sur la famille," Documentation Catholique, 72 (1975), p. 518 (my translation).
4. The range of the "whole story" is well presented in R. and R. N. RAPOPORT, and Z. STRELITZ, Fathers, Mothers and Society. Towards New Alliances (New York: Basic Books, 1977).
5. The "experts" generally agree that the passage from the state of culture referred to in the text to the one which has been reached by a majority of people in Western societies is relatively recent. See P. BELTRAO, Sociologia della famiglia contemporanea (Rome: Università Gregoriana Editrice, 2nd ed., 1977), pp. 28-54.
6. E. W. BURGESS, H. J. LOCKE, and M. M. THOMES, The Family. From Institution to Companionship (New York: American Book, 3rd. ed., 1963). It should be noted that the two types of families described in this book represent theoretical constructions. Existing families are never found which fully verify either one of them. They come closer to one or the other type.
7. T. PARSONS and R. BALES, Family, Socialization and Interaction

Process (Glencoe: Free Press, 1955). This social system has also been called the "conjugal family" by W. J. GOODE, World Revolution and Family Patterns (New York: Free Press, 1963), in particular pp. 6-17.

8. P. LASLETT (ed.), Household and Family in Past Time. Comparative Studies in the Size and Structure of the Domestic Group Over the Last Three Centuries in England, France, Serbia, Japan and Colonial North America, with Further Materials from Western Europe (Cambridge: University Press, 1972). - R. L BLUMBERG and R. F. WINCH, "Societal Complexity and Familial Complexity: Evidence for the Curvilinear Hypothesis," American Journal of Sociology, 77 (1972), pp. 898-920, have also shown that in 500 societies about which household data is available, a curvilinear relationship is reported between societal complexity and the family structure. In the simplest societies on the one side and the most complex societies on the other, the nuclear family predominates.

9. C. B. STACK, All Our Kin. Strategies for Survival in a Black Community (New York: Harper and Row, 1974), p. 31. We would argue that Stack defines household rather than family. Properly speaking, household refers to people living together whether related or not. Family refers to relatives whether or not living together. We could speak of domestic family when we wish to designate related persons living together. See R. F. WINCH and R. L. BLUMBERG, "Societal Complexity and Familial Organization," in A. S. SKOLNICK and J. H. SKOLNICK (eds.), Family in Transition. Rethinking Marriage, Sexuality, Child Rearing, and Family Organization (Boston: Little, Brown, 1871), p. 126.

10. Theologians who attempt, like Leo XIII did in his 1880 encyclical letter Arcanum Divinae, ASS, 12 (1894), pp. 385-402, to describe the "Christian concept" of the family, merely show that they are not in touch with reality.

11. STATISTICS CANADA, Canada's Families (Ottawa: Statistics Canada, 1976). Pages are not numbered.

12. A. TOFFLER, The Third Wave (New York: Bantam, 1981), pp. 230-231.

13. M. DURKIN, "Intimacy and Marriage: Continuing the Mystery of Christ and the Church," Concilium, 121 (1979), pp. 74-81.

14. E. SHORTER, The Making of the Modern Family (London: Collins, 1976).

15. B. J. BOELEN, "Personal Maturity...," p. 35.

16. GS, par. 52 (p. 1073; tr., p. 257).

17. GS, par. 50 (p. 1070; tr., pp. 253-254).

18. See J. GROOTAERS, "Histoire...," p. 153.

19. GS, par. 50 (p. 1071; tr., p. 254).

20. ASSEMBLÉE DES ÉVÊQUES DU QUÉBEC, "Lettre...," p. 518: The family "constitutes an irreplaceable affective milieu for receiving the child and lavishing on him or her, through parental care, the tenderness and warmth which are needed for his or her equilibrium and psychological development" (my

translation).
21. <u>GS</u>, par. 51 (p. 1072; tr., p. 255).
22. L. MACARIO, "Ruoli...," pp. 122-124. This is one of the reasons why there has been a general tendency to go back to a conjugal form of family education; see A. I. RABIN, "The Sexes. Ideology and Reality in the Israeli Kibbutz," in G. H. SEWARD and R. C. WILLIAMSON (eds.), <u>Sex Roles in Changing Society</u> (New York: Random House, 1970), pp. 285-307; also M. GERSON, <u>Family, Women and Socialization in the Kibbutz</u> (Lexington: Lexington Books, 1978), who shows that kibbutz parents follow their children's development more closely than is generally believed and that they remain the key socializers of their children.
23. H. MALEWSKA and G. AMZALLAG, <u>L'apprentissage du comportement sexuel</u> (Tournai: Casterman, 1974), p. 26; E. J. HAEBERLE, <u>The Sex Atlas</u>..., pp. 146-147. At the International Symposium on the sexuality of children held in Montreal in 1979, this point was often made by the participants. See the proceedings edited by J.-M. SAMSON, <u>Childhood and Sexuality</u> (Montreal: Études vivantes, 1980).
24. M. LEGRAIN, <u>Le corps</u>..., p. 95. See the important book of A. MONTAGU, <u>Touching. The Human Significance of the Skin</u> (New York: Harper and Row, 1972). This point has already been made by S. FREUD, <u>Three Essays on the Theory of Sexuality</u> (1905), in J. STRACHEY (ed.), <u>The Standard Edition of the Complete Psychological Works of Sigmund Freud</u> (London: The Hogarth Press and the Institute of Psycho-analysis, 1953-1966), Vol. VII, p. 223.
25. S. JOURARD, "An Exploratory Study of Body Accessibility," <u>British Journal of Social and Clinical Psychology</u>, 5 (1966), pp. 221-231: the findings reveal that the subjects who see themselves as attractive were touched more often and that a relationship existed between the subjects' feeling for their bodies and parents' feelings about the bodies of their children.
26. J.-L. FLANDRIN, <u>Familles</u>..., pp. 150-152, 155-156.
27. THOMAS AQUINAS, <u>In decem libros Ethicorum</u>... L. X, lect. 6, pp. 527-529.
28. See A. GRANOU, "Capital, salaire et famille," <u>Lumière et Vie</u>, 25/116 (1976), pp. 23-32.
29. The link between the lack of physical pleasure and every conceivable form of violence has been demonstrated by a good number of serious studies. For a review of the literature, see J. W. PRESCOTT, "Body Pleasure and the Origins of Violence," <u>Bulletin of the Atomic Scientists</u>, 31/9 (1975), pp. 10-20.
30. T. PARSONS and R. F. BALES, <u>Family</u>..., p. 10.
31. V. ELWIN, <u>The Muria and Their Ghotul</u> (Bombay: Oxford University Press, 1947); <u>The Kingdom of the Young</u> (Bombay/London: Oxford University Press, 1968).
32. Over a quarter of a century ago, studies on touching from a developmental perspective made this point: see L. K. FRANK,

"Tactile Communication," Genetic Psychology Monographs, 56 (1957), pp. 209-255.

33. S. M. JOURARD and J. E. RUBIN, "Self Disclosure and Touching. A Study of Two Modes of Interpersonal Encounter and Their Interrelation," Journal of Humanistic Psycholgy, 8 (1968), pp. 39-48; E. ROBERTS, D. KLINE, and J. H. GAGNON, Family Life and Sexual Learning (Cambridge: Population Education Inc., 1978); N. BLACKMAN, "Pleasure and Touching. Their Significance in the Development of the Preschool Child - An Exploratory Study," in J.-M. SAMSON (ed.), Childhood and Sexuality (Montreal: Études Vivantes, 1980), pp. 175-202.

34. J. W. SANTROCK and R. A. WARSHAK, "Father Custody and Social Development in Boys and Girls," The Journal of Social Issues, 35/4 (1979), pp. 112-125.

35. The "empty nest syndrome" affects most parents only minimally and transitorily. Only those parents who have been overprotective and overinvolved with their child suffer major negative effects. See E. B. HARKINS, "Effects of Empty Nest Transition on Self-report of Psychological and Physical Well-being," Journal of Marriage and the Family, 40 (1978), pp. 549-556; A. G. KAPLAN and M. A. SEDNEY, Psychology and Sex Roles. An Androgynous Perspective (Boston: Little, Brown, 1980), p. 287.

36. X. THÉVENOT, "Christianity...," p. 55.

37. See review of the research literature in L. L. CONSTANTINE, "The Impact of Early Sexual Experiences. A Review and Synthesis of Outcome Research," in J.-M. SAMSON (ed.), Childhood and Sexuality (Montreal: Études Vivantes, 1980), pp. 150-172.

38. See, e.g., A. W. BURGESS et al., Sexual Assault of Children and Adolescents (Lexington: Lexington Books, 1979); D. FINKELHOR, Sexually Victimized Children (New York: The Free Press, 1979); R. L. GEISER, Hidden Victims. The Sexual Abuse of Children (Boston: Beacon Press, 1979). According to the 1983 Canadian National Child Protection Survey, only 1% of all cases of sexual abuse of children involve a person unknown to the child; in 45.8% of cases, the offender is a parent, a sibling or a grandparent; in 67.2% of cases the offender is a family member or holds a guardianship position. See REPORT OF THE COMMITTEE ON SEXUAL OFFENCES AGAINST CHILDREN AND YOUTHS, Sexual Offences Against Children (Ottawa: Canadian Government Publishing Centre, 1984), Vol. I, p. 217. - For a general view of incestuous behaviour today and counseling, see: B. JUSTICE and R. JUSTICE, The Broken Taboo. Sex in the Family (New York: Human Sciences Press, 1979); K. C. MEISELMAN, Incest. A Psychological Study of Causes and Effects with Treatment Recommendations (San Francisco: Jossey-Bass, 1979).

39. Experts are sounding the alarm: see B. De MOTT, "The Pro-incest Lobby," Psychology Today, 13/10 (1980), pp. 11-18. - K. C. MEISELMAN, Incest..., p. 31, suggests that "it is realistic to think of incest as an event that occurs in one or

two lifetimes out of a hundred." Other students of incestuous behaviour offer similar "educated guesses."

40. See, e.g., the "do's and don'ts for parents" offered by B. JUSTICE and R. JUSTICE, The Broken Taboo..., pp. 214-217.
41. Ibid., p. 210.
42. S. G. LUTHMAN, Intimacy..., pp. 28-29.
43. This is the teaching of THOMAS AQUINAS, ST, I^a-II^{ae}, q. 64, a.2. In the case of justice, the "mean of virtue" is set by reason in reference to some external thing: the other's due, no more, no less. In the case of all other moral virtues, which deal with interior feeling, the mean is one which is set by reason in reference to the agent himself "as affected by passions," as capable of unique emotional responses.
44. On this score, the bulky REPORT OF THE COMMITTEE ON SEXUAL OFFENCES AGAINST CHILDREN AND YOUTHS (1984), commissioned by the Federal Government of Canada, is cause for some concern. Persons in a position of trust towards a young person "who commits a sexual touching with, on, or against such young person is guilty of an indictable offence and is liable to imprisonment for ten years." "'Young person' means a person under the age of 18 years" and "'a sexual touching' includes both direct and indirect physical contact" (p. 59, rec. 9). Are sexual "direct or indirect physical contacts" clearly identifiable physical aggressions as the medico-legal REPORT so readily implies? Is it reasonable to assume that an adult who touches a child or an adolescent "sexually" is ipso facto "abusing" him or her? The 1314-page REPORT does not discuss such decisive questions. They might have been considered if professionals from relevant disciplines other than health care and law had also been appointed to the Committee.
45. M. S. CALDERONE, "Childhood Sexuality. Its Nature, Its Importance," in J.-M. SAMSON (ed.), Childhood and Sexuality (Montreal: Études Vivantes, 1980), p. 25; T. LANGFELDT, "Child Sexuality. Development and Problems," ibid., pp. 105-110.
46. See good summary presentation of this classical view by D. OFFER and W. SIMON, "Sexual Development," in B. J. SADOCK, H. I. KAPLAN, and A. M. FREEDMAN (eds.), The Sexual Experience (Baltimore: Williams and Wilkins, 1976), pp. 132-134. Even in criticisms of Freudian theory, these basic ideas have not been discarded. See, e.g., P. CHODOFF, "A Critique of Freud's Theory of Infantile Sexuality," American Journal of Psychiatry, 123 (1966), pp. 507-518.
47. R. G. SLABY and K. S. FREY, "Development of Gender Constancy and Selective Attention to Same-sex Models," Child Development, 46 (1975), pp. 849-856; R. G. SLABY, "The Self-Socialization of Boys and Girls. How Children's Developping Concept of Gender Influences their Sex-Role Behavior," in J.-M. SAMSON (ed.), Childhood and Sexuality (Montreal: Études Vivantes, 1980), pp. 123-127.
48. This, at least, is a plausible interpretation of the insight which gave rise to the discarded notion of "latency." See C.

SARNOFF, Latency (New York: J. Aronson, 1976).

49. See again the good overview of D. OFFER and W. SIMON, "Sexual Development..."

50. For an overview of sexual activities during the developmental stages of infancy, childhood, and adolescence, and of parental reactions, see: F. M. MARTINSON, "Eroticism in Infancy and Childhood," Journal of Sex Research, 12 (1976), pp. 251-262; W. H. MASTERS, V. E. JOHNSON, and R. C. KOLODNY, Human Sexuality..., pp. 182-198.

51. THOMAS AQUINAS does not exclude chastity (sexual integration) from the list of virtues which are acquired exclusively through practice: see ST, I^a-II^{ae}, q. 51, aa. 2-3; q. 63, a. 2.

52. VATICAN II, Declaration on Christian Education (Gravissimum educations), par. 1, in W. M. ABBOTT (ed.), The Documents..., p. 639, and GS, par. 49 (p. 1070; tr., p. 253); CONGREGATION FOR THE DOCTRINE OF THE FAITH, Declaration..., par. 13 (pp. 94-95); SBF, prop. 28 (p. 164); JOHN PAUL II, FC, par. 37 (p. 128; tr., pp. 73-74). A recent intervention by American Bishop L. WELSH illustrates the official Church position today on this matter: "Education for Human Sexuality," Origins, 13 (1983), pp. 81-84.

53. M. CHAMPAGNE-GILBERT, La famille et l'homme à délivrer du pouvoir (Ottawa: Leméac, 1980), p. 223.

54. See, e.g., A. YATES's comments on the difficulty experienced by so many parents in naming the clitoris in sexual education because it has no other function than that of pleasure, in "The Effect of Commonly Accepted Parenting Practices on Erotic Development," in J.-M. SAMSON (ed.), Childhood and Sexuality (Montreal: Études Vivantes, 1980), p. 371.

55. SBF, prop. 30 (p. 165). Unfortunately, this insightful perception of the episcopal college is lost in the use made of it in FC, par. 37 (p. 217; tr., p. 72).

56. M. MALDAGUE, "The Decade of the 80s May Be a Failure Without a Decisive Effort in Environmental Education," The Environmentalist, 1 (1981), pp. 123-126.

57. FC, par. 21 (p. 106; tr., p. 41). See also GS, par. 50 (p. 1070-1071; tr., pp. 253-254): "Children are really the supreme gift of marriage and contribute very substantially to the welfare of their parents."

58. See, e.g., H. L. CLINEBELL, Jr., and C. H. CLINEBELL, The Intimate Marriage..., pp. 121-122, 170-173.

59. See P. TOINET, L'homme en sa vérité. Essai d'anthropologie philosophique (Paris: Aubier, 1968), pp. 295-319; R. MAY, The Courage to Create..., pp. 58-63, 92-93, 124-135.

60. See THOMAS AQUINAS, In decem libros Ethicorum..., Bk. II, lectio 8 (p. 96, no. 342) and Bk. III, lectio 21 (p. 177, no. 630-631); ST, II^a-II^{ae}, q. 142, a. 1. For a review of the research on sexual fantasies, see W. H. MASTERS, V. E. JOHNSON, and R. C. KOLODNY, Human Sexuality..., pp. 244-259; for a treatment of their morality, see A. GUINDON, The Sexual

Language..., pp. 223-249.
61. J. LE DU, Jusqu'où iront-ils? L'éducateur piégé par la morale (Lyon: Chalet, 1974), p. 37.
62. L. BEINAERT, "Régulation...," p. 28 (my translation).
63. In her research concerning the moral dilemma of women contemplating abortion, C. GILLIGAN, "In a Different Voice. Women's Conception of Self and of Morality," Harvard Educational Review, 47 (1977), pp. 481-517, shows how many unwanted pregnancies manifest the ambivalence of the mothers' desires. W. PASINI, Désir d'enfant et contraception (Tournai: Casterman, 1974), is filled with examples of pregnancies which function as cure-all, punishment, competition.
64. B. SCHULLER, "Die Personwürde des Menschen als Beweisgrund in der normativen Ethik," Theologie und Philosophie, 53 (1978), pp. 538-555, shows that the Kantian ethical maxim which forbids the treatment of others as means belongs to the domain of intentionality and of attitudes rather than to that of deontology, i.e., the domain of permitted or forbidden acts according to their objects.
65. "Immortality through children" is an intention which is alien to the Christian Creed. We confess the resurrection of the flesh, not immortality in a descent.
66. The Synodal Fathers make an inaccurate statement, it seems to me, when they state that "by freely giving themselves to procreation, the spouses make a simple and fundamental choice for life rather than against it" (SBF, prop. 36, p. 165). Is this not another telling example of the shortcoming of the fecundity-fertility view in terms of moral assessment? First, this statement implies a rash judgment, namely that spouses who do not place themselves at the service of reproduction make a choice against life. How can this be demonstrated? Second, the mere fact of accepting freely to reproduce does not guarantee that a choice has been made "for life" ... at least if, by "life," the bishops mean more than mere biological life.
67. E. H. ERIKSON, Childhood and Society (New York: W. W. Norton, 2nd ed., 1963), pp. 266-268; Insight and Responsibility. Lectures on the Ethical Implications of Psychoanalytic Insight (New York: W. W. Norton, 1964), pp. 130-132; Identity, Youth and Crisis (New York: W. W. Norton, 1968), pp. 138-139.
68. This truth concerning the real "birth" of a human person is being repeated over and over again in a wide variety of approaches: see, e.g., P. GORDON, L'initiation sexuelle et l'évolution religieuse (Paris: Presses Universitaires de France, 1946), pp. 123-130. See also S. G. LUTHMAN, Intimacy..., p. 74; A. DONVAL, Un avenir ..., p. 56; M. LEGRAIN, Le corps..., pp. 75-76; L. TIGER, Optimism. The Biology of Hope (New York: Simon and Schuster, 1979), p. 30; P. AUDOLLENT et al., Sexualité..., p. 28.
69. M. SCARF, Unfinished Business. Pressure Points in Lives of Women (New York: Doubleday, 1980), pp. 137-170.

70. FC, par. 21 (pp. 105-106; tr., p. 41).
71. J. HALEY, interviewed by M. PINES, "Restoring Law and Order in the Family," Psychology Today, 16/11 (1982), pp. 60-69. Recent books on raising children show a new awareness of this need of the child for a well-defined family structure. See, e.g., T. LICKONA, Raising Good Children. Helping Your Child Through the Stages of Moral Development (Toronto: Bantam, 1983).
72. P. GREVEN, The Protestant Temperament. Patterns of Child-Rearing, Religious Experiences, and the Self in Early America (New York: New American Library, 1979).
73. Ibid., pp. 339-341.
74. R. DENIEL, Une image de la famille et de société sous la Restauration (1815-1830). Étude de la presse catholique (Paris: Éditions Ouvrières, 1965).
75. B. J. BOELEN, "Personal Maturity...," pp. 38-39.
76. R. and R. N. RAPOPORT and Z. STRELITZ, Fathers..., pp. 20-21. The impossible attempt to satisfy all the needs of their children is a trap parents should avoid: see D. M. REED, "Traditional Marriage...," p. 222.
77. J. GRAND'MAISON, "The Modern Family, Locus of Resistance or Agency of Change," Concilium, 121 (1979), p. 53.
78. ASSEMBLÉE DES ÉVÊQUES DU QUÉBEC, "Lettre...," p. 518 (my translation).
79. R. and R. N. RAPOPORT and Z. STRELITZ, Fathers..., pp. 26-27.
80. M. CHAMPAGNE-GILBERT, La famille..., p. 37.
81. See a review of the literature on children and role models in D. I. RIDDLE, "Relating to Children. Gays as Role Models," Journal of Social Issues, 34/3 (1978), pp. 46-49. - Though many competing theories exist on the modalities of family influences on sex-role development, no one disputes the fact that such influences exist and that they are strong. See a good summary of the literature in A. G. KAPLAN and M. A. SEDNEY, Psychology..., pp. 179-209.
82. See T. GORDON, Parent Effectiveness Training. The Tested New Way to Raise Responsible Children (New York: P. H. Wyden, 1970); P. E. T. in Action (New York: P. H. Wyden, 1976). Even though some assumptions of Gordon's philosophy could be disputed, I believe that one of these books should be "required reading" for every parent.
83. R. and R. N. RAPOPORT and Z. STRELITZ, Fathers..., p. 14.
84. C. OLIVIER, Les enfants..., p. 15. See also from a historical perspective, J. DONZELOT, The Policing..., pp. 216-217.
85. R. and R. N. RAPOPORT and Z. STRELITZ, Fathers..., p. 26.
86. M. RUTTER, "Dimensions of Parenthood. Some Myths and Some Suggestions," in The Family in Society. Dimensions of Parenthood (London: HMSO, 1974), p. 21.
87. V. HELD, "The Equal Obligations of Mothers and Fathers," in O. O'NEILL and W. RUDDICK (eds.), Having Children. Philosophical and Legal Reflections on Parenthood (New York: Oxford University Press, 1979), p. 229. See the perceptive statement

of SBF, prop. 16 (p. 118): "The Church can help today's society by examining the value of housework and childrearing, whether it is done by husband or by wife. All this is important for the education of children, because the distinction between different types of work and professions disappears if everyone clearly shares the same rights and responsibilities in whatever they work at." This message has not been picked up in FC.

88. See, e.g., N. D. GLENN and S. McLANAHAN, "The Effects of Offspring on the Psychological Well-Being of Older Adults," Journal of Marriage and the Family 43 (1981), pp. 409-421.

89. See, e.g., R. A. FEIN, "Men and Young Children," in J. M. PLECK and J. SAWYER (eds.), Men and Masculinity (Englewood Cliffs: Prentice Hall, 1974), pp. 54-62; J. LEVINE, Who Will Raise the Children? New Options for Fathers (and Mothers) (New York: Bantam, 1977).

90. R. A. FEIN. "Research on Fathering. Social Policy and an Emergent Perspective," Journal of Social Issues, 34 (1978), pp. 122-135.

91. B. J. BOELEN, "Personal Maturity...," p. 45.

92. R. and R. N. RAPOPORT and Z. STRELITZ, Fathers..., pp. 19-20, report that one third of the women in the USA are the principal family breadwinners.

93. M. MEAD, Culture and Commitment. A Study of the Generation Gap (Garden City: Natural History Press/Doubleday, 1970), pp. 51-76. Most adults would be astonished to find out what children know and have to say if they really listened to them instead of automatically assuming the role of teacher: see G. MATTHEWS, Dialogue with Children (Cambridge: Harvard University Press, 1985).

94. H. L. CLINEBELL, Jr., and C. H. CLINEBELL, The Intimate Marriage..., p. 162.

95. See G. DUPERRAY, "La communication de la foi dans la vie familiale," Lumière et Vie, 25/126 (1976), pp. 59-71.

96. See some good pages on this topic in M. LÉGAUT, L'Homme à la recherche de son humanité: "et homo factus est" (Paris: Aubier/Montaigne, 1971), pp. 62, 78, etc.

97. See, on this notion, P. TILLICH, The Courage To Be (London: Nisbett, 1952).

98. FC, par. 18 (p. 100; tr., p. 34).

99. FC, par. 17 (p. 100; tr., p. 33).

100. FC, par. 18 (pp. 100-101; tr., p. 34).

101. FC, par. 18 (p. 101; tr., p. 34).

102. FC, par. 22 (p. 106; tr., p. 42).

103. FC, par. 36 (p. 126; tr., pp. 70-71).

104. FC, par. 36 (pp. 126-127; tr. p. 71).

105. SBF, prop. 30 (pp. 164-165).

106. J. SHEA, "A Theological Perspective.:.," p. 93.

107. M. LEGRAIN, Le corps..., p. 83, notes how socio-economic conditions of families bring about a lack of vital space which creates major difficulties for sexual education.

108. Quoted by M. CHAMPAGNE–GILBERT, La famille..., p. 398 (my translation).
109. SBF, prop. 26 (p. 164).
110. D. CURRAN, Traits of a Healthy Family (New York: Winston Press, 1983).
111. See the beautiful "Letters" of M. CHAMPAGNE–GILBERT, La famille..., pp. 263–277.
112. B. LASLETT, "The Family as a Public and Private Institution. An Historical Perspective," Journal of Marriage and the Family, 35 (1973), pp. 480–492. For the history of childhood, see the well-known study of P. ARIES, Centuries of Childhood. A Social History of Family (New York: Random House, 1962).
113. See, e.g., N. F. COTT, The Bonds of Womanhood. "Woman's Sphere" in New England, 1780–1835 (New Haven: Yale University Press, 1977). In her study, she shows how the separation between the public sphere and the domestic sphere (a phenomenon that began with the advent of industrialization) profoundly affected sex roles, particularly in the emerging middle class.
114. SBF, prop. 30 (p. 164).
115. This indictment is brought against early American evangelicals by P. GREVEN, The Protestant Temperament..., p. 26. It could also be brought against the XIXth-century French Catholic traditionalists: see P. BRÉCHON, La famille. Idées traditionnelles et idées nouvelles (Paris: Le Centurion, 1976), pp. 15–55.
116. E. H. MUDD, H. E. MITCHELL, and S. B. TAUBIN, Success..., p. 212.
117. J. RÉMY, "The Family. Contemporary Models and Historical Perspective," Concilium, 121 (1979), pp. 7–8.
118. R. J. LIFTON, The Broken Connection. On Death and the Continuity of Life (New York: Simon and Schuster, 1979).
119. The literature on this point has been surveyed and analyzed by a student of mine, G. H. WALTERS, "The Nuclear Image 1960–1982: A Study of the Psycho-spiritual Impact of the Threat of Nuclear War on Children, Adolescents and the Family in the United States" (unpublished master's degree seminar paper in the Faculty of Theology. Saint Paul University, Ottawa, 1983). I thank him for this contribution.
120. W. BEARDSLEE and J. MACK, "The Impact on Children and Adolescents of Nuclear Developments," in Psychological Aspects of Nuclear Developments (Washington D.C.: American Psychiatric Association, Task Force Report, no. 20, 1982), p. 89.
121. S. ESCALONA, "Growing Up With the Threat of Nuclear War. Some Indirect Effects on Personality Development," American Journal of Orthopsychiatry, 52 (1982), p. 607.
122. This mythology characterizes much of the ecclesiastical discourse on family. See P. BRÉCHON, "Les valeurs familiales: mythes et réalités," Lumière et Vie, 25/126 (1976), pp.

33-47.
123. "Nuclear numbing" is mere avoidance of moral responsibility. See R. J. LIFTON, "Beyond Nuclear Numbing," Teachers College Record, 84/1 (1982), pp. 15-29.
124. W. BEARDSLEE and J. MACK, "The Impact...," p. 91.
125. Even the studies of popular celebrations and rituals point to this fact. See W. HEIM, "Religious Practice within the Family. A Contribution to the Theology of Intimate Belonging in the Light of Popular Beliefs and Customs in the Past," Concilium, 121 (1979), p. 86.
126. See E. H. ERIKSON, Childhood..., pp. 246-251; Identity..., pp. 96-97, 103-104.
127. UNITES STATES CATHOLIC CONFERENCE, "The Challenge of Peace: God's Promise and Our Response," Origins, 13 (1983), p. 28. This letter is, in my opinion, the best R. C. Church document which has been written on war and peace in the nuclear age.
128. See G. D. KAUFMAN, "Nuclear Eschatology and the Study of Religion," Journal of the American Academy of Religion, 51/1 (1983), pp. 3-14.
129. See the superb text of THOMAS AQUINAS, SCG, Bk. III, c. 69 (Vol. III, p. 96, no. 2445) quoted in epigraph to the foreword.
130. UNITED STATES CATHOLIC CONFERENCE, "The Challenge...," p. 30.
131. A. MYRE, "Et les béatitudes évangéliques," in Le Bonheur menacé. Journées universitaires de la pensée chrétienne (Montreal: Fides, 1976), pp. 101-112.
132. SBF, par. 30 (p. 164).
133. See W. J. GOODE, The Family (Englewood Cliffs: Prentice-Hall, 1964), pp. 4-5; F. A. BEACH, Human Sexuality in Four Perspectives (Baltimore: The Johns Hopkins University Press, 1976), p. 9; M. LEGRAIN, Le corps..., p. 161.
134. J. LACROIX, Force..., p. 73. In this sense it is still exact to call even the present-day family the "social cell," contrary to the opinion of R. MEHL, Society..., p. 23.
135. See, e.g., VATICAN II, Declaration on Christian Education..., par. 3 (p. 641); GS, par. 52 (p. 257; tr., p. 1073); FC, par. 37 (p. 127; tr., p. 72) and par. 43 (p. 134; tr., pp. 82-83).
136. See, e.g., L. GRÉGOIRE, "En civilisation occidentale," in P. De LOCHT (ed.), Mariage et sacrement de mariage (Paris: Le Centurion, 1970), p. 61; C. ROGERS, Becoming Partners..., p. 8; J. BERNARD, The Future of Marriage (New York: Bantam, 1972), p. 127; M. NARBAITS, "Comment les garçons et les filles vivent-ils l'amour aujourd'hui?" Échanges, 109 (1973), p. 2; J. P. MONTGOMERY, "Toward an Understanding of Cohabitation," Dissertation Abstracts International, 33 (1973), pp. 7059-7060; H. PELLETIER-BAILLARGEON, "Avons-nous encore une éthique sexuelle?," Cahiers de Recherche Éthique, 3 (1976), pp. 5-12; L. ROUSSEL and O. BOURGUIGNON, Générations nouvelles et mariage traditionnel. Enquête auprès de jeunes de 18 à 30 ans (Paris: Institut National d'études démographiques, 1979); A. BÉJIN, "Le mariage extra-conjugal

d'aujourd'hui," in Sexualités occidentales. Communications No. 35 (Paris: Seuil, 1982), pp. 138-146; S. CHALVON-DEMERSAY, Concubin..., p. 130; F. and P. LAPLANTE, Jeunes couples aujourd'hui (Montreal: Éditions du Méridien, 1985).

137. GS, par. 47 (p. 1067; tr., p. 249).

138. A. McCUMBER, "Development...," pp. 221-222.

139. SBF, par. 30 (pp. 164-165, specifically points b, c, d, e, j, and l).

140. JOHN PAUL II, Homily of September 26, 1980, in AAS, 72 (1980),p. 1010. English text in Origins, 10 (1980), p. 260.

141. Reported by W. McCREADY, "The Family and Socialization," Concilium, 121 (1979), p. 121.

142. This is clearly underlined by the ASSEMBLÉE DES ÉVÊQUES DU QUÉBEC, "Lettre...," p. 517. See also the remarks of L. MACARIO, "Ruoli...," pp. 106-107.

143. J. ISAAC, Réévaluer..., p. 103.

144. See SBF, par. 30 (p. 165, point e, g, h) and FC, par. 44 (pp. 135-136; tr., pp. 84-85).

145. M. LEGRAIN, Le corps..., p. 165.

146. JOHN PAUL II, Homily of September 26, 1980..., p. 1008.

147. SBF, par. 5 (p. 141).

148. J.-P. AUDET, Structures..., p. 91; see also pp. 80-81.

CHAPTER SEVEN

GAY FECUNDITY or LIBERATING SEXUALITY

In 1960, Michael Buckley wrote a standard anti-gay manifesto entitled: Morality and the Homosexual: A Catholic Approach to a Moral Problem. In the introduction, the reader is instructed to bear in mind,

> that we condemn any religious bodies, as well as individual moralists, who in defending the practice of contraception by confusing the purposes of matrimony, put sexual fulfillment and mutual help and companionship on an equality with the primary purpose of procreation. Such views play into the hands of homosexuals. If sexual pleasure and companionship are regarded as equally primary, and if procreation may be legitimately prevented by artificial means, the force of the argument against homosexual unions where there is genuine affection is enormously weakened.[1]

Five years later, Vatican II purposely left aside the late Scholastic distinction between the primary and secondary ends of matrimony, presented marriage as "a whole manner and communion of life,"[2] and insisted on the parents' ultimate responsibility to decide in the sight of God whether they ought to prevent reproduction or, on the contrary, plan it. In so doing, the Council did indeed weaken enormously the strength of what had gradually become the argument in Catholic moral theology against gay sex. Thomas Aquinas's embarrassed and atypically incoherent attempts to find rational grounds for condemning a life style which an order-seeking, thirteenth-century society came to regard as intolerable sexual nonconformity were decisive.[3] Lesbians were most likely spared much of the antigay feelings and condemnations found henceforth in the Christian literature precisely because their sexual activities did not imply "wastage of semen."[4]

Though some moralists continue to brand all homosexual acts at least ontically or premorally evil because they are never open to the specific value of the production of children,[5] more and more one finds others who consider this aspect of the moral analysis irrelevant.[6] After all, why would infertile sex be more "unnatural" and blameworthy for gay partners than for nongay spouses who are naturally, accidentally, or artificially sterile?[7] Any answer to this question must necessarily call upon an element of explanation foreign to the notion of reproductivity.

As critical methods are being applied to Christian sources, it is also becoming more and more manifest that the few indictments contained in the biblical file against gays are, at best, inconclusive.[8] Considering, moreover, the whole thrust of Jesus' ministry, so alien to a religious world-view in which the word of God is used to clobber people, Christian moralists must ponder whether they have been conducting a proper assessment.[9] As long as we find, among the Christians whom they have instructed, those who pray for "pervert faggots" while they slip on their hoods, light up their crosses, and organize their murderous pogroms against gays, we must seriously question what we have done with the Gospel.

In ethical discussions, gay behaviour is controversial as a sexual reality and in no other capacity. Lesbians and gays are not taken to task for their food preferences, their driving habits, their political views, or their working patterns. Christian ethicists have traditionally postulated that, other things being equal, heterosexuality is "what ought to be." Therefore, they have posed the notion of heterosexual activity as ethically normative and they have counselled gay persons accordingly. One may wonder, today, whether this is not like offering women male ethical models, spouses monachal standards of chastity, or Africans European moral sexual patterns.

I do not deny, though, that when conducted with the needed sensitivity and subtlety this discussion may prove of some usefulness, mainly, perhaps, for educational and social purposes. It may even help lesbians and gays to discern their values and to formulate developmental strategies. Nevertheless, we must also realize that the intended focus of such a discussion is usually not the moral life of gay people themselves. It is meant for heterosexuals who ought to choose to be who they are and act accordingly. This discussion is the tributary of a pre-twentieth century view that there are homosexual acts, not homosexual persons. The use of the word "sodomy" in the ethical literature before our own century illustrates this outlook: it designated heterosexual copulation outside the vagina (anal sex, oral sex, etc.) as well as homosexual copulation.[10] Homosexuality, as such, was not yet a clearly identified reality. What was known was the "deviated" sexual activity of persons believed to be uniformly heterosexual.[11] The traditional view was really saying, then, that homosexual activity is "unnatural" to the heterosexual person.

This way of construing the moral problematic leads to the formulation of perplexing predicaments. Does a gay's moral dilemma consist in choosing between being a gay (the immoral

choice) and not being a gay (the moral choice)? Is this a
reasonable choice for one who is irreversibly a homosexual?[12]
There are enough gay bibliographies nowadays to convince anyone
who is not incurably prejudiced that for many persons gayness is
their only sane choice.[13] Have moralists also considered the
seriousness of the moral objections raised against therapies aimed
at converting gays into nongays: the ghastly cost of years of
therapy in quest for cures which are often less than probable;[14]
ethically objectionable treatments including brain tampering and
physical punishment;[15] deeply ingrained self-hatred and guilt
resulting from unsuccessful therapies aiming at freeing the
patient from what is construed as a sickness, an aberration, a
perversion?[16]

From this first Shakesperean quandary, to be or not to
be a gay, flows another unsolvable question raised by the
classical, heterosexual-normativeness approach: to act or not to
act as a gay. When ethicists commonly held that one could not be
gay they judged that one should not act like one either. Then,
some ethicists began to admit that some people were perhaps
irreversibly gay. Yet these ethicists kept saying that even such
persons ought not to act like they were because their conditon was
still an aberration.[17] Gradually, the logic of the common-sense
philosophy traditionally used in Christian theology which holds as
a self-evident maxim that one should act in accord with who one is
(agere sequitur esse) began to impose itself. An increasing number
of theologians, while they still hold that heterosexuality is
ideal and normative for all sexual behaviour, nevertheless argue
that the homosexual acts of gays may receive a positive moral
evaluation.[18] Under all the fancy language of the trade, the basic
idea is that all human acts, being the acts of finite,
historically situated, and developing beings, cannot really
pretend to more than a limited perfection. Aristotle's "virtuous
man," Lawrence Kohlberg's "stage-6 moral judge,"[19] or William
Perry's "position-9, committed college graduate"[20] are super-
men/women. You never find one in real life.

No human activity produces a fully perfect result
because it necessarily proceeds from an embodied, contextually
situated, sexually differentiated and oriented, idiosyncratic, not
fully actualized being. It therefore lacks the perfection it could
have had if... if the agent had been a woman instead of a man, if
the agent had been more knowledgeable, if the agent had had more
imagination, if the agent lived in the year 3000, if sin had never
affected human relationships, and so on. Because one is a
homosexual person something may not be present in his or her
performance, something which would have been there had she or he
been a heterosexual. But is this "lack" an evil? Is the lack of
biological parenthood an evil for couples who have chosen social
commitments which are incompatible with child-rearing? Is the lack
of lifelong covenant love with another human person an evil for

celibates? Is the lack of the wherewithal for philanthropy an evil for poor people? Is the lack of intense erotic affection for a same-sex friend an evil for a heterosexual person? Unless we call "evil" what is lacking to an act because of a creature's limitations, none of the acts described above are, of themselves, evil. This is the reason why many Christian ethicists argue today that the lack of a heterosexual quality in gay relationships is not an evil.[21] I am more and more inclined to agree with them.

We must understand that there is no such thing as a moral project which does not lie in the agent's executive power, which is unattainable in the real world in which she or he lives. Even in the most classic moral theology, an <u>intention</u> properly so called, the very soul of moral decision-making, is directed toward an end <u>as attainable by concrete means</u>.[22] The elaboration of any moral project does not and cannot proceed when this intention cannot be realistically formed. Is this not mere common sense? How could a real moral project exist in the absence of any foreseeable commitment of the self? One wonders what ethicists are thinking about when, addressing their gay audience, they are content to tell gays and lesbians what they <u>cannot</u> do and how they <u>cannot</u> live but stop short of proposing any realistic sexual project for them. The only options they seem to be able to offer them (a heterosexual or an asexual life style) are, as they themselves must recognize, unachievable for healthy homosexual persons.

This, in turn, opens up another question: Does the classical way of debating the moral issue of homosexuality in terms of "to act or not to act" not remain, even with the recent shift towards a more positive evaluation, a rather limited operation? Ethicists are merely telling gays and lesbians whether their "sexual activity" can be considered moral. (It should be noted that few ethicists dare to specify what they really mean by "sexual activity" because the fragility of much of the reasoning would become still more glaring: Are holding hands and kissing "sexual acts?" Where does one draw the line? Following what rationale? Moreover, is this approach which focuses on "sexual acts" not the result of a typical male fixation?[23]) Where do gay persons go from there? Reviewing this literature, David Blamires observes with perspicacity that "it leaves the self-perceived homosexual high and dry in an ethical limbo."[24] If many intelligent and creative gays and lesbians invest so much in art and culture, it may well be, as Seymour Kleinberg suggests, that they find in these values a substitute for the loss of traditional morality which has nothing more to offer than blind condemnations.[25]

Real life gay sex calls for the formulation of an entirely different ethical question, one which addresses the fundamental issue of the moral development of gay persons. I submit that we enunciate it in terms of human sexual fecundity:

Can the gay sexual language be fruitful for the human community, i.e., for both gays and nongays? I am not blind to the fact that this approach implies a number of built-in assumptions, notably that some people have gay identities and that this identity of theirs is, for all practical purposes, irreversible. However, I consider that sex research and clinical practice bear these assumptions out.[26] These assumptions also limit the scope of this chapter. It will not address other legitimate problems concerning, for instance, adolescent homosexual practices,[27] pedophiliac behaviour, bisexuality, or dysfunctional gays.[28]

I readily admit, therefore, that the search for an answer to the question I propose to investigate will not resolve every issue connected with the homosexual debate. My proposal even abstracts from the question of knowing whether "genital acts" (whatever that really means) between gay persons are morally or only ontically evil, or perhaps not evil at all. One could hold any one of these views and still find what will follow acceptable or unacceptable. Depending on one's belief or judgment on the kind of sexual acts which are licit or not, one may give gay interactions and gay relationships whatever "content" one deems fit. Nor, for that matter, will my proposal culminate in the fabrication of a set of sexual prescriptions that gays ought to learn and practice. However, it might help them acquire a clearer awareness of their own moral limits and assets as gay persons. They would then be in a much better position to discern the means of expressing their sexual selves in ways which are meaningful.

With the human fecundity approach, we focus on the task of each individual to grow, through the sexual language, into a whole self. Hence, in the case of gays and lesbians, the main ethical issue lies in their willingness (or unwillingness) to achieve the truth of their existence by creatively expressing themselves in the light of their living options, and by wisely discerning appropriate means. If the moral task consists in making one's own truth or in making sense of one's own life, then we are finally coming to grips, in this approach, with the crucial question of an ethical project for lesbians and gays.

Nongays also have much to learn from this approach. If gay fecundity is something other than a second rate, defective replica of heterosexual fecundity, if it is an original source of humanization on its own terms in our society, then it should bring to the human sexual concert novel tonalities which enrich the quality of everyone's performance.

It seems imperative, therefore, that we set out to verify if and how the essential components of human sexual fecundity are found in gay sex. While allowing for diversity in the way the sexual language will be spoken by different gay persons, it will nevertheless be possible to characterize a style of gay fecundity which the community of Christian women and men may come to recognize as having significance for their lives. Then, perhaps, we will move beyond mere tolerance toward reconciliation and toward a factual recognition of the gay, my neighbour and my beloved sister or brother in Christ.

1. SENSUOUS EXPERIENCE

So many creative artists are known to have been homosexual that, as George Weinberg observes, the myth of the special creativity of gays has become widespread.[29] Apologists of homosexuality capitalize on this belief, gathering and advertising the names of illustrious lesbians and gays throughout history.[30] Those who look upon gay liberation with suspicion downplay the number and the significance of creative gay personalities.[31] Counting heads on both sides strikes me as another version of the childish game, "Mine is better than yours." Since no serious doubt can exist that gays are creative too, would it not be more constructive to find out whether gayness gives human creativity special tonalities? Empirical researchers have yet to seriously investigate this field.[32] In the meantime, a reflection on the gay experience of sexuality may help to identify some traits of their possible contribution to human sexual fecundity.

The Bible itself presents us with a few telling examples of healthy and fruitful gay partnerships. In a socio-religious context where homosexuality is considered an abomination, exegetes can hardly bring themselves to recognize the very existence of the gay relationships of biblical heroes. But the facts are there. One does find in the Bible poignant accounts of same-sex love. The Book of Ruth is generally presented to Jewish and Christian congregations as a touching love story between the young widow Ruth and the older, righteous Boaz. Yet the text says otherwise: the love story is really between Ruth ("the beloved") and Naomi ("my fair one"), her mother-in-law. They have pledged each other a covenantal love till death do them part (1: 16-18).[33] The village women recognize that, even after Ruth's reproductive union with Boaz, the bride loves Naomi more than anyone else (4: 15). Hence Ruth's son is born for Naomi (4: 16-17). The whole account of the two women's relationship is one of deeply expressed affection for one another and of festive thanksgiving.[34]

Interestingly enough, Ruth's and Naomi's son, Obed, is the grandfather of David, the most celebrated hero of the Old Testament, the illustrious ancestor of Jesus, and the lover of King Saul's eldest son, Jonathan.[35] Of Jonathan, it is said that his "soul became closely bound to David's and Jonathan came to

love him as his own soul" (1 S 18: 1 and 3). After Jonathan's
death, David laments; "Very dear to me you were, your love to me
more wonderful than the love of a woman" (2 S 1:26). The narrative
contains traces of deep and physically-expressed, emotional ties
(e.g., 1 S 18: 1-4; 19: 1-7; 20: 3-4, 11-17, 34, 39-42; 2 S 1:
17-27). Jonathan's father, Saul, is not unaware of the sexual
nature of the young warriors' mutual attraction (1 S 20: 30-34).
Here again the sensuous affection of the relationship is stressed
and is, as James Nelson remarks, a cause for celebration.[36] Little
compares to it in the historical accounts of heterosexual love in
the Old Testament. It is matched only by some treatments of
heterosexual love found in Wisdom literature, especially in The
Song of Songs, where the sexual love of a partner is celebrated
for its own worth.

This gratuitous celebration of love is characteristic
of gay sexuality. More than any other group, practicing gays and
lesbians come face to face with their sensuality because same-sex
attraction has no other source than mutual attraction. A woman
does not make love to another woman or a man to another man
because that is what is expected of everyone; or because that is
what must be done to get a provider or a homemaker; or, again,
because that is how babies are made. Healthy gay persons are
sexually active with a partner because they wish to express their
affection to someone to whom they are attracted. Though nongays
may obviously seek the same goal, lesbians and gays display, as a
group, a sensual approach to sex. The ethically relevant question
about gay sex has little to do with the level of sexual activity
or with its techniques.[37] It should rather address the issue of
the properly human quality and significance of this sensuous
celebration.

In Christian tradition, there has always been a
formidable Docetist tendency to underestimate Christ's sensuous
humanity and love's sexual body. For the benefit of us all, gay
people should, as Matthew Fox states, be "expert at sensuality."[38]
In the search for significant sexual integration within a given
socio-cultural context, gays and lesbians can play a special role
in helping the whole community rediscover sensuousness. They
remind us to reclaim our sensual bodies and to learn from them who
we are and how to act humanly. How many people today seek to
disown their bodies and their sensual realities? They act as if
they were not their bodies, as if their bodies were not their own
intimate selves whom they are supposed to love as God does. Some
Christians seem to act on the premise, which is certainly not
Jesus' premise (Mt 22: 39), that self-hatred is the path leading
to the love of others. They spend their life taking revenge on
their own flesh, denying its every need, cultivating successive
illnesses, overfeeding or underfeeding it. They must be taught to
look at their body, to know it, to touch it, to reclaim what is
theirs. This is a basic condition for communicating intimately and

165

truthfully with others.[39] One cannot be a stranger in one's own house and still let a friend in. To touch a partner, to let the warm rush of loving feelings flow through one's body, to let oneself be overwhelmed by the other's presence within oneself, is to experience sexual, intimate communication. Only a sensualized and personalized body is capable of this basic, human experience of sharing one's life. And let us not kid ourselves: human bodies are primarily contact oriented. They need to touch each other in order to communicate intimately.

Gay males have a special vocation, in this respect, to teach North American males how to experience the quickening of loving feelings and how to let the sexual action flow from that experience of the other's sensuous and amorous indwelling.[40] Most males in our culture are still being programmed to produce "things" and to value themselves in terms of performance.[41] Since physical performance is based on biological youth and fitness, sexual "performers" increasingly strike out with age. Males who have learned to speak the sexual language well, to speak it as an expression of inner, sensuous communion, should, like old wine, get much better with age. We have yet to learn what males are capable of sexually.[42] Gay males who are attentive to their own sexual experience and work at humanizing their sensuality through their tenderness can be of great help in this common quest to discover who we are as sexual selves.

Like every other Christian, gays must avoid sexual disintegration by giving into either corporealism and its hedonistic ethics or spiritualism and its purity ethics. Overpowered by sensuality, some may refuse to receive any other cues for their conduct than genital pruriency and instantaneous pleasure. These gays end up "having sex" as one "has" a cheese-burger and a milkshake. In the cruising world of John Rechy's The Sexual Outlaw,[43] or the market mentality of numerous patrons of gay baths who seek a social structure "where everyone is attractive and available at minimal expense,"[44] gays merely "have sex," as if they bought it off the shelf at their nearest shopping center. Sex which produces mere "sexual outlets" soon becomes toxic for human persons who are capable of more than the behaviour of chirping birds or lever-pressing mice in the Skinner Box. At least, this is what we hold in a Church which believes that the Spirit will set our bodies free (Rm 8: 23).

Frightened by their socially deviant sexuality, other gays and lesbians refuse to acknowledge, on the contrary, that their sensuality is the incarnational law of their tenderness. They easily fall prey to the teaching of one of the purity ethics. Following a dualistic philosophy, these hold that the spiritual forces inside or outside of us should rule over the body and its evil, erotic yearnings. Instead of fostering a mutual irrigation of flesh and spirit so that we may become whole, this ethical current preaches the salvation of the soul by the damnation of the body. Those senseless efforts, nourished by a sick religiosity which bargains with a scarecrow-god instead of celebrating the God of the agape Covenant, produce homosexual neurotics - those gays psychiatrists know and oftentimes carelessly generalize about.

This is not to deny that gay persons, like nongay persons, may validly choose celibacy, even religious or priestly celibacy.[45] Religious and priests are sexual beings and many of them have a homosexual orientation.[46] But, as Marcel Eck points out, it should not be une vocation refuge, an escape from their sexual life and from the sexual tasks that lie ahead.[47] Church spokespersons who advocate celibacy for all homosexual Christians are up against at least two major difficulties. First, while most of them, particularly in the Roman Catholic tradition, would readily admit that celibacy is a special and charismatic vocation, they turn around and impose it indiscriminately on all gays and lesbians, whether or not they have a celibate vocation.[48] Secondly, while many would acknowledge that celibates are sexual beings with a sexual life of their own, they propose celibacy as a solution to gay persons' sexual problems.[49] But are sexual problems more easily resolved (at least if this is understood as a positive integration) in a celibate life style than in a partnered life style?

Responsible gays and lesbians should come to grips with who they are as sexual beings, choose to be fully who they are, and discern whether this will be better achieved as celibates or as partnered. Celibates will witness to another form of sexual fecundity. This is the topic of the next chapter. Partnered gay persons have the opportunity to deepen the sensuous experience and to liberate sensuality from the shame which weighs upon it. In so doing, they help the Christian community discover how the word, in order to live among us, is made flesh. God's glory is not seen otherwise nor is love rightly sought through other mediations.

2. NONVIOLENT STYLE OF PARTNERSHIP

Partnered gay persons... Is a gay relationship wholly relational? Does it bear original sexual products of a relational nature? These questions raise what I believe to be the most fundamental theoretical question concerning the homosexual pattern of sexuality. Some who champion gay partnership as an acceptable Christian and ethical choice often skip over the issue too lightly.[50] In so doing, they lessen their own chances of laying out an ethical project for gay persons which is fully lucid and realistic. No life style is without its own limits, its inherent drawbacks, its characteristic pitfalls. Think about the celibate by choice in search of a non-coital, sexual expression of herself in a Church still caught up in all kinds of sexual stereotypes and hang-ups; about a male, socially pushed into a role of dominance, searching for conjugal and parental fecundity; about a couple, trapped in a Parsonian family model of relationship, in search of socially relevant sexual fecundity; about a parent trying to raise a family in a culture which displays a lack of desire for children. To be limited is the definition of human choices. To merely tell gays that everything is fine with loving gay relationships is not much more helpful, albeit less destructive, than to tell them that everything is wrong with what they do. Since every way of life has its assets and its liabilities, why not face gay partnerships as objectively and as truthfully as possible?

To be fruitful, sexual relationships between human beings presuppose both sameness and differentness. No one communicates sensuously and tenderly his or her intimate meaning to another unless they share a decoding system. The more sameness there is between the two, the easier it is to decipher the other's messages. Partners who share sameness of religion, education, social status, moral conviction, aesthetical taste, age, ethnic background, village origin, etc., are very comfortable with their mutual signals. The sources of misunderstandings are few. In fact, these may be too scarce. When there is little to discover in the other, interaction finds little stimulus. Too much comfort is an obstacle to conversion and to human development.

Fecund sexual relationships between human beings, then, also presuppose differentness, that whereby the other is really other. Otherness is the basic condition of real mutuality. The other is, by definition, one who is different from myself, therefore one who may unsettle me, disturb me, astonish me, challenge me. Conflict, its negotiation through interaction and reconciliation, is the very law of moral development.[51] If no one stands before me with a certain firmness, inviting me lovingly to hear a voice different from my own, how am I ever redeemed from my interior poverty and from my self-assumptions? Is Jesus' salvific therapy anything other than a divine challenge to our too comfortable, earthly positions?

All human sexual relationships, whether they be heterosexual or homosexual, may, obviously, bring together partners who are too similar to provide the necessary challenge for growth-producing exchanges or who are too different for meaningful exchanges to even take place. A certain balance of sameness and differentness is needed. Unlike all other differences which constitute the other's otherness, the male-female difference does not establish just another degree of differentness such as being black, white, or yellow; Chinese, German, or Canadian; rich, middle class or poor. The male-female difference cuts through humanity itself: human beings would not be who they are (would they even exist?) if this difference were to disappear. This difference establishes a basic sexual differentness between persons whereby one partner is challenged by the other in his male or in her female assumptions concerning human existence. Male-female sexual interactions do not automatically produce well-identified females or males because many other ingredients must be added to the relationship. Yet, the other's otherness in the male-female sexual dialogue carries within it a potential for self-discovery in one's male-female humanity which is not present in the same-sex otherness of the other.[52] It is difficult to contend that these are not hard facts. The question is: Do they carry moral implications for gay partners?[53]

The atypical ability to communicate well, sexually, with one's own sex rather than with the other sex should not be dismissed, it seems to me, as ethically irrelevant. Who could argue convincingly that, if the task of morality is to liberate humanity in us, individually and socially, the gay style of relating to others has no influence on this liberating process? It has. And it is the job of an ethicist to assess its limits, to propose moral strategies of liberation, and to suggest the potential it holds for creativity in the realm of sexual relationships.

A lucid gay person should acknowledge the fact that the sameness of same-sex relationships represents a potential deficiency in terms of other-sex challenge. He or she should become aware of the potential threats to personal development this may represent when not compensated by other acquired abilities. Same-sex partners are generally not as competent as other-sex partners to confront female or male self-assumptions creatively. I know very well that there are macho gay males and "nellies" as there are "butches" and "femmes" among lesbians. I am also aware that the same categories can be found among nongays. This line of argumentation merely shows that much more than sexual orientation contributes to our total sexual make-up. Yet, the fact remains that no male can, through the sexual language, reveal to me the female mystery of my humanity as well as a female can.

A gay person who does nothing to compensate for her or his lack of other-sex feedback may also find some difficulty with self-assertiveness because an unchallenged self does not grow strong in a confident way. Anger or compensatory aggressiveness in conversation are poor substitutes. To argue for gay sex against the conflictual nature of heterosexual relations is more often than not an illusion.[54] Courage is a pivotal virtue for moral life and ego strength, as psychologists call it, is born out of well-resolved relational conflicts.

Finally, a lesbian or a gay may in her or his sexual

relationship, gradually lose sense of the mystery of the other's otherness; think, after a while, that she or he has the other completely "figured out;" minimize, therefore, the length of the road we must all travel before achieving a community of loving but different and autonomous persons.

Again, I am neither claiming that nongays do not experience similar difficulties nor am I arguing that those dangers are unavoidable for gays. I merely state that these are the kinds of traps lesbians and gays should particularly look out for. The best way to avoid being caught in them is to develop strategies to make up for what the homo-sexual language does not, of itself, foster. If, on the contrary, one were to seek total sameness through gay partnerships; if one wished to abrogate the other's difference so as to make the other conform to one's desire, one would obviously be giving into sexual solipsism, the vice against sexual language as relational. This would amount to sheer immorality.[55] The gay people I know may have indulged themselves at times at the expense of a partner's own good just as the nongay people I know may have done occasionally. Anybody who did not would have to be considered a sexual non-sinner, a rare bird indeed! But the majority of my acquaintances have more moral vitality and are seeking moral, developmental strategies.[56]

Unless a gay person suffers from some kind of pathology (and some do), she or he is capable of warm and significant friendships with gay or nongay persons of the other sex. If this gay person has a real homosexual orientation, many sexual messages received in this dialogue with persons of the other sex will be decoded somewhat differently than they are meant and some of them may not even register. But we should not push this point too far. First, because it is well known (at least since Alfred Kinsey's prestigious reports) that the extremes of exclusive heterosexual activity (scale 0) or exclusive homosexual activity (scale 6) are not the "normals" from a statistical viewpoint. Though gays and lesbians are people who experience a steady and nearly exclusive erotic preference for members of their own sex, few of them, are incapable of some degree of erotic attraction to members of the other sex. Secondly, we should recognize the fact that this dialogue between the sexes also contains non-sexual components and modalities.[57] A gay or a lesbian who entertains such a dialogue and learns from the "different voice" is certainly in a healthier situation than one who encloses him/herself in a same-sex world and keeps hearing the "same voice" all the time. The former is a situation which offers better potential for growth in male-female humnity. Gays and nongays alike should, therefore, learn to choose their close friends by criteria which cut across sexual boundaries and preferences.[58]

Similar comments should be made, it seems to me,

concerning relationships with nongays. Few who have any realistic knowledge of gay life in our present-day atmosphere of social ostracism and ecclesiastical condemnation, would deny gays and lesbians the right to seek support for psychological, social, legal, recreational, religious and political reasons, from gay groups or/and organizations.[59] As long as they are rejected by heterosexual societies the need for supportive affiliations is perfectly understandable. Who can live happily and creatively without the support of those who, under some aspect (work, religion, politics, sports, ethnicity, etc.), represent sameness? On the gay scene, gay people find a vital space, one in which they have the privilege of being themselves comfortably, of spontaneously acting out their sexual identity, of sharing common feelings, linked identities, and intimate experiences. Critics of the gay bars, for instance, too easily overlook their positive function and offer lesbians and gays no realistic alternatives.[60]

This is not to say that all is well on the gay scene. Based on consumerism, much of this scene offers few opportunities for significant interactions.[61] Many gay persons get hooked on it, not realizing that it, too, is a closet, imposing its gay stereotypes and encouraging phony role-playing[62] and competitive cruising.[63] Glen, a thirty year-old gay, speaks for many experienced gays when he says that the scene is "a ghetto, and like all ghettos it narrows your vision of yourself and the rest of the world."[64] When a gay or a lesbian becomes totally absorbed in gay society – and according to research very many do[65] – he or she begins to construct a world unto itself, one which alienates from authentic social intercourse. How will someone who is trapped in such an environment become healthily self-assertive and grow strong enough in his social identity to function normally in the human community? As important as they are, "loving relationships" alone are no substitute for a lack of inner identity and ego-strength.

This brings us to a third relational strategy which, beyond the ongoing dialogue with good friends of the other sex and of the other sexual orientation, seeks to promote the kind of progressive conversion and change of which responsible, adult morality is made. This strategy is fundamentally a mental attitude. We could call it openness to growth.

The doctrinaire, psychoanalytic position which presents homosexuality as an arrest in development is, today, highly questionable.[66] In view of the available data, I would hesitate at the present time to elaborate any kind of general argument with a built-in "immaturity" assumption.[67] The openness-to-growth strategy need not imply that gay people should try to become heterosexuals. I can appreciate Marc Oraison's argument against a panicky, self-given homosexual label following some acute case of adolescent, same-sex attachments and erotic experiences.[68] We should not deny the existence of pseudo-homosexual identities any more than the existence of pseudo-[69] heterosexual ones. Both may serve as self-fulfilling prophecies. What openness to growth does imply, therefore, is the readiness to discover one's genuine sexual orientation (whether this be homosexual or heterosexual) and to become responsible for one's true sexual identity.

However, there is more to openness to growth than seeking the truth about one's sexual orientation. Gays and lesbians who are mature and truly homosexual should not, in the name of a certain gay sincerity and authenticity, decide to close their own developmental file, never question their feelings again, and justify their every act by saying: "We are made like that." By each of our human choices we make ourselves be who we are. To abdicate this dominion over ourselves, to lose the ability to even wish to be different (I am not referring to heterosexuality here), is to forsake our privilege to be moral. Gayness does not include a shorter way to moral maturity.[70] One should resist the suggestion, often found in excessively apologetical, gay literature, that gay is good without discernment, conversion, and growth. Eden is lost to gays as well as to nongays.

At this point, we have spelled out possible shortcomings of gay fecundity and suggested remedial strategies. To envisage the relational aspect of gay fecundity exclusively in these terms, however, would be shortsighted or biased. The gay experience of relating might prove of value for any community which is open enough to learn from it. After all, nongays should also cultivate an openness to growth.

A recent discovery of nongays concerning gays is that gay partners are not bound to play conventional husband and wife games and roles in order to have a meaningful and enduring partnership. Experienced gay counsellors are urging lesbians and gays to choose partnership patterns which fit the real-life situation of the partners involved rather than to copy stereotyped conjugal roles.[71] In fact, lesbians and gays, being freer from strictly assigned marital roles, do have the opportunity to invent new forms of partnerships. Married people may indeed learn something from them in terms of sharing as equal persons.[72] Gay men are often very threatening to other men and gay women to other women precisely because they challenge a deeply internalized, sexist dualism with its contestable assignment of roles. Those who, for some reason or other, have vested interest in the patriarchal status quo react by falsely branding lesbians as manly and gays as effeminate.[73] They should perhaps replace this unfounded and therefore rash name-calling with some honest self-appraisal: What kind of women and men are they themselves? Are they enough their own persons to become sexually fecund towards one another or are they playing stifling roles?

In addition to the gay relationship's potential for experimenting with democratic rather than despotic models of partnership, an active nonviolent style of human relationships must also be counted as a plus of the gay experience. The sameness implied in gay mutuality is, perhaps, too summarily appraised negatively.[74] If it is true to say that sameness does not foster growth-producing conflicts, is it not equally true to state that it averts some destructive ones? In Totem and Taboo, Sigmund Freud suggested that, after they had banded together in order to overcome their father who possessed all the women, the brothers of the original horde were enabled to renounce the possession of women through their homosexual feelings and acts. Same-sex attraction and affection kept them from fighting among themselves over the women. Social organization was thus rescued. This would have been the germ of the institution of matriarchy later replaced by the patriarchal organization of the family.[75] If one reads Freud not for historical accounts nor therapeutic techniques but for insights into humanity, one might find that, here again, there is more than meets the eye.

If anything is more difficult than being a gay male, in our own patriarchal organization of the family, it is perhaps to be a nonviolent, caring, and tender heterosexual male.[76] I have already mentioned a well-known fact that half the crimes in North America are perpetrated on the victims by members of their own heterosexually structured families. Contrary to the widely diffused belief among "concerned parents" that gay men are child molestors, current research has also established over and over again that the usual rapist of both girls and boys, his own and his neighbours', is statistically the heterosexual male.[77] Most men who have sex with boys from twelve to sixteen, for that matter, are more heterosexual than homosexual.[78] To whom do we owe our empty parks, our empty streets, our cities empty every evening of the year because packs of young hoodlums mug everyone in sight? Is this the outcome of the gay scene? Are these ruffians not the product of the heterosexual scene where successful males are pictured and constantly advertized as greedy, conquering, aggressive beings who prey on female sex objects and on any other male who does not have a killer instinct?

John Money and Anke Ehrhardt state that, despite the non-uniformity of traits in the gay personality, there is one that is shared by the majority of irreversibly gay males: "As boys, they were not fighters. They avoided challenges to compete for dominance in the dominance hierarchy of boyhood."[79] The gay literature of the past ten years seems to bear this out. It also bears witness to the fact that gay friendships and gay behaviour, contrary to the allegations of David Reüben in his Everything you always wanted to know about sex but were afraid to ask, are characterized by nonviolence. If there is an obvious attempt on the male gay scene to construct macho types of homosexuality (cowboy, truck driver, athlete, etc.),[81] this is mostly a reaction to the feminization of gays (an image imposed upon gays by the heterosexual view) which incites a number of them to stress virility. However, as Freud realized, same-sex attraction does not push gays to make war on each other but to make love to each other.

Violence and active nonviolence are two opposite strategies, indeed two contradictory ethical styles. They permeate all social transactions. From the start of the gay liberation movement, lesbians and gays have chosen, tellingly enough, to follow the Gandhian tradition of active nonviolence. It has been the method employed by Troy Perry, founder of the Universal Fellowship of Metropolitan Community Churches, in the demonstrations he organized to support gay persons treated unjustly in San Francisco.[82] Homosexual organizations, such as the Gay Activist Alliance, have been unswerving in their dedication to active, nonviolent methods.[83]

I have qualified nonviolence by the word "active," because nonviolent attitudes and behaviour can be highly ambiguous. When nonviolence refers to a passive pacifism, resulting from a lack of ego-strength and of lucid social commitment or, perhaps worse of all, from a need to become a victim in a self-punishing rite for one's own repressed aggressiveness and guilt, then nonviolence functions as a blinder and is itself disguised violence. Gandhi and all his followers teach that active nonviolence rests on "home rule," a self control which requires interior strength and the acquired ability to handle confrontations smoothly.[84]

Because of the way they relate to same-sex persons and because of what they are up against in our society, lesbians and gays are in a unique position to liberate sexual relationships from stereotypical, aggressive styles and to develop an active, nonviolent style of partnership which we badly need at the present time if we want to survive as human beings.[85] This, at least, is at the heart of the Christian creed for which the very content of interrelationship is love.

3. CELEBRATION OF GRATUITOUS LOVE

In their study, Homosexualities, Alan Bell and Martin Weinberg observe that those in the Churches who propose a new, positive view of homosexuality argue that sexual relationships involving "mutual respect, genuine affection, and an enduring commitment cannot be viewed as morally reprehensible."[86] I think this quite accurately summarizes a widespread position. When gay sex is loving (and here qualifications are sometimes added: committed, hopeful, giving and receiving, responsible, etc.), it is difficult to discover, in the words of Leonard Barnett, what Christian law is broken.[87]

I recognize that this argument often lacks depth and sophistication. Hence, it leaves itself open to refutation: granted that a gay sexual relationship is "loving," is it sexually integrating, constructive of male-female humanity and of community? A Christian can hardly dispute the fact, however, that the basic law of human relationship is love (Mt 22: 37-40; Mk 12: 28-31; Lk 10: 25-28; Jn 13: 34-35; Rm 13: 8-10; Ga 5: 14): love covers a multitude of sins (1 P 4: 8); it makes one learn to value the things that really matter (Ph 1: 9-10); it binds all the rest together and makes them perfect (Col 3: 14); it alone will never come to an end (1 Co 13: 8). Hence, as "orthodox" a theologian as Thomas Aquinas deduced that moral life can only be destroyed in someone when love, whereby one is united to God, is destroyed. There is no other way one can turn from the ultimate goal of the whole, concrete moral order.[88] When Thomas inquires whether injustice, for instance, is a deadly sin, a sin properly so called, one which destroys Christian life, he merely argues that, since injustice consists in doing harm to another, it strikes at love, "which gives life to the soul."[89] In other words, all possible shortcomings and deformities found in a human act may well be called "moral faults" because of deficiency or excess in reference to a certain ideal of human excellence (whether the definition follows Aristotle's or Maslow's descriptions and prescriptions) but none of this is automatically a sin in the Christian sense of the word of love is not destroyed thereby.

I am dumbfounded to find professional Christian ethicists who deal with homosexuality writing so much about reproductivity and the male-female structure of humanity and so little about love. I have yet to hear from many of them how the homosexual language, spoken between consenting gay partners with "mutual respect, genuine affection, and an enduring commitment" constitutes an unloving act against him or her or against anybody else. In twelfth-century England, St. Aelred, "the gay Abbot of Rievaulx," utilized his own gay experience of love to write some of the best Medieval dissertations on friendship and on the love of God.[90] When it is authentic and generous of self, gay love is fruitful.

Are gay persons in a position in our own cultural context to celebrate true love in a special fashion? In Saint Paul's hymn to love (1 Co 13: 1-13), two expressions put across features which could well characterize gay people's contribution to the Christian experience of love in our own society: "there is no limit to love's power to endure," and "love does not brood over injuries." These are expressions of love's gratuitousness, that whereby love is love, establishing between human beings an economy of gift based ultimately on God's gift of the Spirit in Jesus the Christ.

"Love's power to endure" is the definition of fidelity. Relational sexual fidelity is a fundamental disposition to maintain through time the quality and intensity of a loving and sexually creative presence between two persons. Strange as it may sound, I believe that such a fidelity is an aspect of loving gratuitousness which gays and lesbians vouch for in a very unique way. Many defenders of the gay scene are arguing, on the contrary, that, since gay people should not be assimilated to heterosexual spouses, promiscuous sex is the essence of a gay commitment.[91] I believe they are wrong.

First, attitudinal surveys have established that gays and nongays are generally very similar in the satisfaction they derive from their love relationships and in their general expectations regarding commitment, intimacy, and personal freedom. The bottom line of Letitia Anne Peplau's survey on twenty features a relationship might have is that the differences in expectations is really not between gays and nongays, but between men and women.[92] Then, there is strong evidence to believe that faithful gay partners form the best adjusted and happiest gay group. Alan Bell and Martin Weinberg's study, the most extensive research on homosexualities yet completed in America, reports that "Close-Coupleds" (their "happily married" gays and lesbians) not only demonstrate superior adjustment compared with all other gay groups but "could not be distinguished from the heterosexuals on various measures of psychological adjustment and actually scored higher on the two happiness measures."[93] Even allowing for Edward Malloy's cautionary methodological remarks on the above study,[94] the fact remains that serious data exist to back up the position which holds that sexual fidelity is part and parcel of gay sexual fecundity.[95]

These studies confirm, on the other hand, the widely known fact that gay partnerships are statistically less liable to survive than nongay marriages. However, researchers rightly observe that gays and lesbians encounter fewer social barriers than married nongays to calling it quits. When same-sex relationships are in trouble, family and friends rarely encourage the partners to work out differences. There are usually no children to worry about, no legal formalities to negotiate, no financially dependent partner to look after.[96] This is precisely the point which supports my case for the special social value of gay fidelity. Theirs can hardly be a case of loveless, institutional fidelity. Lesbians and gays who remain in a partnership generally do so by the strength of their mutual love and dedication because of highly qualitative, relational sexual fidelity.

Sexual fidelity cannot be more optional for gay Christians than for nongay Christians because, for human beings who become who they are through time, fidelity is the historical condition of sexual fecundity. To experience relational fidelity is to experience the redeeming power of love. In life-long, interpersonal commitment, loving partners maintain alive in each other's heart the hope that lasting love is possible, that it exists and that it is godly. In that sense, relational sexual fidelity is the test of Covenant love in our lives.

Gay persons should, therefore, seek to avoid the corruption of sexual fidelity through excess or deficiency. Affective entrapment is the name of the excess. It happens when a partner becomes a life buoy, one from whom the other expects everything. This, I suspect, is a trap of which lesbian lovers should be particularly made aware. Happily, this does not appear to be typical of gay women and men in North America today. Recent surveys have shown that they are apt to have more close friends than nongays generally do.[97] This is a sign of health for gay relationships because a human project which is lived as bondage instead of liberation cannot be moral. Authentic sexual fidelity, on the contrary, creates room for the other to be himself or herself, to be self-trusting because of the other's full acceptance.

Where sexual fidelity is lacking, we find promiscuity. Although they may agree about little else, most students of homosexuality agree that there is a much higher rate of promiscuity in the male than in the female gay world.[98] One-night stands make orgasms, rarely love. And when a person is habitually looked at by hungry eyes, eyes showing only a desire to "eat" him, how will he ever believe and hope in the covenant love of God when there is no living witness to vouch for it? "Samaritans," prostitutes, "tax collectors," adulterers, all those for whom no one really cares are reborn to themselves and to others when Jesus looks at them with life-giving eyes. Having finally seen and been looked at tenderly by one who loves in earnest, they can finally believe that there is, after all, a Father in heaven (Jn 14: 9).

Norman Pittenger justly observes that people who engage in one-night stands do so, most of the time, not because they are selfish and wicked but because they are lonely, seeking some attention, however imperfect, in a casual release from sexual tension.[99] Craving some affection, one feels an overwhelming need for some skin contact, since tenderness is never human when it is not enfleshed. Research data confirm the fact that, oftentimes, gay partners picked up in cruising are involved in more interaction than mere impersonal sex.[100] However, an individual easily falls into the habit of putting himself in the path of anyone (significantly called "trade" on the cruising scene) who is willing to put his hands on him. If he is young or attractive, he even finds strangers who are quite willing to pay something, in kind or money, to do just that and nothing more. After his body has been touched and used in this context of fast tricking, he has generally not received the expected care. He feels worse about himself and his loneliness merely increases. Hence, another fortuitous partner is sought with the same results. As the need to be stimulated grows with each encounter, confidence in himself and trust in others diminish until he cannot recognize and accept the caring even when it is there because sensuality is completely divorced from tenderness.[101] He is well on the way to fitting Otto Kernberg's description of a pathological, promiscuous narcissist, in whom self-hatred is stronger than self-love. He has lost the capacity to fall in love and to enter a long-term commitment.[102]

Though promiscuous, dysfunctional gays are probably not more numerous, proportionally, than promiscuous, dysfunctional nongays. Heterosexism ("an ideology that assigns a person to inferior status and lack of human dignity because his or her sexual orientation is toward persons of the same sex"[103]) depicts all gay persons as depersonalized, immoral beings and treats them with ridicule and injustice. This well-known and much commented upon situation[104] is the basis for my second suggestion: if love's gratuitousness can be characterized in the life of Christian gay persons by sexual fidelity toward a gay partner, it can also be characterized by forgiveness toward nongays and by a compassionate life style.[105]

In her reaction against persecution, Ruth Simpson retaliates by a massive attack against heterosexual women, families, the world at large, feminist organizations, the Catholic Church, psychiatrists, journalists, police officers, and the courts of justice.[106] This and similar indictments are, it seems to me, a road which Christian gay persons should not follow. I do not wish to insinuate that gay-haters have legitimate grounds for their hate and their injustices. They do not.[107] "To all who are pure themselves, everything is pure" (Tt 1: 15). Nor am I suggesting that passivity, indifference, or submission are the answer. The oppressed gay world is a choice sector for liberation theology in North America.[108] And gay liberation will be attained only where courageous lesbians and gays denounce injustices while being actively involved in modifying the extant social situation.

While stereotypes can be exposed, injustices denounced, and rights vindicated, those who trespass against us should be forgiven. It often helps to remember that many a gay-hater is himself a victim in need of help: a sexually rigid person threatened by guilt about his or her own sexual impulses;[109] an individual threatened by the fear of his or her same-sex inclinations;[110] or a man threatened in his stereotyped male identity.[111] "Saint" Peter Damian, the most vocal spokesman for the antigay campaign in the history of the Church, the author

of the only extant ecclesiastical tract against homosexuality, the
eleventh-century Liber Gomorrhianus,[112] was a battered child,
rejected by his mother, beaten constantly, and treated as a slave
by an older brother and his cruel wife during the first twelve
years of his life.[113]

Forgiveness is a celebration of life over death, of
existence over nothingness, of love over hatred. It alone has the
spiritual power which is needed to break, at some point, the
spiral of hostility. Out of one's experience of the fragility of
all things human, of anguish, of loneliness and of hurt, one can
find in one's heart a basis for initiating (for-giveness) new
relationships of love, of that whereby we are all redeemed from
our finitude and from our sins. The passion to exist and to share
our life in love is never better affirmed than in the celebration
of forgiveness.

To forgive is divine. There is perhaps no parable in
the New Testament which speaks more eloquently of the Heavenly
Father than that of the "prodigal son": it is a celebration of
life by a forgiving parent (Lk 15: 11-32). In his own dealings
with "sexual sinners," Jesus demonstrates, by an identical
attitude, how much he is the true Son of God. Lesbians and gays
who wish to be Jesus' disciples in renovating the earth by loving
their enemies and praying for their persecutors so that they might
be sons and daughters of the Father in heaven (Mt 5: 44-45), have
their own "sexual sinners" to forgive in the person of all gay-
haters. To speak a sexual language in which hostility is conveyed
to persons whose sexual orientations is not one's own is the
epitome of sexual sinfulness. To respond in the same fashion would
make lesbians and gays no better than their oppressors. Because
lesbians and gays are so constantly the target of gay-haters,
those among them who have learned to make their peace and for whom
forgiveness has become a way of life contribute much to liberate
sexual expressions of love from fear, guilt, and anger. Having
grown through pain (is there any other way?), they have acquired,
as Matthew Fox remarks, a "sensitive vulnerability" that allows
them "to identify with the sufferings of other oppressed persons."
They can be genuinely compassionate. Their suffering becomes
redemptive.[114]

Gay persons whose sexual language is fruitful in
faithfulness to a partner, in forgiveness towards their enemies,
and in compassion for the oppressed have indeed mastered the art
of sexual love in a way which can only build Christian community.
They celebrate love with a gratuity which testifies to the fact
that their love is indeed Christian love.

4. A SOCIAL SEXUAL PRAXIS

Sexual fecundity may take the historical form of parenting. Some gay persons have children of their own, either through a former marriage or, in the case of lesbians, through casual heterosexual coitus or artificial insemination.[115] Others, relatively few, are granted permission to adopt or to become foster parents.[116] As their "patron saint" they could claim Ruth who got a child from Boaz for Noami and herself.[117]

When the ethical implications of this form of gay fecundity are examined dispassionately, they prove to differ little in their nature from those of parenting for heterosexual persons. Those who disagree with this statement will, in all likelihood, raise the objection: "But can we really say that being raised by gay parents is in the child's best interest?" The problem with this question, however, is that the case of an abstract child raised by abstract gay parents does not exist. What does exist is Peter or Helen in the parental care of John and Paul or Mary and Jane.

In the case where Peter or Helen are presumably heterosexual children, the most reasonable answer seems to be: "Who are the best available parents?" At this point in time, it seems as arbitrary to assume that a heterosexual parent will automatically do a better job of parenting than a gay parent[118] as to assume that a female is _ipso facto_ a more qualified parent than a male.[119] This is not to deny the fact that, given certain social conditions, the parent's gayness, like the maleness or the femaleness of a divorced parent, may be one factor which should go into the decision-making process concerning custody. Should it be the decisive one? The current research on children in custody of gay divorcees, notably males, reports little effect of the parent's sexual preference on a child's sexual orientation.[120] The new, major study conducted by the Kinsey Institute on the development of homosexuality in men and women finds little or no support for traditional theories concerning the role of parents in sexual preference.[121] Is it not somewhat hard to believe, therefore, that a child is better off with an irresponsible or neurotic heterosexual parent than with a responsible and healthy homosexual one? Why speculate on whether, "all things being equal," the gay or the nongay is the better parent? The truth of the matter is that "all things" are always unequal because they are so very circumstantial. Ethicists ought, therefore, to avoid sweeping statements on this issue.[122] As Brenda Maddox rightly suggests, custody should be decided "on observable factors like the parents' devotion to their children, their good sense in managing them, their general ethical standards and their children's love for them."[123]

In the case where Peter or Helen are presumable homosexual children, the foregoing remarks still apply. If some gay organizations sponsor fostering programs by gays and lesbians for children or adolescents who are themselves homosexually oriented, it is because there are literally thousands of such youngsters who have run away from (when they have not been thrown out and disowned by[124]) heterosexual parents who cannot deal with the gayness of their own children, regardless of the beautiful qualities of these children.

Though there can be little doubt that twelve- or fifteen-year olds may already have an irreversible homosexual orientation, ascertaining whether Peter or Helen is such a child remains, it seems to me, highly problematic.[125] This is the Achilles' heel. But, again, I am convinced that a run-away child who, rightly or wrongly, labels himself gay or has all the symptoms of gayness is better off with healthy gay parents who care enough about the child's own good to help him or her discern his or her sexual orientation and to live creatively with the outcome than with uptight heterosexual parents who give their homosexually inclined child a negative self-image; who refuse their child a much needed supportive love; or who are so threatened by their child's tendencies that they let all their opportunities to guide the child slip away. This is not to mention the fact that socialization of the homosexual child by heterosexual parents is problematic in itself. Parents of a black child in a white society can communicate to their child that he or she is black and what it is like to be a black in a white society. Few nongay parents are able to perform the same task for their homosexual child.[126] For street kids who have oftentimes become professional hustlers, the problem may obviously have become too complex for any normal parenting formula. Different categories of group homes may well be, as Robin Lloyd suggests, the best solution.[127]

When we shift the focus from the child's point of view to that of the gay parents, the moral problems that might possibly arise are again akin to those faced by heterosexual parents. Antigay campaigners may argue that some gay foster parents may nourish a seductive intent. They may even quote certain gay literature which, calling on the Greek tradition of pederastic education, promotes overt same-sex activities between adults and children.[128] However, the alarming increase of heterosexual incestuous behaviour and the incipient literature defending the practice[129] show that the problem which can be identified in the gay world is no different from the one found in the nongay world. For most prospective parents, gays as well as nongays, the fundamental ethical issue is really one of motivation: "Why do I want a child?" Gay men who wish to have a child to solve their own problem of loneliness or to strengthen their partnership, as well as lesbian, feminist activists who wish to score a point against

the "patriarchal, heterosexual power" by begetting a child through
artificial insemination are all sinning against this child. Gays
as well as nongays should not consider parenting where the primary
concern is not the child's own good.

There is obvious truth in the gay slogan, "Two-four-
six-eight, we don't overpopulate." Parenting is not the way most
lesbians and gays develop the historical implications of their
sexual fecundity. They characteristically exercise the latter, it
seems to me, through a social sexual praxis. I take "praxis" to
refer to the regime of human activity and reality precisely as
historical. Action becomes praxis when it is critically committed
to the making of history in a community. We are becoming aware of
the fact that, through their very sexual identity and practice,
gay people are critically among us. Contrary to many other groups,
the North American homosexual community represents a sense of
shared values and a willingness to assert sexuality as part of the
whole of life.[130] Their sexual fecundity does have a
characteristic social exposure and should contribute to society's
own renewal.

Psychotherapist Clarence Tripp is probably right when
he claims that "the socially integrated homosexual [...]
consistently defines himself as a regular member of society -
refusing to see himself or to let others see him as set apart from
it."[131] Even the authors of The Joy of Gay Sex reassure young gay
men with the picture of "well-adjusted older gay men."[132] And the
latest scientific studies confirm the fact that many avowed
lesbians and gays have stable and satisfying work records.[133]
Without a certain degree of social integration and effectivenes,
one has, except under very exceptional circumstances, a weak basis
for a valid critique of society - one lacks the required
credentials. Rollo May evokes, on this score, the pseudoinnocence
of the flower-children type of social criticism.[134] Who will ever
take seriously the social indictments of insignificant, social
parasites whose very survival hinges on the technological advances
they pretend to denounce?

It is true that a social critique through active
commitment to human affairs also presupposes that one keeps one's
distance from certain social practices and that one contests them
by being and acting in a way that produces other social meanings
and values.[135] If, therefore, "moral integration" is tantamount to
the disappearance of gay identity, gay people will be in no
position to debunk prevalent sociosexual prejudices and
insanities. The disquieting otherness of lesbians and gays plays a
prophetical role to the extent that they are perceived as
committed citizens.

Richard Woods has compared gay people to "clowns," not
to the powerless circus-clown who amuses children but to the clown

182

reinstated where he belongs, in the public place and in the king's courtroom and council chamber. He is the clown who is ready to face the king's wrath and the citizen's vindictiveness for telling them, in jest, their truth.[136] In this sense, Georges Rouault's crucified Christs capture well the Clown's sacred mission. The paradigmatic story of the Exodus, that of "a rabble of people" (Nb 11: 4), "People of various sorts" (Ex 12: 38) which later became Israel, already spoke of God's predilection for those who are powerless minorities, those whose visionary nonconformity is disturbing to their oppressors. The Crucified Christ is the ultimate symbol of God's redemptive love for "what is foolish by human reckoning" (1 Co: 26-31). In him, the lowly are exalted (Lk 1: 52).

While Jews, the former minority of Christian society, repossessed Israel and became the new majority; Blacks, the White society's minority, repossessed Africa (well... most of it!) and became the new majority; French Canadians, Canada's minority, repossessed Québec and became the new majority; because the man/woman difference is not accidental like those above gay people will never become a majority. They will forever stay a minority in the midst of human society – the "disquieting others."[137] By this very fact, their's will always be the role of "the opposition." Their's is the function of critically appraising society's sexual options and practices. Lived in faith by a Christian, the gay sexual praxis is a committment in the service of the larger enterprise of liberating the human so that God's image can shine forth in it.

Is it possible to be more specific about this gay social critique? It is highly plausible that, as Seymour Kleinberg seems to argue, some gays and lesbians fabricate secret values which run counter to everything the heterosexual society believes in.[138] In this sense, "camp" would still be an adequate, coded language of subversive gay outsiders.[139] The question is whether we can expect any more from this than from the sterile contestation of overgrown hippies? I am of the opinion that there are more positive and fundamental contributions to expect from lucid and Christian gay people than the outrageously colorful extravaganzas of an atypical assortment of nellies and leather-clad ruffians.

By their social commitment through a sexual identity (since this is that whereby they are socially contested), gay women and men challenge a widespread contemporary trend, denounced by social analysts like Wilhelm Reich and Herbert Marcuse, to separate sexual communication from social endeavours. For many people in our society today, sex has become the paradise of personal harmony, a private space where individuals withdraw from the rest of the world and enjoy humanized interactions.[140] Outside this guarded Eden, where young and old take refuge occasionally from the lonely crowd, too many encounters are anonymous, manipulative, and dehumanizing transactions. Asocial, private, sexual happiness is a myth Christians cannot buy without betraying their hope in the construction of a loving community. Sexual fecundity must humanize social interactions.

Present to the world as persons in their own right, unsupported by influential family credentials, gays and lesbians question a certain social use of sexual bonds to gain power. Christian gays and lesbians should become conscious of the fact that they confront an anti-evangelical hierarchy of values which appraises social worthiness by one's race, one's family ties, one's influential friends (see Mt 11: 2-5). The powerful of this world side with stable, patriarchal families because in them,[141] individuals are taught conformity to law and order. History teaches that, structured by private property and male authority, such families have more often than not resisted social changes even when these were needed for the common good.[142]

This factual tendency of families to "take care" of their own in this world at the expense of the larger fellowship's well-being may explain the radical Evangelical criticism concerning the relative significance of family loyalty,[143] because, like all those who take up the cause of the poor, the outcast, the marginalized, Jesus appears much more as a "family breaker" than as a family person. The only one whom he ever calls "Abba" ("papa") is God. This Father's house is the only one to which he feels bound (Lk 2: 49. See Mk 3: 20-21). Those whom he calls upon to follow him are warned that this commitment will bring about family tensions (Mt 10: 34-36). Disciples should abandon all claims to family ties (Mt 19: 29; Lk 14: 25-26), place the affairs of the Kingdom before filial devotions (Lk 9: 60), and be more attached to Jesus' fellowship than to mothers, fathers, sons, and daughters (Mt 10: 37). The "forgiving father" whom Jesus praises so highly in Luke 15 does everything a good Jewish father of the time who cared for "family life" would not have done: that is, show so much comprehension for a young son who squandered his inheritance and so much indifference toward an elder son who took such good care of the family patrimony. No, Jesus is conspicuously not a family promoter. To call on the "holy family" as a model of family ties and virtues is a mere pious figment of the imagination. Nothing is known of Jesus' "family life" apart from the fact that, one day, the good little boy ran away from home to prepare the urgent revolutionary task which lay ahead and, in so doing, broke his parents' hearts (Lk 2: 41-50). If one thing is clear in Jesus' attitudes and sayings, therefore, it is that pedigrees and clan affiliations are not that whereby society is redeemed from its lack of soul.[144] Human creativity, in Jesus' book, is not necessarily linked with the family principle. Gays and lesbians are capable of a fecundity which contributes to liberating sexuality from family appropriation as a force to dominate others.

Finally, through their sexual social praxis gay people dispute the widely held notion of heterosexual society that humanity is ultimately reconciled within the couple.[145] This is an old story. The Sadducees had not understood, either, that at the resurrection marriages are irrelevant (Mt 22: 30) because they had not understood that Christ is the only locus of the reconciliation of human nature (Ga 3: 23-29). Only that which is redeemed by liberating love has eternal value. This is the truth which gay Christians could act out in a heterosexual society which tends to absolutize conjugal and family values and, in so doing, deforms them.

For gay sexual praxis to have a social impact, it must obviously enjoy a certain amount of visibility. This presupposes that its gay practitioners are decloseted. The concrete decision to disclose or conceal one's homosexual identity is a difficult one for most gays and lesbians in North America. Since disclosure always implies some painful effects, I will voice my position concerning "coming out" in the framework of the classical moral theory of an act with a double effect: a gay person ought to disclose his or her sexual orientation unless disproportionate harm is foreseen.[146]

Before looking at some of the benefits of disclosure (warranting my opinion) and at some causes of disproportionate harm (calling for qualification), we should realize that the very concept of disclosure is relative. Many persons hide their gayness from themselves using one or many systems of denial: "How," Peter keeps repeating to himself, "can I be a homosexual when I am so masculine?;" "I'm innocent," muses Mary, "since I only answer to homosexual advances from others;" "Between Helen and myself," says Jane, "there's only a very special friendship;" "It's merely temporary," reflects Richard, "a holdover from what I did when I was younger."[147]

For centuries, the "good name" of anyone committing the "unmentionable vice" has been undermined. This led to a loss of self-respect and to the crippling emotions of fear and anxiety.[148] Guilt contributes to divorcing many gay persons from their original history. They forsake who they are because they have been told that gayness could not be part of it. To become free as all of God's true children, gay persons must learn to transfer their guilt into an awareness of human finitude and a celebration of the Liberator's redemptive love. Now is perhaps the best time for lesbians and gays to reflect on the meaning of human limitations and boldly teach a North America, which has also lost its "good reputation" in the face of Nations and is reacting with overwhelming fear to its loss of innocence, how to become peacefully "just human" when the dice are no longer loaded to one's advantage.

"Coming out" is best understood as a process, one through which a homosexual person establishes contact with her true self, recognizes her sexual preference, chooses to integrate this knowledge into her personal life and to make her public self congruent with her true self.[149] When the step of self-disclosure has been taken, other steps may or not follow: one may disclose one's sexual preference to gay partners, to some close heterosexual friends, to some family members.[150] When neighbours, employer and work associates know about one's homosexuality, overtness is usually complete. The few reflections which follow apply, to a great extent, at all levels of disclosure.

Why should we consider "passing" (the gay word for hiding one's homosexuality) as merely a "lesser evil" in given circumstances and "coming out" as the better option? The basic reason is that, as a rule, the virtue of sexual integration requires a sexual activity which is expressive of one's own truth, of one's real sexual identity. New York's famous Dr. Howard J. Brown,[151] in an address delivered in November, 1973, to the Gay Academic Union of Hunter College, said: "I have found that I can associate much more honestly and clearly with the straight faculty members. I had not realized how many things about myself I really hid, and how many times during the day I was still programmed to be a shadow of the way I am."[152] Liberated from a false identity and from a phony expression of oneself to others, one may start speaking the sexual language as one's mother tongue, not as a foreign language. By the same token, others are given the chance to relate intimately with a real person, not with a fantasy-person.

Lesbians and gays who are not known as homosexuals must continually strive to present a false image of who they are and of how they really feel.[153] If this is not alienation, I do not know what is. Moreover, the fear of exposure, of seeing their way of life ruined at any moment, forces them to continually devise strategies of disguise.[154] The lie can sometimes go so far as faking heterosexual love and taking another person "for a ride," using him or her as a means to protect oneself without any concern for this other person's integrity and future.[155] It is not astonishing to find, therefore, that self-hatred is much stronger among covert, "passing" homosexuals than it is among overt gays.[156]

To come out partially, partially solves the problem. However, there might be an added daily energy drain inevitable for one forced to live a double life with different sets of people. One has to start functioning as though one had many different identities. Shirley Luthman remarks that "that kind of constant shifting must take its toll in energy consumption that could otherwise be put to use for growth and creativity."[157] Since one is fragmented, one cannot operate as an integrated, organic self. Hence, one cannot realize all of one's human potential.

Researchers are agreed that the majority of homosexual persons "pass" as a means of avoiding social sanctions throughout most of their lives.[158] Publicly-avowed gays and lesbians are often frustrated by closet-bound homosexuals because they, in a certain way, "must pull the weight for those who are still hidden."[159] No one can doubt that, as people are learning that a daughter, a son, sometimes a parent, often a close friend is homosexual[160] the social attitude toward lesbians and gays is changing. If all those who are homosexual were known, if only to themselves, to friends and relatives, antigay laws and procedures could not be upheld and social attitudes would change radically.

The situation being what it is, however, no sensible person should yield to the pressure of militant lesbians and gays before weighing the stakes. At this point in time, North American society still coerces lesbians and gays into investing much energy defending their acceptability. Through its various door-closing discriminations, it also often deprives them of many social, religious, political, legal, and economic opportunities.[161] One must therefore assess whether one is strong enough to support the psychological pressure and, perhaps more decisively, whether some of the practical consequences in terms of this or that career and social life do not represent a disproportionate harm. This weighing is never a mathematical operation and cannot be done, therefore, in a merely abstract manner.[162] Whatever conclusion is reached regarding public disclosure, lesbians and gays should consider that family members and close friends are usually worth the consideration and the trust of being told who one is as a sexual being.

Considering the potential or actual shortcomings of their sexual fecundity, lesbians and gays must also acknowledge their own poverty and expect from God his gracious gift of love and from the Christian community life-giving values which others' fecundity can produce in them. Nongays should also be ready to do more than merely understand and support their gay sisters and brothers. For their love to be genuine, nongays must recognize, in the gay children of God, original versions of God's own inexhaustible fecundity. There is, in an authentic Christian experience of gay fecundity, a liberating potential which is very much in tune with some of the most significant evangelical passages concerning the Christian experience of loving community.

NOTES

1. (Westminster: Newman Press, 1960), p. xv.
2. GS, par. 50 (p. 1072; tr., p. 255).
3. One of the most enlightening studies of Aquinas's atypically incoherent position on gay sex is found in J. BOSWELL, Christianity, Social Tolerance, and Homosexuality. Gay People in Western Europe from the Beginning of the Christian Era to the Fourteenth Century (Chicago: University of Chicago Press, 1980), pp. 318-330. Though the reproductive aspect is also used in some Protestant discussion, it does not normally hold the place it occupies in Catholic thinking, both Roman and Anglo: see D. S. BAILEY, "Homosexuality and Christian Morals," in J. T. REES and H. V. USILL (eds.), They Stand Apart (London: Heinemann, 1955), p. 49; T. W. JENNINGS, "Homosexuality and Christian Faith: a Theological Reflection," in H. L. TWISS (ed.), Homosexuality and the Christian Faith: a Symposium (Valley Forge: Judson Press, 1978), pp. 60-61.
4. S. HANLEY et al., "Lesbianism: Knowns and Unknowns," in B. SCHLESINGER (ed.), Sexual Behaviour in Canada (Toronto: Toronto University Press, 1977), p. 126.
5. Among Roman Catholics: P. S. KEANE, Sexual Morality..., pp. 86-87; G. D. COLEMAN, Homosexuality - An Appraisal (Chicago: Franciscan Herald Press, 1978), p. 74; E. A. MALLOY, Homosexuality and the Christian Way of Life (Washington, D.C.: University Press of America, 1981), p. 227. The argument is also found in non-Roman Catholic theologians: e.g., R. GORDIS, "Homosexuality and the Homosexual," in E. BATCHELOR (ed.), Homosexuality and Ethics (New York: Pilgrim Press, 1980), p. 56; W. MUEHL, "Some Words of Caution," in L. T. TWISS (ed.), Homosexuality and the Christian Faith: A Symposium (Valley Forge: Judson Press, 1978), p. 83; É. FUCHS, Sexual Desire..., p. 216.
6. Even as unyielding a psychiatrist and theologian as Anglican R. T. BARNHOUSE, who classifies homosexual acts as "intrinsically evil," does not believe that the reproductive argument can be successfully employed today against gay sex: Homosexuality: a Symbolic Confusion (New York: Seabury Press, 1977), pp. 174-175. See also R. C. theologian M. A. FARLEY, "An Ethic for Same-Sex Relations," in R. NUGENT (ed.), A Challenge to Love. Gay and Lesbian Catholics in the Church (New York: Crossroad, 1983), p. 93.
7. H. K. JONES had already argued this point well in Toward a Christian Understanding of the Homosexual (New York: Association Press, 1966), p. 99.
8. D. S. BAILEY, Homosexuality and the Western Christian Tradition (London: Longmans, Green, 1955); A. J. R. BRUSSARD, "La Bible et l'homosexualité," in H. WITTE (ed.), Dieu les aime tels qu'ils sont. Pastorale pour les homophiles (Paris: Fayard, 1972), pp. 43-58; J. J. McNEILL, The Church and the Homosexual

(Kansas City: Sheed, Andrews and McMeal, 1976), pp. 37-66; T. M. HORNER, Jonathan Loved David. Homosexuality in Biblical Times (Philadelphia: The Westminster Press, 1978); V. P. FURNISH, The Moral Teaching of Paul (Nashville: Abington Press, 1979), pp. 52-83; J. BOSWELL, Christianity..., pp. 91-117; W. WOGGON, "A Biblical and Historical Study of Homosexuality," Journal of Religion and Health, 20 (1981), pp. 156-163; M. A. FARLEY, "An Ethic...," pp. 94-95; R. SCROGGS, The New Testament and Homosexuality. Contextual Background For Contemporary Debate (Philadelphia: Fortress Press, 1983); G. R. EDWARDS, Gay/Lesbian Liberation. A Biblical Perspective (New York: Pilgrim Press, 1984). Fundamentalist interpretations of Scripture as found, e.g., in G. L. BAHNSEN, Homosexuality: A Biblical View (Grand Rapids: Baker Book House, 1978), are as good a corroboration as one can find of the inconclusiveness of the biblical case against homosexuality.

9. From this point of view, see L. SCANZONI and V. R. MOLLENKOTT, Is the Homosexual My Neighbor? Another Christian View (San Francisco: Harper and Row, 1978). This essay may lack depth of analysis, but it has the merit of asking the relevant question.

10. This use of the word "sodomy" is still found in P. PALAZZINI, "Homosexualitas," in P. PALAZZINI (ed.), Dictionarium Morale et Canonicum (Rome: Catholic Book Agency, 1965), Vol. II, pp. 559-560.

11. P. ARIÈS, "Réflexions...," p. 58.

12. It is interesting to note that THOMAS AQUINAS (ST, I^a-II^{ae}, q. 31, a. 7), following ARISTOTLE (Nicomachean Ethics, VII, 6: 1148b25 - 1149a3) answered negatively to this very question. Both held that the sexual acts of those who were constitutionally gay escaped moral qualification.

13. See, among others: J. KATZ, Gay American History. Lesbians and Gay Men in the U.S.A. (New York: T. Y. Crowell, 1976); C. ISHERWOOD, Christopher and His Kind, 1929-1939 (New York: Farrar, Straus and Giroux, 1976); H. BROWN, Familiar Faces, Hidden Lives. The Story of Homosexual Men in America Today (New York: Harcourt, Brace, Jovanovich, 1977); J. BABUSCIO, We Speak for Ourselves. Experiences in Homosexual Counselling (Philadelphia: Fortress Press, 1977); T. D. PERRY, The Lord Is My Shepherd and He Knows I'm Gay. The Autobiography of the Reverend Troy D. Perry as told by C. L. LUCAS (New York: Bantam, 1978); M. BOYD, Take Off the Masks (Garden City: Doubleday, 1978); L. FADERMAN, Surpassing the Love of Men. Romantic Friendship and Love Between Women from Renaissance to the Present (New York: Morrow, 1981); C. CHARRON, Désobéir (Montreal: VLB, 1983); A. BORDEN, "Growing Up Lesbian and Catholic," in J. GRAMICK (ed.), Homosexuality and the Catholic Church (Chicago: The Thomas More Press, 1983), pp. 45-59; B. McNAUGHT, "Reflections of a Gay Catholic," ibid., pp. 21-44; J. GREEN, Jeunes années (Paris: Seuil, 1984). Some novels also

depict what many gays recognize as true to life: e.g., P. N. WARREN, The Front Runner (New York: Bantam, 1975); L. Z. HOBSON, Consenting Adult (Garden City: Doubleday, 1975); M. Z. BRADLEY, The Catch Trap (New York: Ballantine, 1979).

14. W. CHURCHILL, Homosexual Behavior Among Males (New York: Hawthorn, 1967), pp. 282-291.

15. E. M. SCHUR, Crimes Without Victims. Deviant Behavior and Public Policy: Abortion, Homosexuality, Drug Addiction (Englewood Cliffs; Prentice-Hall, 1965), pp. 104-107; G. H. WEINBERG, Society and the Healthy Homosexual (Garden City: Anchor Books, 1973), pp. 41-68; M. RIORDON, "Capital Punishment: Notes of a Willing Victim," The Body Politic, 17 (January/February, 1975), pp. 14-21; C. A. TRIPP, The Homosexual Matrix (New York: New American Library, 1976), pp. 243-267; G. C. DAVIDSON, "Homosexuality. The Ethical Challenge," Journal of Consulting and Clinical Psychology, 44 (1976), pp. 157-162, reprinted in Journal of Homosexuality, 2 (Spring 1977), pp. 195-204; C. SILVERSTEIN, "Homosexuality and the Ethics of Behavioral Intervention," ibid., pp. 205-211.

16. J. J. McNEILL, The Church..., p. 121. From this point of view, some recent theological discourses on the "homosexual perversion" can only succeed in achieving similar negative results: see, e.g., G. L. BAHNSEN, Homosexuality..., and K. PHILPOTT, The Gay Theology (Plainfield: Logos International, 1977).

17. For over a quarter century, J. F. HARVEY has been defending this theoretical position while trying to find "pastoral responses" to the gays' plight: see, again, in J. R. CAVANAGH, Counseling the Homosexual (Huntington: Our Sunday Visitor, 1977), pp. 222-238. Presbyterian J. R. KIRK holds a similar position in The Homosexual Crisis in the Mainline Church (New York: T. Nelson, 1978).

18. See, e.g., C. E. CURRAN, "Homosexuality and Moral Theology: Methodological and Substantive Considerations," The Thomist, 35 (1971), pp. 447-481, with further clarifications in "Moral Theology, Psychiatry and Homosexuality," in Transition and Tradition in Moral Theology (Notre Dame: Notre Dame University Press, 1971), pp. 59-80 and in "Moral Theology and Homosexuality," in J. GRAMICK (ed.), Homosexuality and the Catholic Church (Chicago: The Thomas More Press, 1983), pp. 138-168; J. F. DEDEK, Contemporary Medical Ethics (New York: Sheed and Ward, 1975), pp. 80-86; A. GUINDON, The Sexual Language..., pp. 365-368; P. S. KEANE, Sexual Morality..., pp. 84-90; L. S. CAHILL, "Moral Methodology: A Case Study," Chicago Studies, 19 (1980), pp. 171-187. Among Protestant theologians, see H. THIELICKE, The Ethics of Sex (London: J. Clarke, 1964), pp. 269-292; H. K. JONES, Toward a Christian Understanding..., pp. 97-100; R. K. SHINN, "Homosexuality: Christian Conviction and Inquiry," in R. W. WELTGE (ed.), The Same Sex. An Appraisal of Homosexuality (Philadelphia: Pilgrim Press, 1969), pp. 43-54. From a Jewish perspective a similar

view is held by H. MATT, "Sin, Crime, Sickness or Alternative Life Style: A Jewish Approach to Homosexuality," in Judaism, 27 (1978), pp. 13-24.

19. See, e.g., L. KOHLBERG, "Moral Stages and Moralization. The Cognitive-Developmental Approach," in T. LICKONA (ed.), Moral Development and Behavior. Theory, Research, and Social Issues (New York: Holt, Rinehart and Winston, 1976), pp. 31-53.

20. W. G. PERRY Jr., Forms of Intellectual and Ethical Development in the College Years. A Scheme (New York: Holt, Rinehart and Winston, 1968).

21. Among Catholics: G. BAUM, "Catholic Homosexuals," Commonweal, 99 (1974), pp. 479-482; J. J. McNEILL, The Church...; A. KOSNIK et al., Human Sexuality..., pp. 186-218, specifically pp. 214-215; G. MÉNARD, De Sodome à l'Exode. Jalons pour une théologie de la libération gaie (Montreal: Univers, 1980). Among theologians who are not Roman Catholics: N. SECOR, "A Brief for a New Homosexual Ethics," in R. W. WELTGE (ed.), The Same Sex. An Appraisal of Homosexuality (Philadelphia: Pilgrim Press, 1969), pp. 67-79; N. PITTENGER, Time for Consent? A Christian Approach to Homosexuality (London: SCM Press, 1967); L. P. BARNET, Homosexuality. Time To Tell the Truth to Young People, Their Families and Friends (London: V. Gollancz, 1975), pp. 88-99; T. W. JENNINGS, "Homosexuality...," pp. 57-68; J. B. NELSON, "Homosexuality and the Church," Christianity and Crisis, 37 (1977), pp. 63-69; and Embodiment..., pp. 181-210; B. W. HARRISON, "Misogyny and Homophobia. The Unexplored Connections," Integrity Forum, 7 (Lent 1981), pp. 7-13.

22. THOMAS AQUINAS, ST, I^a-II^{ae}, q. 12, a. 1, ad 4um.

23. See M. E. HUNT, "Lovingly Lesbian: Toward a Feminist Theology of Friendship," in R. NUGENT (ed.), A Challenge to Love. Gay and Lesbian Catholics in the Church (New York: Crossroad, 1983), pp. 135-155.

24. D. BLAMIRES, "Recent Christian Perspectives on Homosexuality – the Context for the Debate," in M. MACOURT (ed.), Towards a Theology of Gay Liberation (London: SCM Press, 1977), p. 16.

25. Alienated Affections. Being Gay in America (New York: St. Martin's Press, 1981), p. 43.

26. See, e.g., the conclusion of M. T. SAGHIR and E. ROBINS, Male and Female Homosexuality. A Comprehensive Investigation (Baltimore: Williams and Wilkins, 1973), pp. 112, 318, etc. Those who resist the idea most are still to be found among psychiatrists. W. C. ALVAREZ, Homosexuality and Other Forms of Sexual Deviance (New York: Pyramid Books, 1974), lists numerous studies that reinforce his advocacy of extended psychoanalysis for gays. But most of the resources he quotes were published before 1950. Even the most fierce advocates of the orthodox, psychoanalytical dogma today must qualify the success of their "cure." L. J. HATTERER, Changing Homosexuality in the Male. Treatment for Men Troubled by Homosexuality (New York: McGraw-Hill, 1970), p. 86, warns that

therapists must be realistic in their expectations: "In treatment of a patient who is past 35 and whose homosexual past is extensive, goals have to be modest and limited." C. W. SOCARIDES, Homosexuality (New York: J. Aronson, 1978), backs up his own statement, "There is at present sufficient evidence that in a majority of cases homosexuality can be successfully treated by psychoanalysis, or at least that its symptoms and suffering can be greatly alleviated" (p. 3), by ten clinical cases (pp. 195-397). They are persons who, aside from their homosexual adventures, are profoundly disturbed, who have been followed regularly by him during an average of 4 or 5 years (imagine the prohibitive costs for the rank and file gay!) and who end up with doubtful heterosexual "adaptations." The case for reversibility is, at present, poorly defended. Moreover, contemporary findings contradict the view that pre-homosexual boys have an unusually strong maternal identification, an assumption which is at the heart of the psychoanalytic theory. See A. P. BELL, M. S. WEINBERG, and S. KIEFER HAMMERSMITH, Sexual Preference. Its Development in Men and Women (Bloomington: Indiana University Press, 1981), pp. 41-51. The dominant view on the goals of therapy for gays is that it should seek to help the client become better adjusted as a gay or lesbian when a person discovers him/herself to be one.

27. A. P. BELL, M. S. WEINBERG, and S. KIEFER HAMMERSMITH, Sexual Preference..., p. 200-202 (males), 207-208 (females): their findings seem to suggest that "exclusive homosexuality tends to emerge from a deep-seated predisposition, while bisexuality is more subject to influence by social and sexual learning." (p. 201).

28. For this last expression, I am using the typology proposed by A. P. BELL and M. S. WEINBERG, Homosexualities. A study of Diversity Among Men and Women (New York: Simon and Schuster, 1978).

29. G. H. WEINBERG, Society..., p. 126. See P. ROSENFELS, Homosexuality. The Psychology of the Creative Process (Roslyn Heights: Libra, 1971).

30. E.g., B. GRIER and C. REID, Lesbian Lives (Baltimore: Diana Press, 1976); A. L. ROWSE, Homosexuals in History (New York: Macmillan 1977).

31. E.g., A. KARLEN, Sexuality and Homosexuality. A New View (New York: W. W. Norton, 1971), pp. 104-123; R. T. BARNHOUSE, Homosexuality..., pp. 25-27.

32. M. POLLAK, "L'homosexualité masculine, ou: le bonheur dans le ghetto?," in Sexualités occidentales. Communications No. 35 (Paris: Seuil, 1982), pp. 43-45, compares the results of empirical studies on homosexual life styles and suggests that the concentration of gay men in certain socio-professional categories has little to do with innate artistic gifts. This is rather the result of a social logic. Gays are pushed into careers assigned to them by the milieu.

33. Significantly enough, this pledge of enduring love made by a

woman to another woman is often read at marriage liturgies. Pastors spontaneously recognize in it a hymn to sexual fidelity.

34. See a more detailed analysis with bibliographical references in T. M. HORNER, Jonathan..., pp. 40-46.

35. Even though she comments on the unfruitfulness of Jonathan's homosexuality, the Jewish author, É. A. LÉVY-VALENSI, in Le grand désarroi. Aux sources de l'énigme homosexuelle (Paris: Éditions universitaires, 1973), clearly acknowledges the homosexual nature of the bond between David and Jonathan. Her interpretation of the unfruitfulness of Jonathan's gay love is highly debatable: 1) it leaves aside important textual elements: is not David's elegy (2 S 1: 19-27), one of the most famous love-songs of world literature, a fruit of this same-sex relationship? 2) the author argues, as proof of her thesis, that Jonathan's seed withers away in the weaklings he has sired. Are Jonathan's parental miscarriages the fruit of his gay love? Is it rather not mighty David's glory?

36. J. B. NELSON, Embodiment..., pp. 185-186.

37. Most nongays who stereotype gays would be astonished to find out how little they differ from themselves in such matters. See A. P. BELL and M. S. WEINBERG, Homosexualities..., pp. 69-72 and 106-111; W. H. MASTERS and V. E. JOHNSON, Homosexuality in Perspective (Boston: Little, Brown, 1979); W. H. MASTERS, V. E. JOHNSON, and R. C. KOLODNY, Human Sexuality..., pp. 324-327.

38. M. FOX, WHEE! We, wee. All the Way Home. A Guide to the New Sensual Spirituality (Wilmington: Consortium Books, 1976), pp. 194-195. A similar point is made by B. W. HARRISON, "Toward a Just Social Order," Journal of Current Social Issues, 15/Spring (1978), p. 67; S. KLEINBERG, Alienated Affections..., pp. 38-69.

39. See the commonsensical advice of D. CLARK, Loving Someone Gay (New York: New American Library, 1977), pp. 109-114.

40. The two most widely known, longitudinal studies of men's developmental stages through adulthood - G. E. VAILLANT, Adaptation to Life (Boston: Little, Brown, 1977) and D. J. LEVINSON, The Seasons..., - point toward the incapacity of white males to experience warm, intimate friendships. See also R. A. LEWIS, "Emotional Intimacy among Men," Journal of Social Issues, 34/1 (1978), pp. 108-116; S. F. MORIN and E. M. GARFINKLE, "Male Homophobia," Journal of Social Issues, 34/1 (1978), p. 41; S. KLEINBERG, Alienated Affections..., p. 67.

41. Women complain about the "performance" atmosphere of sexual encounters. See S. HITE, A Nationwide Study of Female Sexuality (New York: Dell, 1977), pp. 130-131.

42. S. G. LUTHMAN, Intimacy..., p. 11.

43. (New York: Dell, 1978).

44. See M. S. WEINBERG and C. J. WILLIAMS, "Gay Baths and the Social Organization of Impersonal Sex," Social Problems, 23 (1975), pp. 124-136. See the testimony of long-standing

patron, A. KANTROWITZ, "Old-New," The Advocate, August 20, 1981, pp. 15-18.

45. See M. B. PENNINGTON, "Vocation Discernment and the Homosexual," in R. NUGENT (ed.), A Challenge to Love. Gay and Lesbian Catholics in the Church (New York: Crossroad, 1983), pp. 235-244; M. KROPINAK, "Homosexuality and Religious Life," ibid., pp. 245-256.

46. Discussing priestly celibacy, S. BRECKEL and N. M. MURPHY, "Psychological Development...," pp. 46-47, state that, "An individual who senses that his sexual object choice is for a person of the same sex, if he were to become sexually active, is not stricly speaking, a homosexual. Homosexuality is confirmed by genital sexual activity which is preferred and expressed with a partner of the same sex." If this is true, it applies equally to heterosexuality. Then priests and religious women and men who do not engage in coital activities would be neither homosexual nor heterosexual. This implies that they would not have successfully resolved the oedipal crisis, at puberty, through a definite, new objectal choice. This opinion also presupposes, it seems to me, a very restricted notion of "sexual activity." - As for the percentage of homosexual persons among priests and religious men and women, I have not seen statistical studies. However, out of my own counseling experience and the counseling experience of others I have consulted, I would certainly risk a higher percentage than the one which is found in the population at large. See, also, R. NUGENT, "Priest, Celibate and Gay: You Are Not Alone," in R. NUGENT (ed.), A Challenge to Love. Gay and Lesbian Catholics in the Church (New York: Crossroad, 1983), p. 257; and "Homosexuality, Celibacy, Religious Life and Ordination," in J. GRAMICK (ed.), Homosexuality and the Catholic Church (Chicago: The Thomas More Press, 1983), p. 90. R. WOODS, Another Kind of Love. Homosexuality and Spirituality (Chicago: T. More, 1977), p. 103, estimates that 30% of priests and religious in America would be homosexual.

47. M. ECK, Sacerdoce et sexualité (Paris: Fayard, 1973), p. 84. See also G. C. KIESLING, Celibacy, Prayer and Friendship. A Making-sense-out-of-life Approach (New York: Alba House, 1978), p. 177, and A. W. JONES, "When is a Homosexual not a Homosexual?." Anglican Theological Review, 59 (1977), p. 184.

48. The point is well taken in D. C. MAGUIRE, "The Vatican on Sex," Commonweal, 103 (1976), pp. 138-139, and "The Morality of Homosexual Marriage," in R. NUGENT (ed.), A Challenge to Love. Gay and Lesbian Catholics in the Church (New York: Crossroad, 1983), pp. 119-124. Typically, evangelist Billy Graham, who has no other use for celibacy, finds that it is the solution to the gay problem. See T. W. JENNINGS, "Homosexuality...," p. 65. It is also the position of R. T. BARNHOUSE, "Homosexuality," Anglican Theological Review, 6 (1976), p. 128.

49. E.g., G. DURAND, Sexualité..., pp. 251-252 and 274-275; P. S.

KEANE, Sexual Morality..., p. 84. Both these authors have a good chapter on celibacy as a sexual life style.

50. I find this to be the weak point of J. J. McNEILL, The Church...

51. R. SIMON, "Critères pour une hiérarchie des valeurs," Concilium, 120 (1976), pp. 96-97.

52. S. KLEINBERG, Alienated Affections..., p. 85, confesses that "Marie was a foreign country. [...] I understood neither Marie's experience of life nor the quality of her sexuality. [...] All the excitement, the novelty, the gratification came from difference. I never lost awareness of that, and it was clear that that had not been true of my experience with men."

53. In my opinion, they do have ethical implications for social institutions, for educational policies and for so-called bisexuals who have no well-established sexual preference. (I do not have the space to spell those out.) I am concerned, here, with the ethical project of those who have an established gay identity and not with all the ethical implications of this analysis.

54. It is not totally absent from J. J. McNEILL's reflection on homosexuality and the relation of the sexes: The Church..., pp. 135-138.

55. T. W. JENNINGS, "Homosexuality...," p. 60, also warns against what would be the "sheer lust" of homosexuality lived under a form which moral theology would have to call a "vice."

56. I can no longer accept arguments like that of G. D. COLEMAN, Homosexuality..., pp. 57-59, which merely state, without any kind of clinical or theoretical proof that, because homosexual interactions cannot fulfill masculine/feminine mutuality, gays cannot become whole, and that is that. What do we do with the research evidence of many gays who score as high as anybody else on scales of completeness and human integration? Since when is the road to human fulfilment unique? Where is the proof that no other strategies exist, apart from the sexual one, to "ultimate oneness?" Why is the same argument not valid against the celibate life style?

57. Some authors, e.g., L. SCANZONI and V. R. MOLLENKOTT, Is the Homosexual..., p. 130, distinguish merely between "genital relating" and other kinds of "male-female relating." I find this an unacceptable notion of sexual relationships. One could say that, in a sense, all male-female relating is genital (unless one leaves one's genitals in the closet before leaving one's room). If one means "genital play," then many sexual interactions imply no genital manipulations.

58. J. R. ZULO and J. D. WHITEHEAD, "The Christian Body and Homosexual Maturing," in R. NUGENT (ed.), A Challenge to Love. Gay and Lesbian Catholics in the Church (New York: Crossroad, 1983), p. 25. See the good chapter on the heterosexual friendships of gay men in S. KLEINBERG, Alienated Affections..., p. 93-117.

59. They are numerous. Connexions, a bilingual Canadian

publication which assists sharing of information among citizen's groups, grassroot movements and individuals working for social justice in Canada, provides documentation on 68 gay organizations in Canada (Vol. 6, no. 1). It specifies that its listing is not meant to be comprehensive.

60. See similar remarks by J. BABUSCIO, We Speak..., p. 114. Any alternative which does not allow gays and lesbians to say themselves as they are sexually is obviously no alternative.

61. S. CHALIFOUX, "Réflexions sur le vécu homosexuel à l'adolescence," Revue Québécoise de Sexologie, 2 (1981), p. 102.

62. J. R. ZULO and J. D. WHITEHEAD, "The Christian Body...," pp. 27-28, 33.

63. This is not to mention the fact that the gay scene is not immune from all the other forms of racism which characterize a society. See, e.g., J. V. SOARES, "Black and Gay," The Advocate, November 17, 1976.

64. J. BABUSCIO, We Speak..., pp. 121-122.

65. M. LEZNOFF and W. A. WESTLEY, "The Homosexual Community," in J. H. GAGNON and W. SIMON (eds.),. Sexual Deviance (New York: Harper and Row, 1967), pp. 193-195; E. HOOKER, "The Homosexual Community," ibid., pp. 180-181; L. HUMPHREYS, Out of the Closets. The Sociology of Homosexual Liberation (Englewood Cliffs: Prentice-Hall, 1972), pp. 13-41; M. T. SAGHIR and E. ROBINS, Male and Female..., p. 170; M. S. WEINBERG and C. J. WILLIAMS, Male Homosexuals. Their Problems and Adaptation (New York: Oxford University Press, 1974), pp. 18-30; J. H. GAGNON, Human Sexualities (Oakland: Scott, Foresman, 1977), p. 244; M. P. LEVINE, "Gay Ghetto," in M. P. LEVINE (ed.), Gay Men. The Sociology of Male Homosexuality (New York: Harper and Row, 1979), p. 196.

66. The first scientific rebuttal came from E. HOOKER, "The Adjustment of the Male Overt Homosexual," Journal of Projective Techniques, 21 (1957), pp. 18-31. In recent years, Hooker's case has been gaining more and more scientific credibility. See, e.g., M. S. WEINBERG and C. J. WILLIAMS, Male Homosexuals...; A. P. BELL and M. S. WEINBERG, Homosexualities...; L. A. PEPLAU, "What Homosexuals Want in Relationships," Psychology Today, 15/3 (1981), pp. 28-38, a first report on a study to be published at a later date.

67. R. T. BARNHOUSE, Homosexuality..., continually argues from this assumption without ever setting out to prove it. J. G. MILHAVEN, Toward a New Catholic Morality (Garden City: Doubleday, 1970), pp. 59-68, discussed the ethical implications of what he then considered, with the available psychoanalytic literature, an immaturity. I also indulged in this kind of consideration in The Sexual Language..., pp. 342-353. Today, I would not.

68. M. ORAISON, The Homosexual Question (New York: Harper and Row, 1977), particularly the first chapter.

69. See M. SNYDER, "Self-fulfilling Stereotypes," Psychology

Today, 16/7 (1982), pp. 60-68.
70. See the four stages toward mature homosexual identity suggested by J. R. ZULO and J. D. WHITEHEAD, "The Christian Body...," pp. 26-31.
71. R. REECE, "Coping with Couplehood," _The Advocate_, Oct. 19, 1977, pp. 31-32; N. J. WOODMAN and H. R. LENNA, _Counseling with Gay Men and Women. A Guide for Facilitating Positive Life-Styles_ (San Francisco: Jossey-Bass, 1980), p. 95; K. FAHMI, B. GARSIDE, and J. STITT, "Un modèle d'intervention psycho-sociale auprès de la communauté gaie," _Revue Québécoise de Sexologie_, 2 (1981), p. 55.
72. S. F. MORIN and E. M. GARFINKLE, "Male Homophobia...," pp. 43-44; J. McNEILL, "Homosexuality, Lesbianism, and the Future: The Creative Role of the Gay Community in Building a More Human Society," in R. NUGENT (ed.), _A Challenge to Love. Gay and Lesbian Catholics in the Church_ (New York: Crossroad, 1983), pp. 54-60.
73. See A. P. MacDONALD, Jr., _et al._, "Attitudes toward Homosexuality: Preservation of Sex Morality or the Double Standard?," _Journal of Consulting and Clinical Psychology_, 40 (1973), p. 161; M. D. STORMS. "Attitudes toward Homosexuality and Femininity in Men," _Journal of Homosexuality_, 3 (1978), pp. 257-263; and "Theories of Sexual Orientation," _Journal of Personality and Social Psychology_, 38/5 (1981), pp. 783-792; K. FAHMI, B. GARSIDE, and J. STITT, "Un modèle...," p. 51. - It is interesting to recall, here, that sex-role stereotypes already formed the core of the moral criteriology for judging the "normality" of pederastic activities in Ancient Greece: see K. J. DOVER, _Greek Homosexuality_ (Cambridge: Harvard University Press, 1978), pp. 60-109; and more explicitly in Ancient Rome: see P. VEYNE, "L'homosexualité à Rome," in _Sexualités occidentales. Communications No. 35_ (Paris: Seuil, 1983), pp. 26-33: an adult male could not be "passive" during pederastic intercourse anymore than during heterosexual intercourse.
74. Thus, M. LEGRAIN, _Le corps_..., p. 67. See, on the contrary, the positive focus suggested by T. W. JENNINGS, "Homosexuality...,' p. 66.
75. S. FREUD, _Totem_..., p. 144.
76. See R. BRANNON, "The Male Sex Role: Our Culture's Blueprint of Manhood, and What It's Done for Us Lately," in D. DAVID and R. BRANNON (eds.), _The Forty-nine Percent Majority. The Male Sex Role_ (Reading: Addison-Wesley, 1976); A. E. GROSS, "The Male Role and Heterosexual Behavior," _Journal of Social Issues_, 34/1 (1978), pp. 87-107; J. HARRISON, "Warning: The Male Sex Role May Be Dangerous to Your Health," _Journal of Social Issues_, 34/1 (1978), pp. 65-86; J. NICHOLS, "Butcher Than Thou: Beyond Machismo," in M. P. LEVINE (ed.), _Gay Men. The Sociology of Male Homosexuality_ (New York: Harper and Row, 1979), pp. 328-342.
77. See, _e.g._, P. GEBHARD _et al._, _Sex Offenders. An Analysis of_

Types (New York: Harper and Row, 1965), p. 272; V. De FRANCIS, Protecting the Child Victim of Sex Offenders (Denver: The American Humane Association, Children's Division, 1976); A. P. BELL and M. S. WEINBERG, Homosexualities..., p. 230; R. L. GEISER, Hidden Victims..., p. 80.

78. R. L. GEISER, Hidden Victims..., p. 80.
79. J. MONEY and A. A. EHRHARDT, Man & Woman, Boy & Girl. The Differentiation and Dimorphism of Gender Identity from Conception to Maturity (New York: Mentor Book, 1972), p. 243.
80. (New York: D. McKay, 1970), pp. 134–136. Reuben's entire chapter on male homosexuality, pp. 129–151, is a gross, stereotyped caricature with which very few gays would identify.
81. See L. HUMPHREYS, "Exodus and Identity: the Emerging Gay Culture," in M. P. LEVINE (ed.), Gay Men. The Sociology of Male Homosexuality (New York: Harper and Row, 1979), pp. 139–142; M. WALTERS, The Nude Male. A New Perspective (Harmondsworth: Penguin Books, 1979), pp. 270–296.
82. T. D. PERRY, The Lord..., pp. 121–180.
83. R. SIMPSON, From the Closet to the Courts (New York: Penguin Books, 1977), pp. 146–147.
84. See the good advices to gays in C. A. TRIPP, The Homosexual Matrix..., pp. 132–140.
85. See also J. McNEILL, "Homosexuality, Lesbianism...," pp. 58–59.
86. A. P. BELL and M. S. WEINBERG, Homosexualities..., p. 150.
87. L. P. BARNETT, Homosexuality..., pp. 88–99. This is the basic position found, e.g., W. N. PITTENGER, Time..., p. 58; J. J. McNEILL, The Church...; L. SCANZONI and V. R. MOLLENKOTT, Is the Homosexual...
88. THOMAS AQUINAS, ST, I^a-II^{ae}, q. 72, a. 5.
89. Ibid., II^a-II^{ae}, q. 59, a. 4.
90. See on Aelred's gayness: M. GOODICH, The Unmentionable Vice. Homosexuality in the Later Medieval Period (Santa Barbara: ABC-Clio, 1979), pp. 5–6; J. BOSWELL, Christianity..., pp. 221–226; K. RUSSELL, "Aelred, the Gay Abbot of Rievaulx," Studia Mystica, 5/4 (1982), pp. 51–64.
91. See E. A. MALLOY, "Homosexual Way of Life: Methodological Considerations in the Use of Sociological Considerations in Christian Ethics," Proceeding of the Thirty-Fourth Annual Convention of the Catholic Theological Society of America (New York: The Catholic Theological Society of America, 1980), pp. 139–140. In his book, Homosexuality..., Malloy makes the lack of commitment the bottom line of the gay way of life. This position, however, is not convincingly established.
92. L. E. PEPLAU, "What Homosexuals...," pp. 28–38.
93. A. P. BELL and M. S. WEINBERG, Homosexualities..., p. 216; see pp. 195–216, 219–220.
94. E. A. MALLOY, "Homosexual Way...," pp. 131–132.
95. See also case histories given by B. FAIRCHILD and N. HAYWARD, Now That You Know. What Every Parent Should Know About

Sexuality (New York: Harcourt, Brace, Jovanovich, 1979), pp. 126-151.

96. A. P. BELL and M. S. WEINBERG, Homosexualities..., p. 102; L. A. PEPLAU, "What Homosexuals...," pp. 35 and 37; N. J. WOODMAN and H. R. LENNA, Counseling..., pp. 91-100.

97. A. P. BELL and M. S. WEINBERG, Homosexualities..., pp. 171-179. The influence of the feminist movement has balanced the conventional feminine yearning for affective dependency with a desire for personal autonomy: see L. A. PEPLAU et al., "Loving Women: Attachment and Autonomy in Lesbian Relationships," Journal of Social Issues, 34/3 (1978), pp. 7-27.

98. W. SIMON and J. H. GAGNON, "The Lesbians: A Preliminary Overview." in J. H. GAGNON and W. SIMON (eds.), Sexual Deviance (New York: Harper and Row, 1967), pp. 247-282; M. HOFFMAN, "Homosexuality," in F. A. BEACH (ed.), Human Sexuality in Four Perspectives (Baltimore: The Johns Hopkins University Press, 1976), p. 171; C. A. TRIPP, The Homosexual Matrix..., p. 144; A. P. BELL and M. S. WEINBERG, Homosexualities..., pp. 81-102.

99. N. PITTENGER, Love..., pp. 59-60; and "What it Means to be Human," in M. MACOURT (ed.), Towards a Theology of Gay Liberation (London: SCM Press, 1977), p. 89. - L. HUMPHREYS, Tearoom Trade. Impersonal Sex in Public Places (Chicago: Aldine, 1970), states that 54% of the males who indulge in the most depersonalized form of same-sex games, the one taking place in public men's rooms (tearooms), are heterosexually married men.

100. A. P. BELL and M. S. WEINBERG, Homosexualities..., pp. 73-80.

101. D. CLARK, Loving..., p. 141.

102. O. KERNBERG, interviewed by L. WOLFE, "Why Some People Can't Love," Psychology Today, 12/6 (1978), pp. 56-57.

103. L. M. RUSSELL, The Future of Partnership (Philadelphia: Westminster Press, 1979), p. 84.

104. E.g., L. HUMPHREYS, Out of the Closets..., pp. 13-41; M. S. WEINBERG and C. J. WILLIAMS, Male Homosexuals..., pp. 17-30; E. E. LEVITT and A. D. KLASSEN, Jr., "Public Attitudes Toward Homosexuality: Part of the 1970 National Survey by the Institute for Sex Research," Journal of Homosexuality, 1 (Fall 1974), pp. 29-43; K. L. NYBERG and J. P. ALSTON, "Analysis of Public Attitudes Toward Homosexual Behavior," ibid., 2 (Winter 1976-1977), pp. 99-107; P. IRWIN and N. L. THOMPSON, "Acceptance of the Rights of Homosexuals: A Social Profile," ibid., 3 (Winter 1977), pp. 107-121; J. KELLY, "The Aging Male Homosexual: Myth and Reality," The Gerontologist, 17 (1977), pp. 328-332; J. GRAMICK, "Prejudice, Religion, and Homosexual People," in R. NUGENT (ed.), A Challenge to Love. Gay and Lesbian Catholics in the Church (New York: Crossroad, 1983), pp. 3-19.

105. J. R. ZULO and J. D. WHITEHEAD, "The Christian Body...," p. 36, also make a suggestion to this effect. See also M. FOX,

"The Spiritual Journey of the Homosexual ... and Just About Everybody Else," in R. NUGENT (ed.), A Challenge to Love. Gay and Lesbian Catholics in the Church (New York: Crossroad, 1983), pp. 189-204.

106. R. SIMPSON, From the Closet... See also C. WITTMAN, "Refugees from Amerika: A Gay Manifesto," in J. A. McCAFFREY and S. M. HARTING (eds.), The Homosexual Dialectic (Englewood Cliffs: Prentice-Hall, 1972), pp. 157-171.

107. Even moral theologians who hold that "homosexual acts" (whatever that means) are sinful, also denounce the sin of gayhating (which is etymologically more correct than "homophobia"): see, e.g., J. R. KIRK, The Homosexual Crisis..., pp. 125-133.

108. See, e.g., M. MACOURT (ed.), Towards a Theology of Gay Liberation (London: SCM Press, 1977); G. MÉNARD, De Sodome...; G. R. EDWARDS, Gay/Lesbian Liberation...

109. K. T. SMITH, "Homophobia. A Tentative Personality Profile," Psychological Reports, 29 (1971), pp. 1091-1094; J. DUNBAR, H. BROWN, and D. M. AMOROSO, "Some Correlates of Attitudes Toward Homosexuality," Journal of Social Psychology, 89 (1973), pp. 271-279; J. DUNBAR, M. BROWN, and S. VOURINEN, "Attitudes Toward Homosexuality Among Brazilians and Canadian College Students," Journal of Social Psychology, 90 (1973), pp. 173-183.

110. See A. P. MacDONALD, "Homophobia: Its Roots and Meaning," Homosexual Counseling Journal, 3/1 (1976), pp. 23-33; R. G. KARR, "Homosexual Labeling and the Male Role," Journal of Social Issues, 34/3 (1978), pp. 73-83; S. F. MORIN and E. M. GARFINKLE, "Male Homophobia...," pp. 31-33.

111. D. STEFFENSMEIER and R. STEFFENSMEIER, "Sex Differences in Reactions to Homosexuals. Research Continuities and Further Developments," The Journal of Sex Research, 10 (1974), pp. 52-67; A. P. MacDONALD and R. G. GANES, "Some Characteristics of Those Who Hold Positive and Negative Attitudes Toward Homosexuals," Journal of Homosexuality, 1 (1974), pp. 9-28; J. MILLHAM, C. L. SAN MIGUEL, and R. KELLOGG, "A Factor-analytic Conceptualization of Attitudes Toward Male and Female Homosexuals," Journal of Homosexuality, 2 (1976), pp. 3-10; F. A. MINNIGERODE, "Attitudes Toward Homosexuality. Feminist Attitudes and Sexual Conservatism," Sex Roles, 2 (1976), pp. 347-352.

112. This book has recently been translated into English for the first time by P. J. PAYER: P. DAMIAN, Book of Gomorrah. An Eleventh-Century Treatise against Clerical Homosexual Practices (Waterloo, Ont.: Wilfrid Laurier University Press, 1982).

113. See L. K. LITTLE, "The Personal Development of Peter Damian," in W. C. JORDAN, B. McNAB, and T. F. RUIZ (eds.), Order and Innovation in Middle Ages. Essays in Honor of Joseph R. Strayer (Princeton: Princeton University Press, 1976), particularly pp. 322-325 and 335-338.

114. M. FOX, "The Spiritual Journey...," p. 190.
115. At least a fifth of all lesbians and a tenth of all gay men have children according to A. P. BELL and M. S. WEINBERG, Homosexualities..., p. 391.
116. Adoption by homosexual parents is still relatively rare, but it has already begun: see R. GREEN, "Should Homosexuals Adopt Children?," in J. P. BRADY and H. K. BRODIE (eds.), Controversy in Psychiatry (Philadelphia: Saunders, 1978), pp. 813-828; D. HITCHENS, "Social Attitudes, Legal Standards, and Personal Trauma in Child Custody Cases," Journal of Homosexuality 5/1-2 (1979-1980), pp. 89-95; B. MADDOX, Married and Gay. An Intimate Look at a Different Relationship (New York: Harcourt, Brace, Jovanovich, 1982), pp. 68-69.
117. In Ruth 3: 9, Ruth acknowledges quite candidly that she does not seek a lover but that she is looking for a legally acceptable inseminator.
118. The vast majority of gays and lesbians perform quite adequately as parents: see D. I. RIDDLE, "Relating to Children...," p. 49; N. J. WOODMAN and H. R. LENNA, Counseling..., p. 100.
119. See E. M. HETHERINGTON, M. COX and R. COX, "Divorced Fathers," The Family Coordinator, 25 (1976), pp. 417-428; H. A. MENDES, "Single Fathers," ibid., pp. 439-444; D. K. ORTHNER, T. BROWN, and D. FERGUSON, "Single-Parent Fatherhood: An Emerging Family Life Style," ibid., pp. 429-437; I. VICTOR and W. A. WINKLER, Fathers and Custody (New York: Hawthorn, 1977).
120. M. KIRKPATRICK, R. ROY, and K. SMITH, "A New Look at Lesbian Mothers," Human Behavior, 5/8 (1976), pp. 60-61; J. A. LEVINE, Who Will Raise..., pp. 93-94; D. R. COHEN, "Newsline" (reporting on research of R. GREEN), Psychology Today, 12/6 (1978), pp. 44-46; B. MILLER, "Unpromised Paternity: The Life-Style of Gay Fathers," in M. P. LEVINE (ed.), Gay Men. The Sociology of Male Homosexuality (New York: Harper and Row, 1979), pp. 249-250; B. MADDOX, Married and Gay..., pp. 141-142.
121. A. P. BELL and M. S. WEINBERG, Sexual Preference...
122. As we find, e.g., in P. KEANE, Sexual Morality..., p. 89.
123. B. MADDOX, Married and Gay..., p. 142. The resolution on the rights of gay people adopted by the American Psychological Association on September 5, 1976, states that "the sex, gender identity or sexual orientation of natural or prospective adoptive or foster parents should not be the sole or primary variable considered in custody or placement cases."
124. M. T. SAGHIR and E. ROBINS, Male and Female..., pp. 170-173.
125. V. C. CASS, "Homosexual Identity Formation: A Theoretical Model," Journal of Homosexuality, 4/3 (1979), pp. 219-235; M. W. ROSS, "Retrospective Distortion in Homosexual Research," Archives of Sexual Behavior, 9 (1980), pp. 523-532; R. R. TROIDEN and E. GOODE, "Variable Related to the Acquisition of

a Gay Identity," Journal of Homosexuality, 5/4 (1980), pp. 382-392. We find that authors who dare to propose some counseling strategies for children or adolescents with homosexual preferences remain characteristically vague: e.g., S. F. MORIN and S. J. SCHULTZ, "The Gay Movement and the Rights of Children," Journal of Social Issues, 34/2 (1978), pp. 137-148; N. J. WOODMAN and H. R. LENNA, Counseling..., pp. 71-88; K. FAHMI, B. GARSIDE, and J. STITT, "Un modèle...," p. 52. KINSEY's statistics indicate that more individuals engage in some form of homosexual behaviour during childhood and adolescence than they do during adulthood. Extreme caution is therefore needed in labeling any youth a homosexual just because of homosexual activity.

126. B. M. DANK, "Coming Out in the Gay World," Psychiatry, 34 (1971), p. 182.

127. R. LLOYD, For Money..., pp. 178-188.

128. E.g., J. WERRES, "Les homosexuels en Allemagne," in S. De BATSELIER (ed.), Les minorités homosexuelles (Gembloux: Duculot, 1973), pp. 120-121; J. DANET et al., Fous d'enfance (Paris: Recherches, 1979) and the reply of B. LAPOUGE and J.-L. PINARD-LEGRY, L'enfant et le pédéraste (Paris: Seuil, 1980). Needless to say that this represents an extreme position. It rarely appears in the literature. In Los Angeles, the Rene Guyon Society is working to decriminalize pederastic activities, using the slogan "Sex by age eight, or else it's too late!": W. H. MASTERS, V. E. JOHNSON, and R. C. KOLODNY, Human Sexuality..., p. 352.

129. See chapter six.

130. D. ALTMAN, The Homosexualization of America. The Americanization of the Homosexual (New York: St. Martin's Press, 1982).

131. C. A. TRIPP, The Homosexual Matrix..., p. 140.

132. C. SILVERSTEIN and E. WHITE, The Joy of Gay Sex (New York: Crown Publishers, 1977), pp. 111-112. In fact, some research supports this claim: e.g., D. C. KIMMEL, "Adult Development and Aging: A Gay Perspective," Journal of Social Issues, 34/3 (1978), pp. 113-130.

133. E.g., A. P. BELL and M. S. WEINBERG, Homosexualities..., pp. 141-148.

134. R. MAY, Power..., pp. 47-64.

135. The perplexities created for North American gays and lesbians who are at once the product and the critics of a certain kind of society are well analysed by G. BAUM, "The Homosexual Condition and Political Responsibility," in R. NUGENT (ed.), A Challenge to Love. Gay and Lesbian Catholics in the Church (New York: Crossroad, 1983), pp. 38-51.

136. R. WOODS, Another Kind...

137. It is very rare to find de facto minorities which are not also "sociological minorities," that is, groups that are denied access to all the legal and social privileges available to the dominant members of society. This is the

situation of the gay people of America: see J. KATZ, Gay American History...

138. S. KLEINBERG, Alienated Affection...

139. Ibid., p. 42. See the exquisite essay of V. RUSSO, "Camp," in M. P. LEVINE (ed.), Gay Men. The Sociology of Male Homosexuality (New York: Harper and Row, 1979), pp. 205-210.

140. A. DONVAL, Un avenir..., pp. 26-27.

141. W. J. GOODE, The Family..., pp. 2-3.

142. J. DONZELOT, The Policing of Families..., pp. 48-52.

143. B. W. HARRISON, "When Fruitfulness...," p. 483.

144. S. DOTY, "The Christian Family: The New Testament Witness," Listening, 15 (1980), pp. 17-21; É. MORIN, "La famille...," pp. 73-76.

145. This is my central objection to the otherwise beautiful book of É. FUCHS, Sexual Desire...

146. A review of the literature on "coming out" is found in C. De MONTEFLORES and S. J. SCHULTZ, "Coming Out: Similarities and Differences for Lesbians and Gay Men," Journal of Social Issues, 34/2 (1973), pp. 59-72.

147. See C. A. TRIPP, The Homosexual Matrix..., pp. 125-131.

148. This is changing: see, A. P. BELL and M. S. WEINBERG, Homosexualities..., p. 122: "Numerous investigations of homosexuals' attitudes toward their homosexuality have demonstrated that it is a psychological and social burden for some but an energizing influence for others."

149. J. A. LEE, "Going Public: A Study in the Sociology of Homosexual Liberation," Journal of Homosexuality, 3 (1977), pp. 60 and 65.

150. A. P. BELL and M. S. WEINBERG, Homosexualities..., pp. 62-68, found that the order of disclosure in the family is usually: mother first, siblings second, father third. See good advice for such disclosures in G. WEINBERG, Society..., pp. 110-116; J. BABUSCIO, We Speak..., pp. 93-112; R. WOODS, Another Kind..., pp. 83-92; N. J. WOODMAN and H. R. LENNA, Counseling..., pp. 57-70.

151. The author of the autobiographical Familiar Faces...

152. Quoted by J. BABUSCIO, We Speak..., p. 110.

153. See good examples in D. CLARK, Loving..., pp. 87-100.

154. J. BABUSCIO, We Speak..., p. 41.

155. See the good remarks of D. BLAMIRES, "Recent Christian...," p. 12, on the ethical dilemmas of conservative, fundamentalist positions.

156. See the persuasive evidence provided by L. HUMPHREYS, Out of the Closets... See also M. DANNECKER and R. REICHE, Der gewöhnliche Homosexuelle (Frankfurt: Fischer, 1974), pp. 359-360, and A. P. BELL and M. S. WEINBERG, Homosexualities..., pp. 201-203, 210-212: in these two most prestigious studies of homosexual life styles today, we learn that if suicide rates are much higher in the homosexual population as a whole than in the population in general, it is lower than the latter among the group of gays and lesbians

who have fully assumed their sexual orientation. S. KIEFER HAMMERSMITH and M. S. WEINBERG, "Homosexual Identity: Commitment, Adjustment, and Significant Others," Sociometry, 36 (1973), pp. 56-79, also found a positive correlation between acceptance of a commitment to a homosexual identity and positive mental health. H. HENDIN, Suicide in America (New York: W. W. Norton, 1982), pp. 107-123, argues, however, that guilt and shame at being homosexual is not a significant factor in suicidal cases of gays and lesbians. He suggests that unresolved separation anxiety and extreme vulnerability to rejection are better explanations.

157. S. G. LUTHMAN, Intimacy..., p. 65. See also N. J. WOODMAN and H. R. LENNA, Counseling..., p. 58.
158. This assessment of the situation was put forward as early as L. HUMPHREYS, Tearoom... See, more recently, A. P. BELL and M. S. WEINBERG, Homosexualities..., pp. 62-68; S. KLEINBERG, Alienated Affections..., pp. 70-73.
159. R. SIMPSON, From the Closet..., p. 12.
160. J. MILLHAN, C. L. SAN MIGUEL, R. KELLOGG, "A Factor-analytic Conceptualization...," pp. 3-10.
161. J. B. NELSON, Embodiment..., p. 195.
162. See also N. J. WOODMAN and H. R. LENNA, Counseling..., p. 62.

CHAPTER EIGHT

CELIBATE FECUNDITY or RECREATING COMMUNITIES

Were celibacy to be understood, following Webster's definition, as "the state of being unmarried," we would have to consider the sexual language of infants, of dating teen-agers, of involuntary bachelors and spinsters, of voluntary singles, of widowers and widows, of divorcees, of unmarried gays and lesbians, of vowed religious women, men and Roman Catholic clergy, in short, of the majority of us who are not married.[1] The most we could hope for would be to argue the point that, since all these singles are sexual beings they ought to have some kind of fecund sexual life.

Among unmarried people, however, there are some for whom this condition represents a deliberate option. Theological tradition usually reserves the word celibate for unmarried people who have deliberately opted for this condition.[2] Just as some people choose to live their intimate life as partners, so others freely choose to live theirs as celibates. It should be clearly stated at this point that this chapter does not address itself to the issue of mandatory celibacy for priests in the Latin rite of the Roman Catholic Church. Nor does it deal with the very real problem of those who have chosen the ordained ministry in this Church without consciously and freely opting for celibacy as a worthwhile and challenging sexual life style. The question raised here is the following: What are the modalities of sexual fecundity for those who do freely choose to be celibates?

Since different people understand what it means to be a celibate differently, it is important that I establish my own position in the welter of existing interpretations. For some people, celibacy is defined in opposition to marriage understood as a socio-economic reality.[3] Sexual life has little to do with it. If a celibate's private life includes coital relationships, one speaks of "affairs." Sexual encounters themselves are made to sound like commercial transactions. Divorcing human sexuality from a person's socio-economic identity, however, finds rational justification only within a dualistic concept of humanity.

The contrary view, which defines celibacy uniquely in terms of genital abstention, suffers from the same internal vice. Some Roman Catholic priests, for instance, live the integral experience of conjugal life with a female companion except for one aspect of it: convinced that they ought to safeguard their vow of celibacy, they abstain from coital relations with her. In the

second half of the fourth century, John Chrysostom was already
having second thoughts about similar conceptions and their
practical viability.[4]

Other conceptions that appear in the literature for
vowed or consecrated celibates leave aside the very human
substratum of celibate reality and call upon the spiritual
motivations of those who choose this life style. To define
consecrated celibacy as "total self-gift to the Lord for love of
men"[5] may be inspiring. Yet, this and similar generalities equally
well describe religious life in general, priesthood, an active
involvement in a nonviolent resistance movement, martyrdom,
missionary life, married life, and many other forms of Christian
commitment.

In this chapter, celibacy is taken to be a sexual
reality lived in a well defined social context and in a style of[6]
human relationships which is different from that of couples.
Whereas marriage is the institution of sexual dimorphism, celibacy
is the institution of sexual singularity. Donald Goergen is right
in stating that "being single rather than partnered is at the
heart of celibacy."[7] It is also clear in Goergen's treatment of
the sexual celibate that singleness and partnership are not to be
understood as exterior attributes of the self. Before designating
the sociological, juridical or economical status of a person,
celibacy radically qualifies his or her sexual being. Founded[8] on
the unique and autonomous condition of each human being, it
represents a sexual way of being-in-the-world and of living which
is nourished by the mystery of personhood and which enriches
individuals and human communities by the quality of its own
characteristic sexual fecundity.[9]

To state, as Alfons Auer does, that the "essential
significance" of celibacy "does not lie in personal fulfilment"
and that it "can be understood only in relation to Christ and the[10]
Church" is, in my judgment, not exact. If celibacy is not geared
to personal fulfilment, it would be immoral to choose it as a way
of life and any Church recommending it to its constituency should
be denounced publicly.[11] Supernatural motivations cannot make
something which is an obstacle in the way of human development a
worthwhile enterprise. To impede our humanization is the very
definition of immorality.

This is not to say that motivations such as "for the
sake of the Kingdom" cannot account for a person's choice of
celibacy. To the extent that celibacy is the object of a free
choice, it necessarily comes under the influence of the end in
view of which every important option is ultimately taken.
Furthermore, the Church has, in the course of its history,
gradually institutionalized publicly and, strangely enough, even
privately vowed forms of celibate engagements "for the sake of the

Kingdom." When Christian society was papally controlled and systematically organized, one belonged to some juridically well-defined "order" or one simply did not belong anywhere in Church or society.[12] Laymen and laywomen who attempted to live celibacy "for the sake of the Kingdom" outside the recognized structures posed such a threat to the whole ecclesial and secular fabric of society that they were not tolerated.[13] The impact of this institutionalism of celibacy has been so great that today we still find ourselves confronted with a Christian literature that deals with celibacy solely in terms of the religious life and priestly life.

If, therefore, theology wants to retrieve some of the basic insights on celibacy chosen "for the sake of the Kingdom" from the Christian tradition, it ought to address itself, it seems to me, to a much wider range of celibate commitments in our pluralistic society.[14] Whether the context in which these commitments are inserted be ecclesiastical or secular, sexual celibacy ought, nevertheless, to produce effects which are assets for the individuals involved and for their communities. We are, therefore, inquiring about the values of celibacy.

Values are taken here to mean those aspects of the human good which are recognized and sought by a person and/or by a community. A person's good may include, for instance, education. But as long as this aspect of the good is not the object of one's recognizance and intention, it has no effect on one's conduct. In order to act "willingly in view of an end," which is the classic definition of a properly human act, one's will and mind must be under the moving influence of something perceived as desirable. There are economical, historical, social, and psychological conditions which make it impossible for certain persons or communities to value what we might identify as objective aspects of the good. Liberality cannot be practiced by those who have the bare minimum for survival; reproduction cannot direct the conjugal relationships of sterile couples; punctuality, at least as we understand it, cannot be prized by hunters or by nomads; human rights cannot move young children to action. From these and other examples it becomes clear that an ethical discourse is necessarily written for a "cultural being." Man is adam, the earthy, the earthman and the earthwoman, kneaded of the adamah (humus, soil) of a well identified land. He (or she) is moved to concrete action solely by that aspect of the good which he recognizes as worthwhile from the vantage ground which is his.

So much of the theological discourse on celibacy sounds irrelevant because it is talking about a celibacy that is nobody's celibacy.[15] Celibacy is linked with the most profound realities of the life of man and woman in society. To manifest a preference for celibacy is to understand one's significance in one's own society in a certain way. To consciously choose celibacy as a way of life is, therefore, to take a position in the present-day debates on the meaning of sexuality, on our male/female humanity, on the nature of sexual relationships, on the meaning and the future of human communities.[16] The discourse which bears on celibacy as a sign of the Kingdom of God is not immune from this law of cultural incarnation. Signs signify by reference to a culture. As Michel Rondet remarks: "When culture changes, signs also change their meaning: signs that perdure can betray their meaning."[17]

This discourse on the values of celibacy does not claim, therefore, to have more universal validity than the discourse held in the preceding chapters. It represents an endeavor to discover what contribution a well-spoken, celibate sexual language brings to the common effort of women and men in North American society to make sense of their sexual existence. It will be suggested that successful celibates can teach us the value of solitude for the integration of sensuality and tenderness; of androgenous personhood for the reconciliation of human relationships; of liberating friendships for the quality of love; and of social generativity for the revitalization of the communities in which we live as responsible sexual agents.

1. DISCERNING SOLITUDE

According to the Biblical scholar Jacques Guillet, one[18] of the prevailing traits of Jesus' celibacy is solitude. Jesus often escapes from the crowd and leaves even his disciples behind in order to be alone so that he may intensely live his own inner life and deepen the foundational experience of his own identity[19] and mission in the mystery of the fatherhood of God. In fact, the Church is born out of the total solitude of Jesus dying on the[20] Cross in fidelity to the Father. Solitude is likewise a central theme of the meditations on celibacy of the great sixteenth[21] century Spanish mystic Juan de la Cruz as well as[22] of famous twentieth century mystics such as Thomas Merton and Dag Hammarskjöld.[23] In her interviews with eighty celibate Parisian women, Suzanne Mathieu says that the word solitude kept coming back like a leitmotiv.[24] Contemporary authors who have written on[25] vowed celibacy - Fentener Yann van Vlissigen of Taizé in France,[26] Yves Raguin in India, Philip Keane,[27] Janie Gustafson,[28] and Keith Clark[29] in the United States, to name but a few - all muse over the experience of solitude.

In the Communauté de l'Arche, founded in Southern France by Lanza del Vasto, and composed of both members of families and celibates, the latter are called les simples. The French word simple is the opposite of composed, multiple, and complex. This term offers a deep insight into the nature of celibacy. It translates for contemporary ears what was also implied in older terms such as "monk," from the Greek monos, meaning unique or solitary, and "celibate," from the Latin coelebs, to love oneness or unity. To experience solitude is indeed the logical consequence of an option for celibacy.[30] Solitude is perhaps the principal characteristic of celibacy. One must ask, however, if solitude is an asset or a liability in the sexual dialogue with others.

The assumption of responsibility for one's being-a-single is, for the celibate, a task as unavoidable as the assumption of their being-a-couple is for spouses. The great number of failures shows convincingly that neither achievement goes without saying, without saying oneself sexually as a celibate or as a spouse. We cannot dispute the fact that those who have never freely chosen to be celibates and to live consciously the mystery of human singularity run the risk of becoming disheartened loners or devious solitaries. Those who cannot face human aloneness creatively have the choice of two opposite strategies. Using one strategy, spiritualists will be tempted to break away from human fellowship, to withdraw into themselves, and to immerse themselves in this isolation. This self-enclosed, usually embittered and destructive way of being alone is perhaps more aptly called loneliness.[31] This escapism from sexual responsibility represents a grimace of solitude. In fact, it makes fruitful solitude difficult, if not impossible.[32] In its extreme state, it is a neurosis to be dealt with by professional psychologists.[33] In all cases, it runs counter to the relational structure of the sexual self and it betrays love, the moral norm of human sexual language.

The other strategy, the corporealist one, will be to escape not into oneself but from oneself. Some flee solitude like the bubonic plague and develop what Clark Moustakas calls "the anxiety of loneliness," "a defense that attempts to eliminate it [loneliness] by constantly seeking activity with others or by continually keeping busy to avoid facing the crucial questions."[34] These are people who have never graduated from a need-to-be-satisfied to a deeper level of desire or of love. They are like children who feel lost when their mother goes away because they need her. Her presence is perceived as a pleasurable or a useful contact which fades away as soon as she disappears. Children do not experience absence as the interiorization of a presence.[35] As a consequence, unsatisfied needs produce in them an anxiety of loneliness.

One finds celibates, especially those who live in communities and communes, who make every effort to dissolve their loneliness in the group. The latter has the function of providing maternal contact for the satisfaction of peripheral needs to mask the problem of solitude. These celibates have not yet realized that, unlike needs, the desire for love is never totally satisfied because it is nourished by that which is foreign to itself, by that which is never totally possessed. Such persons, therefore, hold on to the group as someone at sea clings to a lifebuoy. If the group is not composed of people who have resolved their anxiety of loneliness, there is the danger that all will drown in despair. In effect, the anxiety of loneliness, like loneliness itself, represents the condition of being alone without love.[36] Both exclude intimate relations with others because no true intimate rapport with oneself has ever been established through fecund solitude.

Solitude I understand to be the experience of being alone, peacefully, with the mystery of one's own life, with the wholeness of one's existence. Evelyn and James Whitehead describe this movement as "a call to bring about a deeper harmony and integration of the variety of things that I am."[37] One is present to oneself as well as to others. In solitude, one seeks to move beyond the ephemeral, the transient, the accidental, the peripheral, the superficial. In the depth of one's self, one discovers this primeval region of eloquent silence where the reality of one's own inner being lies, where core freedom exults, and where real peace and reconciliation take root.

Since the process out of which a person emerges is essentially an inward process, solitude is a road one must take if one wishes to discover one's true identity.[38] Thérèse Lentfoehr quotes Thomas Merton as saying: "If a man can't be alone he doesn't know who he is."[39] In solitude one assists at the birth of the inexplicable within oneself, of the self coming to life in novel and creative ways as the course of events summons one to become who one is. Emmanuel Mounier speaks of the person as both a movement towards others and "the pulsation of a secret life which is the ceaseless spring of its productivity."[40] As one learns to tap this vital source, one is rejuvenated by wonder, by an acute consciousness that casts fresh light on existence, by an expansiveness of the authentic self.

The authentic self I take to be distinct from both a phony self and the actual self. The phony self is a dreamed and illusory version of who we are, a version which will never materialize because we are simply not like that and never will be. Some people spend their lives running after this false image of themselves, dissatisfied and even distressed because they are walking beside themselves on a road which leads nowhere. The person who is journeying on this particular road on this particular day is the actual self. This is the self which exists, in fact, here and now. Yet, there is more in this self than what is actualized at any given point in time. There is extraordinary potential in each one of us. This self "in abeyance," longing for full existence, this person we can realistically beget in this world with time, and with God's grace, for the world to come, I call the authentic self. The greatest obstacle to the birth of the authentic self is generally not, as some ascetical treatises would have us believe, a lack of goodwill or tenacity. Its worst enemy is a lack of self-esteem, of acceptance of the actual self. The actual self is the only viable starting point because in it and nowhere else is the authentic self in gestation.[41] Francis de Sales expresses the fundamental rule of personal development well when he writes to a friend: "Do not wish not to be what you are, but wish to be very well what you are [...] What is the use of building castles in Spain when we must live in France."[42] One must first exercise a ministry of reconciliation with one's actual self before he or she can be admitted, by the constructive use of solitude, to the presence of the authentic self who reigns in one's own castle. One must learn to befriend oneself.

Have we not left the realm of sexuality, of celibacy defined as a sexual reality, and given into spiritualistic interpretations of celibacy? Granted that solitude represents a value, is it a sexual value? It is. For if we claim that we say our intimate self to other intimate selves through the sexual language, how will this ever be done truthfully if "who we really are" is not even disclosed to our own eyes?[43] Or, if what is disclosed is not loved for what it is? "Our love for ourselves," remarks Thomas Aquinas, "is the model and root of friendship; for our friendship for others consists precisely in the fact that our attitude toward them is the same as toward ourselves." He goes on, quoting Aristotle who said that "friendly feelings towards others flow from a man's own feelings towards himself."[44] Contemporary psychologists would agree that persons who have high self-esteem will most likely respond to others in appropriate ways.[45]

Because they are enfleshed spirits committed to the making of history, human beings are not grasped fully by analytical grids, by experimental measurements, by methods which are necessarily reductionist. I have yet to be shown how a person gets in touch with his or her own intimate self, with its originality, its tender and sensuous structure, its internal coherence, and its élan vital (its vital energy and thrust), if not by the constructive use of solitude, by what the monastic tradition calls a "desert experience." I would contest the genuineness of any such experience that would reveal a fleshless and sexless "soul," for no living human self is known to be structured that way. No wonder monks who strove to get in touch with only their "soul" spent the other half of their meditation chasing away the "devils of the flesh," namely, their exacerbated sexual selves craving attention and care.

Just as an unembodied spirit is inhuman, so is an a-relational self. We must also question the validity of an experience that would equate solitude with isolation, for this would be what Thomas Merton referred to as a "fanciful regression to a tepid womb of oceanic feelings" and denounced as "a lonely pilgrimage without fraternal solidarity."[46] From the earliest days of the monastic tradition, even in the epic of the intransigent desert Fathers, solitude has been understood and experienced as leading up to a plenitude of communion.[47] Today's Christian authors who have reflected on solitude are also of one mind on this point. Because we discover our true nature and identity, our authentic self in solitude, we necessarily discover that communion is constitutive of human personhood.[48]

"Pray," advises Dag Hammarskjöld, "that your loneliness may spur you into finding someone to live for, great enough to die for."[49] This warning might have been a better prognostic of 1984 than George Orwell's Big Brother prophecy of mind control. Admittedly, the exorbitant claims of institutions, both civil and ecclesiastical, will always remain a menace to human liberty. Thomas Merton is right in suggesting that solitude gives us the "grace of independence" needed to guard us against the danger of being swallowed up by institutional demands.[50] However, when we observe members of a new subculture of grown-up electronic whiz kids obsessed with interacting with computers or, more generally, the mass of people living amid the constant din of radio and TV and finding it "exceedingly difficult to let insights from unconscious depths break through," as Rollo May rightly deplores,[51] then one wonders if the message for 1984 is not: "Big Person is not watching you. Nobody is watching. Big Person doesn't care about you. She would rather be alone and mind her own business."

We hear social scientists telling us that loneliness is becoming a major social problem.[52] Nearly every journal of the behavioural sciences annually carries a wide variety of studies on the lonelines of senior citizens, spouses, priests, university students, divorcees, refugees, widows and widowers, veterans, gays, young adolescents or children. For the women and men of technologically advanced societies, societies which have the tendency to fabricate exterior and superficial selves, loneliness has become a major enigma. We should not be astonished to find, therefore, that their quest for sexual meaning often turns out to be a fiasco. Since nothing human is shared they are necessarily frustrated.

By their sexual condition, celibates are cut out to become specialists in the necessary experience of solitude. In a culture which promotes sexual games and insipid sex at the expense of sexual integration, successful sexual celibates can teach us that solitude is a key to sexual discernment. It is also the secret of growing old beautifully and freely without being overly preoccupied with our usefulness.[53] To hear the voices in the wilderness is the sine-qua-non to prophecying about the Kingdom where being-with-others in a fecund, loving dialogue is the heart of the matter.

2. PROPHETICAL ANDROGYNY

Gregory of Nyssa, a leading fourth century authority in Christology, speaks of the androgynous Christ unifying within himself what was separated by the sexual split of the original human unity into male and female.[54] Adam is not without Eve; Jesus, the new Adam (Rm 5: 12; 1 Co 15: 22), is alone. Though he is a vir, a male, both the feminine and the masculine attributes of humankind are in him. This is how the renowned Cappadocian Doctor met the objections formulated against Jesus' celibacy from the Christological axiom: Quod non assumpsit, non sanavit (what he did not assume he did not heal). Having assumed in his celibate, androgynous personality the feminine as well as the masculine, he heals all humankind.

Some contemporary authors have called upon this insight of Eastern theology to make a case for Christ's "height and fullness compared with which normal mankind seems fragmentary and imperfect."[55] Others contend that Gregory of Nyssa's characterization of the celibacy of Jesus applies to every successful celibate life.[56] I believe they are right. The concept of androgyny is closely tied to the ideas of autonomy and wholeness which accounts for the reasonableness of a celibate option. This concept is essential for an understanding of the prophetic contribution sexually integrated celibates make to the achievement of full humanization through the sexual dialogue between women and men.

Androgyny is a word which has recently undergone a substantial semantic evolution in the direction of Gregory's hunch. While it was generally used in the past as a synonym of the pathology called hermaphroditism, researchers on sexual differentiation and psychosexual development now use the term to identify a psychological category expressing well-being. Since its emergence is linked with a shift in the thinking on sexual differentiation, this topic must be examined if the concept of androgyny is to be used meaningfully in our attempt to describe celibate fecundity.

The three major trends of the psychology of sex differences over the years can be interpreted dialectically. The original position understands the differences in terms of nature, the genetic, the innate, the biological, the instinctive. This was contradicted by a view in which nurture, the environmental, the acquired, the psychological, the learned are everything. The clash of these competing positions has brought about the formulation of a contemporary theory of psychosexual differentiation in which the basic proposition is not a dichotomization of genetics and environment, but their interaction.

Based on anatomical differences, the naturalistic position has the tendency to posit two human natures and to interpret femininity and masculinity as two different natural products characterizing, respectively, women and men. Since a "nature" is taken to be the specific form of each living thing and the basic principle of its operations, men and women are seen as enjoying different and irreconcilable characteristics, roles, functions, and mystiques.[57] Whether they speak from a feminist or a masculinist context, the authors who entertain this notion have the tendency to indulge in "pseudospeciation," an operation which consists in considering groups which differ from one's own group as pseudo-species and, therefore, as imperfectly human.[58] This trend has focussed on superiority and subordination.[59] Feminist writings by Elizabeth Gould Davis,[60] Elaine Morgan,[61] and Ashley Montague[62] illustrate this point, as do the classical views of Aristotle, Augustine, Knox, Rousseau, or Freud.

More decisive for our own discussion is a second major consequence of the naturalistic view, namely, an understanding of the interaction between women and men as exterior complementarity. If woman and man are two distinct natures, they must be physically brought together for humanity, created male and female in God's image, to become complete. The couple would, therefore, represent this bringing and welding together, as it were, of one half of the human, woman (passive, emotional, tender, altruistic, receptive, and whatever else woman is supposed to be), with the other half of the human, man (active, rational, sensuous, egotistic, aggressive, and whatever else man is said to be). In a marriage perceived as a fusion, a man and a woman rebuild a humanity which was cut in half by the primeval split. The logic of this naturalistic position is that, confronted with man, woman would become more and more "feminine," and man more and more "masculine." As a result of this position, spouses really never learn anything positive about their own humanity from one another;[63] widows, widowers and divorcees are broken-down beings, hardly capable of surviving humanly with only half the qualities and the skills which are required to cope with daily living; and all singles are incompletely human, some of them irremediably so.

During the first half of this century nurture took over from nature. It became fashionable to think that genes, hormones, and gonads had little to do with it all. Males and females can be transformed into nearly anything society makes them to be. "Gender" which indicates masculine and feminine becomes detached from "sex" which makes males and females.[64] During the

1930s, anthropologist Margaret Mead revealed to Westerners that femininity and masculinity are cultural assignments which vary radically from one people to another.[65] More recently, feminist authors like Simone de Beauvoir[66] and Kate Millett[67] have argued that power, analyzed with a Marxist dialectic by de Beauvoir and in a North American context of economic competition by Millett, is the decisive factor.

The main result of this environmentalist position was to challenge attempts to structure and to define femininity and masculinity in essentialist and universal terms. The immediate and far-reaching ethical consequence was to guard us from too glibly discerning the allegedly cross-cultural and meta-historical "natural law" requirements of each gender. By its excessiveness, though, this position leads to a kind of cultural relativism and arbitrariness which seems suspicious to most researchers today. To postulate that being a female or a male would have no impact whatsoever on one's way of being-in-the-world places a great deal of strain on our credibility. The unresolved problems of this reaction have obviously brought about the gradual formulation of the interactionist theory.

Of greater interest for our present concern, however, is the ethical model of relationships between men and women which is generated by an environmentalist view of differentiation. The current theses supporting this view seldom avoid conceiving such interaction as a battle of the sexes. Particularly in the explanation by power in de Beauvoir, Millett, and others, men and women are depicted as competitors entertaining business-like transactions. At the limit, we would all be unisex solitudes faced with the Promethean task of becoming human each for ourselves or, worse, each against the other. In the first instance, we have a case of solipsism that violates the relational character of the sexual language. In the second, we are dealing with perversion that contradicts the loving quality of sexual fecundity. For Christian ethics, those are major drawbacks.

Milton Diamond's 1965 paper, "A Critical Evaluation of the Ontogeny of Human Sexual Behavior,"[68] was perhaps the first attempt to seriously challenge and force a reversal of the strict environmentalist and learning approach to the development of human sexual behaviour. The argument was in tune with a general movement in behavioural sciences to supersede the old nature-nurture controversy. Today a majority of researchers are working within an interactionist paradigm. It postulates that nothing we are and do is exclusively the work of nature alone or of culture alone. Everything is human construction in an interaction between a human organism and its environment. Sexual differentiation is also understood within this framework. Some researchers place stronger emphasis on physiological determinants of gender differences throughout life.[69] Others lay primary responsibility for the final determination for psychosexual differences upon social conditioning from infancy onward.[70] But everyone agrees, in this position, that one is not without the other.

This third position represents an effort to account theoretically for the sum of ever increasing findings concerning the uterine and extrauterine processes of sexual differentiation[71] with different stages of core gender identity establishment, complex apprenticeships of gender role-learning through infancy, childhood and adolescence,[72] numerous tasks to be accomplished during the adolescent passage and young adulthood for the firm establishment of one's sexual identity, orientation, and personal style,[73] and similar data. This life-long process of sexual differentiation and integration seems to represent a passage from the more peripheral to deeper and deeper levels of human relational existence. It progresses through a series of movements between a pole of similarity (males seek masculinity and females femininity) and a pole of dissimilarity (males open up to femininity and females to masculinity).

People who think about sexual differentiation in an interactionist framework generally understand the successful outcome of this lifelong quest for sexual wholeness in terms of androgyny. The complementarity concept of the naturalistic position stresses the pole of dissimilarity too much to be able to account for women's and men's common humanity. The unisex and competitive concept of the environmentalist position, on the contrary, relies too exclusively on the pole of similarity to be able to explain sexual differentiation and the psychosexual dynamic. These would make no sense except, perhaps, for reproductive purposes.

Androgyny is, therefore, a model of human well-being which draws on the typical valued qualities of both men and women.[74] It postulates that man and woman enjoy the very same human nature in two persons created to relate to one another. Beyond the establishment of one's core gender identity, the developmental task consists in discovering ignored dimensions of one's very own male/female humanity through sexual dialogue with the other sex. Under the loving and sexually challenging sight of persons of the other sex, men discover their own femininity, their anima, and women their masculinity, their animus. The content of this anima and this animus is probably more difficult to define abstractly and cross-culturally than Carl Jung might have believed when he coined these terms.[75] It is probably a moving reality, linked with cultural experiences of femininity and masculinity. Nonetheless, the differences are always there and each sex learns from the other to recognize the hidden face of his or her humanity.

The new androgynous personality is not confused about

216

her or his sexual identity. Androgynous males are men and androgynous females are women. But they allow same-sex assumptions and self-interpretations to be challenged and repressions concerning restrictive sexual roles to be lifted. It is not astonishing to find that persons who score high on androgynous scales also score high on a variety of other scales measuring their human potential: they tend to adapt more easily to a wider range of situational demands and to be more socially competent; they are able to perform a much wider range of activities; they are more easily prepared to successfully pursue second and third careers; they interact more comfortably with the other sex; they tend to have higher self-esteem and identity integration; and so forth.[76]

Celibates cannot delude themselves that they will be made whole through the complementarity of the other-sexed spouse. It is characteristic of their sexual life style to seek human wholeness within themselves, to develop androgynous personalities through their interaction with other-sex persons. Today, even authors who represent a classical stream of thought concerning the spiritual formation of vowed celibates recognize that a new interaction between males and females has proven beneficial to them.[77] The tendency of many celibates to avoid relating to persons of the other sex as real sexual beings is a spiritualistic deviation which can only lead to bruised personalities. Anyone who has lived in environments densely populated with vowed celibates has met male specimens who are either rough, macho bachelors, totally incapable of sensuous tenderness, of empathy, and of affectionate caring, or, on the contrary, affected individuals, incapable of exercising a masculinity confirmed by approving female eyes. Their female counterparts either look like insecure young girls in outgrown bodies or, on the contrary, aggressive creatures, incapable of assertively and elegantly living a femininity valorized by admiring male eyes. In order to avoid this masquerade of celibacy, others are tempted to seek mere complementarity by the creation of a mock-marriage situation or by the setting up of common-life arrangements in which women and men play stereotyped sexual roles. This is the corporealistic deviation. Candidates for life-long celibacy who are encouraged to follow one of these two roads rather than that of androgyny cannot be successfully trained, it seems to me, "to make a celibate life [...] part of the richness of their whole personality."[78] Learning to interact as sexual beings with the other sex may prove difficult for some celibates;[79] but it is a necessary task. This is particularly true for male celibates who, as Kathleen Kelley remarks, are called to minister in Holy "Mother" Church in ways which, in our culture, are characterized as feminine: to be present to others, to listen, to care, to console.[80]

Successful androgynous celibates stand in the midst of the Christian community as living witnesses to the extraordinary human potential of each human person created male/female in God's image. Moreover, because the feminine and the masculine are reconciled in their personalities they are prophetic signs of the eschatological reconciliation of all in Christ in whom "there are no more distinctions between [...] male and female" (Ga 3: 28). The practice of androgyny establishes a humanity reconciled in its most fundamental difference. For a symbol to effectively signify realities of another order, a real basis for its evocative powers must exist in the order in which the symbol functions as symbol. If they are to foreshadow the communion of saints, androgynous celibates must contribute actively to the community pursuit of a renewed experience of living together creatively as men and women. This they do concretely by their free attitude vis-à-vis sexual stereotypes, by their whole life style, by their rich and diversified competencies cutting through sexual roles. In a world where so many factions are at war with each other, the reconciliation of male and female is a basic condition for our hope in the growth of the Kingdom of God.

3. LIBERATION OF FRIENDSHIP

Since celibacy does not focus on one partner, traditional Christian literature describes it as a condition in which dedicated persons are freed to bestow love on many individuals and to mediate God's covenant love for all men and women. The insightful aspect of this view eludes us today because of the angelical, asexual, and unrealistic ways in which it is generally proposed.[81]

Thomas Aquinas's long questio on the "order of charity" should have warned us against lofty discourses on the universality of celibate love. Asked whether we love everyone equally, Thomas replies that inasmuch as we wish everyone their ultimate good, which is God himself, our Christian love is universal. However, since we have closer relationships with some persons than with others, we do not love everyone with the same degree and the same intensity of affection.[82] This is sheer common sense. As Mary Hunt remarks, "wholesale love does not exist; we love concretely."[83] Because we are enfleshed, we maintain a diversity of relationships which call for different kinds and levels of intimacy with a necessarily restricted number of people. The basic problem each one of us must seek to resolve is that of devising the forms of sexual communication which most adequately express the reality of who we are for them and they for us.

Celibates do not belong to another human species. They too are called to love and must love as human beings do. Even those who have taken a vow of celibacy have not given up love. How could they? Love is Christian perfection. What celibates have given up is loving as spouses do. Celibates too are committed to loving others, their "neighbour," in a way which is liberating. It should be characteristic of their sexual fecundity to develop life-giving friendships.

In those oversized institutions where prospective vowed celibates are trained in the art of loving their neighbour, a disembodied atmosphere has often encouraged, paradoxically enough, flight from real, warm, human friendships.[84] At an age when young people are supposed to experience intimacy, to know another human being, and to be known by him or her at a deep level, these candidates are often trained to invest all their energies into taking on a merely "corporate identity." Hence, it is not exceptional to find what Philip Cristantiello[85] calls "protective partnerships" in such "houses of formation."[85] These constitute a subtle spiritualistic deviation. He describes this phenomenon as an unavowed conspiracy of two or more persons to maintain distances and isolation from anything more than a superficial contact with others. Erik Erikson indicates that such distantiation is the counterpart of intimacy. Intimacy is a task which must be accomplished by every young adult.[86] In protective partnerships, the partners merely indulge each other's peripheral sensitivities. Their association relieves them of having to deal with the challenges of sharing real intimacy and protects them from threats of self-disconfirmation. This mechanism protracts, it seems to me, adolescent ego defenses such as asceticism, intellectualization, and the avoidance of sexual communication.

The results can be disastrous because nobody ever gets absolved from reality. Adult living is difficult work and no "miracle" will ever supply for the lack of genuine human growth. If one spends one's young celibate life protecting self-assumptions from being questioned by intimate sharing with others one trusts, the prospects of genuine self-knowledge and self-disclosure are decreased. One may well spend the rest of one's life playing games with oneself and with others and in acting stereotyped roles instead of living authentically and being one's own lovable self.[87] Because of the irresolution of the intimacy question, the celibate is incapable of moving away from self-centeredness toward others. A person who has not been disarmed by the love of others cannot take down her or his own defenses and dare to be vulnerable. Attitudes of suspicion, jealousy, and omnipotence preside over human relationships. Because of affective immaturities, finally, celibates will seek compensatory outlets: some become compulsive eaters, some alcoholics, others indulge in the kind of sentimental pietism which sustains infantilism. Anything to avoid the responsibility of coming to grips with one's sexual self!

Some celibates are scared of intimate relationships

because they feel that if they enter into one, they will have no room to steer this way or that. A moralist must denounce this rationalization and expose it as a myth. We must convince ourselves that the direction our friendships take is always up to us.

If protective partnership has been a largely unrecognized deviation in training centres for vowed celibates, the development of capturing brands of friendship has been, on the contrary, a well-identified corporealistic deviation. This is what spiritual authors of old allude to when they expatiate upon "particular friendships." They often denounce such friendships as being sensual instead of spiritual. True, particular friendships often have unduly strong erotic overtones: not, though, because the partners are too sensuous, but because they are wrongly sensuous. The love versus lust polarity is not equated with spiritual sentiments versus carnal feeling. There is spirit and flesh on both sides of the polarity. But spirit-flesh love is integrative for the partners while spirit-flesh lust is disintegrating and alienating. The difference between particular friendship and elective friendship is that between capturing a person and structuring a person.

Writing in the context of large, self-contained, unisex religious communities, the classic spiritual guides generally had in mind homosexual friendships. However, heterosexual friendships raise the very same issue. In fact, even friendship with God, as Jean Isaac perceives so pertinently, is subject to a similar corruption because it is, fundamentally, a problem of possessiveness and of control, an irresolution of the Oedipus attachment. One has not yet recognized that one's desire to possess the mother and to find one's fulfillment in her is chimerical. God is, therefore, construed as a marvellous surrogate Mother. She represents the fulfilling object par excellence. The celibate has Her all to herself or himself. The literature for celibate priest and religious even plays into the hands of Oedipal yearnings by proclaiming their vocation "objectively more perfect." God would seem to belong to the vowed celibate in a special way. Thus, the scene is set for a "particular friendship" with God. Instead of dying and rising with the Lord, and allowing all creatures to sing the wonders of Being by delivering them from their inhibitions and their fears, deviant celibates adore their own idealistic and narcissistic image in Her. True Christian friendship with God and with others is thus betrayed.[88]

Following in the footsteps of the ancients, contemporary spiritual directors reformulate the rules of discernment for protecting celibate friendships from the foregoing deviation of "particularism."[89] The value of these rules for our discussion lies less in their degree of practicality in given situations than in the analysis of celibate friendship which is

220

implicit in them. Acknowledging that persons deeply concerned about love, as Christians ought to be, score high on a scale measuring the probability of their "falling in love" one or many times during their lives,[90] spiritual mentors exhort celibates-by-choice to attentively examine, day by day, the direction in which an elective friendship is moving. If this direction is one of exclusiveness and totality, this is not the way of celibacy. When a celibate begins to demand more and more from a friend's caring to the point where undivided attention is expected, then celibacy as such has become problematic. One should make new decisions about one's sexual life style as a celibate. Keith Clark is right: "Part of being celibate means that I am owned by no one."[91] Janie Gustafson agrees that "nonpossession is essential to celibate passion."[92]

If one decides to remain celibate and to treat the other as a very close friend but not as a spouse or, if such be the case, not as an active gay partner, then one must respect the truth of his or her respective situation and not create excessive attachments. Otherwise, one must honestly question whether one's primary concern is for a friend's own good or for one's own needs.[93] If, in effect, a celibate maintains a marriage-like relationship without the responsibilities implied in marriage, then one should recognize that one is using rather than loving the other. Egidio Gentili speaks of priests who, in their ministry, have created inopportune affective links between themselves and young women to the point where they hinder the latter's maturational development and the normal fulfilment of their womanly dreams. One day, perhaps too late, these women will realize that they wasted their best years and that they have been "piously" exploited.[94] What is said of priests here applies equally well to any other celibate who indulges in exploitative behaviour.

The blame for such occurrences does not always lie exclusively with the celibate by choice. Immature young men and women, spouses whose marriages are in trouble or have broken down, religious men and women who are going through a vocational crisis sometimes literally throw themselves into the arms of a compassionate celibate and quickly become very emotionally involved with their rescuer. Celibates who wish to follow their option through must wisely select their close friends or, at least, carefully monitor their degree of closeness with people who are looking around for gurus, heroes or saviours.

One of the celibates' most effective ways of discerning the quality of their friendships and the appropriateness of their sexual language is their capacity to live them openly in full view of other close friends and in the midst of the human and/or religious communities to which they belong. Blessed are the celibates who find friends with whom to discuss the matter openly and healthy communities which can supportively witness their love stories. Unfortunately, these are not easy to come by in traditional religious institutions.[95]

How strange that we should have to make such a statement! The ability to communicate truthfully with a wide range of friends as caring, affectionate, tender beings is one of the most valuable testimonies Christian celibates can bring to contemporary society. To diversify one's friendships, to develop rich, intimate fellowships with men and women, children, adolescents, adults, and older persons, with singles and families, ought to be one of the main characteristics of celibate fecundity. Margaret Adam's study of singles shows how their patterns of relationship tend to be more fluid and flexible than the more exclusive attachments most married people have. The sources of their relationships are more varied, reach further in time and across greater geographical distances. This is most valuable for the human community.[96] Celibates should contribute to the opening up of the affective particularisms which urban life has created and foster intercommunication between them.

Sexologists and moralists have thought about human sexuality so exclusively in terms of conjugal and parental relationships, that the sexual language has been dramatically impoverished. Thus, the issue of premarital sexuality has degenerated into a debate over coitus versus noncoitus; the issue of homosexuality stops with a discussion on the morality of homosexual acts; the issue of marital sexuality focusses on such crucial questions as coital positions, simultaneity or number of orgasms, and contraception. All this is so deeply rooted in our psychologies that most people cannot entertain the thought that one can be tenderly sensuous towards a person other than one's own spouse without their minds being invaded by images of child abuse if this person is a child, of sodomy if this person is of the same sex, of adultery if this person is of the other sex. The sexual language has fallen into a state of utter destitution.

This does not mean that coitus is not an important issue. It is and it should also be discussed in the case of celibacy. I would claim that "coital sensuality" (coitus and every other gesture which can be construed as foreplay) is inappropriate behaviour for celibates by choice. To use the coital language is, as we have seen, to speak a conjugal language. To be single rather than partnered is of the essence of celibacy by choice. For a celibate to express sexually his or her warm affection for a friend by a coital language is, therefore, to say an untruth.

A celibate is one who has consciously left aside the conjugal model in order to explore alternate forms of sensuously tender expressions. He or she is an inventor of other languages,[97] of other gestures of friendship, of affection, of communion.

222

This should have concrete repercussions in the lives of celibates. Think, for instance, about the gestures celibate priests make in the exercise of their sacramental ministry. When I was young, a common expression among the French Canadian clergy referred to effective priests as those who "touched souls" ("toucher les âmes"). This idea of a ministry of touching should be rediscovered and revamped: to be able to hold a mourning parishioner in one's arms and allow him or her to cry freely on one's shoulder or to receive with open arms a baby to be baptized and kiss him or her warmly. These and similar life-giving gestures could be sacramental in a less formalized and more effective way than those we usually "perform," since they would really reveal the One in whom the minister believes: a living, warm, caring God.[98]

Our contemporary, Western, sexual indigence may also indicate that our materialism has trained us in the art of acquiring and possessing rather than that of giving and caring. As a consequence, love itself follows the laws of having rather than those of being. The whole thrust of our culture invites us to capture, appropriate, and dominate those who are of our liking. In this sense, as Jean Isaac remarks, the sin of the flesh is, paradoxically,[99] a sin of the spirit: the spirit of possessiveness. Is this not the key to understanding the "vow of chastity" which is taken by religious celibates: the vow of discarding all ascendance over others because this is the greatest obstacle to love?[100]

A well-spoken celibate sexual language is fruitful in liberating friendships from the exclusivity of the conjugal model, from suffocating affective particularisms, from the spirit of domination. By its symbolic contestation of all forms of sexual enslavement, it is an evangelical language which offers all celibates an exceptional[101] opportunity to contribute to the liberation of friendships.

4. REVITALIZATION OF THE COMMUNITY

In his sequence of ego development through eight stages, Erik Erikson reserves three of them for adulthood: intimacy during young adulthood, generativity for maturity, and, in him who has taken care of things and people and has adapted himself wisely to the experience of being, ego integrity. What will be suggested in this fourth point is very much a typical fruit of Eriksonian generativity, defined as "the concern for establishing and guiding the next generation."[102] It also has to do, especially when one's role in the community becomes one of mentor,[103] with ego integrity or wisdom.[104]

If my understanding of these notions of generator and mentor is correct, what the human community has at stake in them is its very revitalization by those who are not content with living in it, let alone of it, but who are actively committed to making it happen by giving of their own selves for it. We are talking about people who have made sense of their own lives, who have come to terms with their society and with who they are, who believe in the future of human fellowship, who have "a passion for life"[105] and want to share it creatively with those who are still groping with personal and social identity problems.

The theme of "celibates for the sake of the Kingdom" as community-producers is a familiar one in the traditional Christian literature. Two variations on this theme recur with remarkable regularity. One stresses the eschatological aspect: to be signs of the Kingdom of Heaven already present and growing among us. The other spells out the apostolic aspect: to be at the service of the community of believers. In listing the traditional reasons brought forth to defend clerical celibacy, for instance, the Second Vatican Council emphasizes "stimulus to charity," "fruitfulness in the world," "the service of God and men," "the service of his Reign and the work of heavenly regeneration," the exercise of "a paternity in Christ."[106] Later Roman documents on the same topic, Paul VI's 1967 encyclical letter on Priestly Celibacy, the 1971 Roman Synod of Bishops, the Guide to Formation in Priestly Celibacy issued by the Sacred Congregation for Catholic Education in 1974, John Paul II's 1979 letter to all the priests on the occasion of Holy Thursday, all reiterate the same twofold consideration.

While these two insistances draw our attention to two levels of significance, both have to do with building the Christian community. Edward Schillebeeckx has shown how the eschatological motive of being "equal to angels," expressed by Luke 20: 35-36, has been wrongly interpreted as bodilessness.[107] Until far into the Middle Ages Christians followed the lead of the synoptic gospels in not regarding angels as fleshless and sexless beings. Angels were seen as "mighty, concentrated personalities, Powers, who stood always in God's presence, prepared to do his bidding swiftly." If celibacy can be designated as an angelic mode of existence, it is only inasmuch as the latter evokes the idea of concentrated force and readiness for the service of God and men. To live eschatologically is to be completely available to the service of the Lord (1 Co 7: 32) for the edification of a loving fellowship, "something that will reach its full development only through the resurrection of the flesh, when we shall be 'sons of God, being sons of the Resurrection' (Lk 20: 36)."[108]

Revitalizing the human community is, I believe, characteristic of all forms of voluntary celibacy. When celibacy fulfills this function, it becomes significant. This is well illustrated by the popularity and success of apostolic religious congregations in the nineteenth century. After the old monarchical and patriarchal system broke down, <u>bourgeois</u> society needed philanthropic strategies to dispense assistance, work, education, and health.[109] New religious congregations met this need. By fulfilling a new role in the community, they were socially significant and, as a consequence, were tremendously appealing to young men and women.

As Edward Schillebeeckx points out, a concerned commitment is phenomenologically contained in the very idea of celibacy.[110] Freed from the demanding tasks of creating the small social cell called "family," celibates should be actively involved in bringing together members of family units in order to form wider communities.[111] In other words, it is characteristic of celibate sexual language to communicate life-enhancing meanings that are liable to bring people together, to form humanly significant social bonds.

Freedom to devote oneself to the Lord's affairs (<u>1 Co</u> 7: 32-35) is easily subject to corporealistic deviations when one loses sight of the true eschatological aspect of celibacy and conceives it merely as a social commodity. Sermons addressed to prospective vowed celibates sometimes make Paul sound like a marketing agent in the service of religious outfits with the following sales pitch: "Why bother with a wife and kids when you can be free to organize your work, your free time and holidays as you please? Join the good life."[112] Celibacy is the opposite of single egocentricity. It implies, among other things, an effective involvement in a concrete community (not an oversized, anonymous institution in which conventual order prevails over conventual persons) with its problems, its interior tensions, its daily difficulties, its hurts and sufferings.[113]

Having begotten schools, hospitals, and all sorts of social agencies which were meant to help a human community develop, religious or clerical celibate associations often refuse to let go of their progeny when the community is ready and willing to take them over. They should keep in mind that these entities, like children, are not begotten to glorify the family name, but for the service and the enrichment of the human and Christian community. The celibate group is no more justified in being incestuous toward its offspring than parents toward their children. Fundamentally, all such behaviour belongs to the same corporealistic deviation.

The spiritualistic deviation, on the contrary, consists in losing sight of the apostolic intentionality of celibacy. Celibacy is seen more as a renunciation for the Kingdom of God than as a service for the Kingdom of God. Though there is solid scriptural basis for linking celibacy with the cross,[114] the whole evangelical inspiration is betrayed when it is defined exclusively as mortification, as some kind of religious suicide. Detachment which does not result in an increased desire for intimacy with God and with others is not Christian.[115] Celibates who get caught in a victim syndrome and trade their generativity for barrenness will often experience a permeating sense of boredom, of stagnation, of interpersonal impoverishment. As Erikson remarks, it is not rare that regression to an obsessive need for pseudo-intimacy takes place. A lack of real concern for others brings about pervasive self-concern. Fruitless, these celibates indulge themselves as if they were their own one-and-only child.[116]

In The Feast of Fools, Harvard theologian Harvey Cox highlights the outstanding social functions played over the centuries by creative communities of religious celibates. In the diversity of their utopian life styles, they often led the historical movements promoting new forms of community living.[117] Fecund celibates can still offer this service today. In an age when privatized family structures begin to show their weaknesses, when individualistic urban life raises insoluble social riddles, when the community's only meeting place is the local shopping centre, celibates have the duty, because they generally have the necessary means, time, and mobility, to challenge the value systems which corrode the human fibers of society. They are called to actively collaborate in creating new models of community. Their main preoccupation should not be to coax others into living the celibate life. Rather, their celibate life style should be an invitation to devise and to socially live out an alternative value system.[118] This is what has to take place if some of our problems, including the disconcerting one of economics, are to find a human solution. When, instead of seeking qualitative social relationships, people subsist by quantities alone and are incapable of letting go of any of what they have out of love for others, human communities necessarily degenerate into lonely crowds and aggressive mobs.

Christian celibates who hope in the final, enduring coming together of the People of God, must be convinced that this Utopian vision will never materialize until we become, with God's grace and our own inventiveness, a Real People. The social regenerative power of sexual celibacy is confronted, in our Western societies, with a tremendous challenge. Celibate Power could change society if celibates dared to love.

NOTES

1. L. H. BEQUAERT, Single Women Alone and Together (Boston: Beacon

Press, 1976), p. xii, estimates that, at any one time, fully one-third of the adult women are not married.

2. C. G. KIESLING, Celibacy..., p. xvii.

3. This is, for instance, the concept which arises from the papers and discussions of the first part of the third Convention of the Centre catholique des médecins français, published under the title, Célibat et sexualité (Paris: Seuil, 1970), pp. 13-40.

4. See Adversus eos qui apud se habent virgines subintroductas, Patrologia Graeca, Vol. 47, col. 495-532.

5. A. SHEEHAN, "Charismatic and Prophetic Roles," Donum Dei, 16 (1971), p. 50.

6. M. RONDET, Le célibat évangélique dans un monde mixte (Paris: Desclée de Brouwer, 1978), p. 15. To speak about "renunciation" of "human sexuality" "for the sake of the Kingdom of Heaven" (as is done in FC, par. 16 [p. 98, tr., p. 29]) is, strictly speaking, incorrect. To renounce "human sexuality" would be humanly destructive and, therefore, immoral. If a celibate renounces anything, he or she renounces a conjugal life style and its sexual expression.

7. The Sexual Celibate (New York: Seabury Press, 1975), p. 108.

8. It is telling that, in three sociological studies of singleness, the idea that people who choose a single life style have a particularly strong interest in and need for psychological autonomy is clearly evidenced. See L. H. BEQUAERT, Single Women...; M. ADAMS, Single Blessedness. Observations on the Single Status in Married Society (New York: Basic Books, 1976); J. L. BARKAS, Single in America (New York: Atheneum, 1980).

9. M. BELLET, Le Dieu..., pp. 234-235, rightly denounces the dualistic trend which sees celibacy and marriage as opposed sexual states which have little to teach each other. This vision fosters a desexualization and an idealization of celibacy. In the R. C. Church, this trend had been reversed in the Vatican II documents and in Paul VI's 1967 encyclical letter, Sacerdotalis Coelibatus: see J. A. KOMONCHAK, "Celibacy and Tradition," Chicago Studies, 20 (1981), pp. 5-39. However, it surfaced again in FC, par. 16 (pp. 98-99; tr., p. 30), which affirms the superiority of the charism of vowed celibacy over that of marriage.

10. A. AUER, "The Meaning...," p. 303. A similar stand is taken by M. W. PABLE, "Priesthood and Celibacy," Chicago Studies, 20 (1981), p. 60: "Of itself, a choice of celibacy is neither virtuous nor sinful. For a Christian, celibacy is virtuous only when it is embraced freely for a motive of faith." This represents a strange view of the rapport between the moral and theologal order.

11. In the decree on the appropriate renewal of the religious life, Perfectae caritatis, par. 12, the second Council of the Vatican warns that candidates to vowed celibacy should "be trained to make a celibate life consecrated to God part of the

richness of their whole personality." W. M. ABBOTT (ed.), The Documents..., p. 475.

12. Y. M.-J. CONGAR, "Les Laïcs et l'ecclésiologie des 'ordines' chez les théologiens des XIe et XIIe siècles," I Laici nella "societas christiana" dei secoli XI e XII (Milan, Vita e pensioro, 1968), pp. 83-117.

13. See, e.g., R. W. SOUTHERN, Western Society and the Church in the Middle Ages (Harmondsworth: Penguin Books, 1970), pp. 300-358, in particular pp. 340-346.

14. X. THÉVENOT, "Les célibats. Risques et chances," Études, 352 (1980), pp. 660-666, also deplores the lack of Christian reflection on nonconsecrated celibacy which, he says, constitutes the situation of the majority of celibates in France.

15. C. G. KIESLING, Celibacy..., pp. xiv and 3. See also A. DONVAL, Un avenir..., p. 95; X. THÉVENOT, "Les célibats...,' pp. 664-665.

16. M. NEUMAN, "Friendships...," pp. 82-83.

17. M. RONDET, Le célibat..., p. 22. See also p. 16.

18. J. GUILLET, "Rejeté des hommes et de Dieu," Christus, 13 (1966), pp. 83-100.

19. M. SIMPSON, "Loneliness and Solitude," The Way, 14 (1974), p. 25; H. J. M. NOUWEN, Out of Solitude. Three Mediations on the Christian Life (Notre Dame: Ave Maria Press, 1974), p. 14.

20. A. PEELMAN, "Fidelity to Christ in the Contemporary Experience of the Church," Église et Théologie, 11 (1980), pp. 108-109.

21. R. P. HARDY, "Solitude: A Sanjuanist Perspective," Église et Théologie, 6 (1976), pp. 5-23.

22. T. LENTFOEHR, "Thomas Merton: The Dimensions of Solitude," The American Benedictine Review, 23 (1972), pp. 337-352; R. CASHEN, The Concept of Solitude in the Thought of Thomas Merton (Unpublished doctoral dissertation, Rome, Pontifical Gregorian University, 1976); R. FARICY, "Thomas Merton: Solitude and the True Self," Science et Esprit, 31 (1979), pp. 191-198.

23. D. HAMMARSKJOLD, Markings (London: Faber and Faber, 1966).

24. S. MATHIEU, Le célibat féminin. De l'image à la réalité (Paris: Mame, 1970), p. 128.

25. Approches psychologiques du célibat. Les images, le corps, la solitude (Taizé: Presses de Taizé, 1969), pp. 107-174.

26. Celibacy for Our Times (St. Meinrad: Abbey Press, 1974), pp. 69-72.

27. "The Meaning and Functioning of Sexuality in the Lives of Celibates and Virgins," Review for Religious, 34 (1975), pp. 268-270.

28. Celibate Passion (San Francisco: Harper and Row, 1978).

29. An Experience...

30. J. GUSTAFSON, Celibate Passion...: after starting her book with oneness and wholeness (pp. 1-10) she is led into a discussion of her desert experience (pp. 11-21).

31. M. SIMPSON, "Loneliness...," p. 24.

32. J. SARANO, La solitude humaine (Paris: Le Centurion, 1968), p. 15.

33. See, e.g., the 5th case of maldeveloped priests in the study on priestly life and ministry commissioned by the NCCB, in E. C. KENNEDY and V. J. HECKLER (eds.), The Catholic Priest in the United States. Psychological Investigations (Washington, D.C.: United States Catholic Conference, 1972), pp. 61-62.

34. C. E. MOUSTAKAS, Loneliness and Love (Englewood Cliffs: Prentice-Hall, 1972), p. 20. See also Loneliness (Englewood Cliffs: Prentice-Hall, 1961), pp. 24-33.

35. D. VASSE, Le temps du désir. Essai sur le corps et la parole (Paris: Seuil, 1969), pp. 19-20.

36. M. SIMPSON, "Loneliness...," p. 24.

37. Marrying..., p. 375.

38. R. FARICY, "Thomas Merton...," p. 193.

39. T. LENTFOEHR, "Thomas Merton...," p. 352.

40. E. MOUNIER, Personalism (London: Routledge & Kegan Paul, 1952), p. 33.

41. This, if I am not mistaken, was the major insight of J. GUSTAFSON's desert experience: Celibate Passion..., pp. 19-21.

42. FRANCOIS de SALES, Oeuvres complètes (Paris: J.-P. Migne, 1861-1864), vol. III, letter 856, p. 714 (my translation).

43. E. E. WHITEHEAD and J. D. WHITEHEAD, Marrying..., pp. 373-388, describe this self-disclosure and the "virtue of self-intimacy" and its practice as a sexual exercise.

44. THOMAS AQUINAS, ST, II^a-II^{ae}, q. 25, a. 4 (Vol. XXXIV, p. 91). The reference to ARISTOTLE is Nicomachean Ethics, IV, 4 (1166 a 1 and 1168 b 5).

45. E.g., S. BRECKEL and N. M. MURPHY, "Psychosexual Development ...," p. 55.

46. T. MERTON, Contemplation in a World of Action (Garden City: Doubleday, 1971), p. 237.

47. A. LOUF, "Solitude pluralis," Collectanea Cisterciensia, 38 (1976), pp. 29-39.

48. D. HAMMARSKJOLD, Markings..., p. 107; Y. RAGUIN, Celibacy..., pp. 69-71; M. SIMPSON, "Loneliness...," pp. 24 and 27; H. J. M. NOUWEN, Out of Solitude..., p. 22; see also by the same author: "Solitude and Community," Worship, 52 (1978), pp. 13-23, and Clowning in Rome. Reflections on Solitude, Celibacy, Prayer, and Contemplation (Garden City: Image Books, 1979), p. 29; R. FARICY, "Thomas Merton...," p. 191; M. FOX, A Spirituality Named Compassion and the Healing of the Global Village, Humpty Dumpty and Us (Minneapolis: Winston Press, 1979), p. 93; T. J. TYRELL, Urgent Longings..., p. 41. I find R. WILD, "I Am in the Desert," Studies in Formative Spirituality, 1 (1980), pp. 207-216, more enigmatic: see, e.g., p. 208.

49. Markings..., p. 85.

50. T. MERTON, Contemplation..., p. 246, has extremely harsh words for "incompetent officials" in the Catholic Church who over-control and literally drive Catholics away from the

visible Church.

51. See R. MAY, The Courage to Create..., pp. 66-67.
52. It was already becoming a popular theme in the 1960s: e.g., E. E. MANNIN, Loneliness. A Study of the Human Condition (London: Hutchinson, 1966); J. SARANO, La solitude...
53. H. J. M. NOUWEN, Out of Solitude..., p. 23.
54. M. BELLET, Le Dieu..., p. 67, merely mentions the fact without quoting a text. I have the impression that the idea is diffused in Gregory's works: e.g., In Scripturae verba, Faciamus hominem and imaginem et similitudinem nostram, Oratio I, Patrologia Graeca, Vol. 44, col. 274D-275C.
55. E.g., I. F. GORRES, Is Celibacy Outdated? (Westminster: Newman Press, 1965), p. 34. Her portrayal of celibate priests as knights, playing the role of St. Michael towards helpless women, presupposes a view of masculinity and femininity which fewer and fewer North American men and women would accept.
56. E.g., A. LOUF, Seigneur, apprends-nous à prier (Bruxelles: Foyer Notre-Dame, 1972), pp. 100-109; J. GUSTAFSON, Celibate Passion..., pp. 89-93; Y. RAGUIN, "Regards sur le célibat consacré," La Vie des Communautés Religieuses, 39 (1981), p. 72.
57. See A. GUINDON, "L'être-femme...," pp. 103-141.
58. See E. H. ERIKSON, Gandhi's Truth. On the Origins of Militant Nonviolence (New York: W. W. Norton, 1969), pp. 431-434. It is interesting to note that in scholastic philosophy and theology, "natures" are thought of as occupying different ranks of perfection in the hierarchy of being: see THOMAS AQUINAS, ST, I^a, q. 47, a. 2. Great "metaphysical theories," like great "moral principles," are often, in my opinion, little more than rationalizations of cultural biases.
59. K. E. BORRESEN, Subordination et équivalence. Nature et rôle de la femme d'après Augustin et Thomas d'Aquin (Oslo: Universitetsforlaget, 1968.)
60. The First Sex (Harmondsworth: Penguin Books, 1971).
61. The Descent of Women (New York: Bantam Books, 1972).
62. The Natural Superiority of Women (New York: Collier Book, 1977).
63. See J. PUYO and J. Le DU, Quand est venu le temps d'aimer (Limoges: Droguet et Ardant, 1974), p. 193; R. GRIMM, Ce qu'aimer veut dire?..., p. 28; E. E. WHITEHEAD and J. D. WHITEHEAD, Marrying..., p. 103.
64. R. J. STOLLER, Sex and Gender. On the Development of Masculinity and Femininity (New York: Science House, 1968), p. 9, was expressing this view when he wrote: "Gender is a term that has psychological or cultural rather than biological connotations. If the proper terms for sex are 'male' and 'female,' the corresponding terms for gender are 'masculine' and 'feminine'; these latter may be quite independent of (biological) sex."
65. See, in particular, Sex and Temperament in Three Primitive Societies (New York: Morrow, 1963 [the first edition appeared

in 1935]).

66. The Second Sex (New York: Knopf, 1953).

67. Sexual Politics (Garden City: Doubleday, 1970).

68. In Quarterly Review of Biology, 40 (1965), pp. 147-175.

69. E.g., M. DIAMOND, "Human Sexual Development. Biological Foundations for Social Development," in F. A. BEACH (ed.), Human Sexuality in Four Perspectives (Baltimore: Johns Hopkins University Press, 1976), pp. 22-61.

70. E.g., J. MONEY and A. A. EHRHARDT, Man & Woman... A clear statement of the interactionist position as regards sexual differentiation is found in J. MONEY, "Human Hermaphroditism...," pp. 83-84.

71. See R. G. SLABY and K. S. FREY, "Development...," pp. 849-856; R. G. SLABY, "The Self-Socialization...," pp. 123-127.

72. See, e.g., D. Z. ULLIAN, "The Development of Conceptions of Masculinity and Femininity," in B. LLOYD and J. ARCHER (eds.), Exploring Sex Differences (London: Academic Press, 1976), pp. 25-47; M. GUTTENTAG and H. BRAY, Undoing Sex Stereotypes. Research and Resources for Educators (New York: McGraw-Hill, 1976).

73. See, e.g., E. H. ERIKSON, Identity..., ; P. BLOS, The Adolescent Passage. Developmental Issues (New York: International Universities Press, 1979); P. Y. MILLER and W. SIMON, "The Development of Sexuality in Adolescence," in J. ADELSON (ed.), Handbook of Adolescent Psychology (New York: J. Wiley, 1980), pp. 383-407.

74. See, e.g., A. G. KAPLAN and J. P. BEAN (eds.), Beyond Sex-Role Stereotypes. Readings Toward a Psychology of Androgyny (Boston: Little, Brown, 1976), pp. viii and 383-392; J. SINGER, Androgyny. Toward a New Theory of Sexuality (Garden City: Anchor Books, 1977), pp. 3-14; M. GUTTENTAG and H. BRAY, Undoing..., pp. 9-11; A. G. KAPLAN and M. A. SEDNEY, Psychology..., pp. 5-12.

75. See how very few psychological differences can be "fairly well established" in E. E. MACCOBY and C. N. JACKLIN, The Psychology of Sex Differences (Stanford: Stanford University Press, 1974), pp. 351-352. For Carl Jung's thought on this point, see A. B. ULANOV, The Feminine in Jungian Psychology and in Christian Theology (Evanston: Northwestern University Press, 1971), pp. 212-285.

76. See, e.g., J. H. PLECK and J. SAWYER (eds.), Men and Masculinity (Englewood Cliffs: Prentice-Hall, 1974); J. T. SPENCE, R. HELMRICH, and J. STAPP, "Ratings of Self and Peers on Sex Role and Their Relation to Self-Esteem and Conceptions of Masculinity and Femininity," Journal of Personality and Social Psychology, 32 (1975), pp. 29-39; M. GUTTENTAG and H. BRAY, Undoing..., pp. 9- 27; many of the articles in A. G. KAPLAN and J. P. BEAN (eds.), Beyond Sex-Role..., e.g., pp. 47-62, 89-97, 223-231, 239-271, 281-292, 319-337; J. L. ORLOFSKY, "Sex-role Orientation, Identity Formation, and Self-esteem in College Men and Women," Sex Roles, 3 (1977),

pp. 561-575; J. I. BERZINS, M. A. WELLING, and R. E. WETTER, "A New Measure of Psychological Androgyny Based on the Personality Research Form," Journal of Consulting and Clinical Psychology, 46 (1978), pp. 126-138; W. ICKES and R. D. BARNES, "Boys and Girls Together - and Alienated. On Enacted Stereotyped Sex Roles in Mixed-Sex Dyads," Journal of Personality and Social Psychology, 36 (1978), pp. 669-683; A. G. KAPLAN and M. A SEDNEY, Psychology..., pp. 24-29.

77. See, e.g., E. GENTILI, L'amour dans le célibat (Gembloux: J. Duculot, 1970), p. 73; J. LAPLACE, "La relation homme-femme vécue dans la vie consacrée," La Vie des Communautés Religieuses, 34 (1976), pp. 226-251; M. RONDET, Le célibat..., pp. 59-61, 66-71.

78. Vatican II's Decree on the appropriate renewal of the religious life, Perfectae caritatis, par. 12, in W. M. ABBOTT (ed.), The Documents..., p. 475.

79. S. C. CALLAHAN, "Personal Growth and Sexuality: Adolescent and Adult Developmental Stages," Chicago Studies, 20 (1981), pp. 36-37.

80. In "Human Sexuality and the Ordained Priesthood. A Workshop for Priests," held at Saint Michael's College, Vermont, June 21-25, 1982.

81. Even where there is recognition of the need for elective friendships between celibate men and women, some contemporary authors still have the tendency to discuss the issue in vague and spiritualistic terms: e.g., C. G. KIESLING, Celibacy..., pp. 133-171; P. M. CONNER, Celibate Love (Huntington: Our Sunday Visitor, 1979). There are still traces in the literature of oppositions to the very idea of real celibate love. M. TRÉMEAU suggests, in Le célibat consacré. Son origine historique, sa justification doctrinale (Paris: C. L. D., 1979), p. 80, that the only women priests ought to love with affection are their mothers and sisters. But Trémeau also describes the body as a wild animal which, when not kept under close watch, is always on the prowl for sexual prey (p. 82)...

82. THOMAS AQUINAS, ST, II^a-II^{ae}, q. 26, specifically article 6. R. MEHL, Society..., p. 154, warns, moreover, that "all human relationships are selective. When they are not, they sink into banality."

83. M. E. HUNT, "Lovingly Lesbian...," p. 145.

84. M. W. PABLE, "Priesthood...," p. 71.

85. P. D. CRISTANTIELLO, "Psychosexual Maturity in Celibate Development," Review for Religious, 37 (1978), pp. 645-663. What the author writes applies as well to young celibates who are not in a seminary or in a religious community.

86. E. H. ERIKSON, Identity..., pp. 135-138.

87. See E. C. KENNEDY and V. J. HECKLER (eds.), The Catholic Priest..., pp. 55-106. Though the authors are careful not to blame celibacy for the lack of emotional development these priests display, it is obvious that their inadequate training for celibacy is very much part of the problem.

88. J. ISACC, Réévaluer..., pp. 91-159, in particular pp. 127-129 and 137-138.
89. E.g., D. GOERGEN, The Sexual Celibate..., p. 172; M. NEUMAN, "Friendships...," pp. 81-93; P. S. KEANE, "The Meaning...," p. 297; M. RONDET, "Hommes et femmes, dans le célibat pour le Royaume," Spiritus, 16 (1975), pp. 408-412; C. G. KIESLING, Celibacy..., pp. 153-217.
90. M. NEUMAN, "Friendships...," pp. 85-87, is very perceptive on this point.
91. An Experience..., p. 111.
92. Celibate Passion..., p. 85.
93. This point is well taken in Y. RAGUIN, "Regards...," pp. 76-81.
94. L'amour..., p. 59.
95. M. NEUMAN, "Friendships...," p. 91; M. RONDET, Le célibat..., pp. 65-66.
96. M. ADAMS, Single Blessedness...
97. See M. RONDET, Le célibat..., p. 28; M. FOX, WHEE!..., p. 193.
98. I want to thank Albert ROY for his 1982 unpublished paper, "Sexualité humaine et ministère pastoral," in which these ideas are expressed.
99. J. ISAAC, Réévaluer..., p. 121. Also pp. 143-144.
100. Ibid., pp. 134-135.
101. See also A. DONVAL, Un avenir..., pp. 91 and 94.
102. E. H. ERIKSON, Childhood..., p. 267; Identity..., p. 138.
103. See D. J. LEVINSON et al., The Seasons..., pp. 97-101.
104. E. H. ERIKSON, Childhood..., pp. 268-269; Identity..., pp. 139-141. See also E. E. WHITEHEAD and J. D. WHITEHEAD, Marrying..., pp. 252-268.
105. J. GUSTAFSON, Celibate Passion..., p. 73.
106. Lumen Gentium, par. 42 and Presbyterorum Ordinis, par. 16. See a brief presentation of the birth and evolution of traditional arguments in J. A. KOMONCHAK, "Celibacy and Tradition...," pp. 5-39.
107. This precise point has been well documented by J. BUGGE, Virginitas...
108. E. SCHILLEBEECKX, Celibacy (New York: Sheed and Ward, 1968), pp. 55-56.
109. J. DONZELOT, The Policing of Families..., pp. 48-95.
110. Ibid., p. 85.
111. This is acknowledged by S. C. CALLAHAN, "Personal Growth...," p. 38.
112. This is obviously contrary to Pauline thinking: see M. THURIAN, Marriage and Celibacy (London: SCM Press, 1959); and X. LÉON-DUFOUR, "The Theological Meaning of Marriage and Consecrated Celibacy," Man Before God. Readings in Theology, by A. ALFARO et al. (New York: P. J. KENEDY, 1966), pp. 131-145.
113. J. ISAAC, Réévaluer..., pp. 110-111.
114. L. LEGRAND, The Biblical Doctrine of Virginity (New York: G.

Chapman, 1963), pp. 53-88. For other traditional sources, see
J.-M. PERRIN, Virginity..., pp. 17-24.

115. J. GUSTAFSON, Celibate Passion..., pp. 85-88.

116. E. H. ERIKSON, Childhood..., p. 267; Identity..., p. 138.

117. H. COX, The Feast of Fools. A Theological Essay on Festivity
and Fantasy (New York: Harper and Row, 1970), pp. 88-90.

118. D. GOERGEN, The Sexual Celibate..., p. 112.

"But," some readers may object, "have you not written a book on a subject which is much broader than sexual fecundity? We have read about identity crisis, solitude and silence, relationships and growth, conflicts and nonviolence, covenant love and elective friendship, fidelity and mercifulnes, ecology and nuclear image, social commitment and contestation. Are not such topics beyond the scope of human sexuality?"

If sex is a question of flesh and bone and mechanical devices, most of what has been written is this book is, I am ready to admit, not a discourse on sexuality. Most sexologists would not write about many of the things I have dwelt on in this volume. But then, if sex is no more than orgasms, we should not expect a sexual revolution, either the liberal kind which increases choices or the reactionary kind which multiplies taboos and interdictions to bring about anything significant. Sexual revolutions which merely affect the mores in their materiality will initiate as many troubles as they solve. Experienced therapists could enumerate a long list of casualties which have resulted from naive expectations of heavenly happiness from the quantitative sort of sexual revolution brought about in the 1960's. They know from experience that adolescents who sleep with more partners than they can remember or couples who open their coital intimacy to third parties merely end up, most of the time, with a pervading sense of disappointment, suspicion, antagonism, betrayal, contempt, and anger instead of the deep satisfaction they sought. The deep impression of the dirtiness of sex with which they are left exceeds the pessimism of their Puritan forebears.

Nothing will ever change this sad experience in the case of those who cling to a corporealist or a spiritualist interpretation of human sexuality. They cannot understand that sex which is not integrative, relational, loving, and socially responsible lacks humanity and cannot, on a long-term basis, produce anything that is humanly fulfilling. To speak about sex in terms of fun, orgasms, baby-production, or religious ecstasy is to describe a disintegrating activity, not a life-enhancing one. To spell out the mechanics of sexual outlets without attending to the necessity and quality of human relationships is to invite anonymous and meaningless solipsistic behaviour. To discuss sexual conduct which is not created by love is to dabble in human perversions. To treat sexual life as an asocial reality is to peddle an illusion.

If the latest "sexual revolution" has brought so

little to so many, it is not that they have expected more than
sexuality could give, but that they have given less to sexuality
than expected. Where human sexuality is recognized for the rich
source of humanness which it is, the sexual creators will deliver
the goods.

The agenda for the forthcoming revolution of the
sexual creators outlined herein is simply an agenda, my own. No
doubt there are other items to be suggested, perhaps more
worthwhile than mine. If the discussion that ensues from this book
gravitates toward these and away from my own, that in itself will
be the proof that it has accomplished something.

ABBREVIATIONS

AAS — Acta Apostolicae Sedis.

ASS — Acta Sanctae Sedis.

DS — H. DENZINGER and A. SCHONMETZER, Enchiridion symbolorum, definitionum et declarationum de rebus fidei et morum (Rome: Herder, 1976).

FC — JOHN PAUL II, Familiaris consortio (1981), in AAS, 74 (1982), pp. 81–191. The English translation quoted is from the Canadian Conference of Catholic Bishops.

GS — SECOND COUNCIL OF THE VATICAN, Gaudium et spes (1965), in AAS, 58 (1966), pp. 1025–1120. English translation: W. A. ABBOTT (ed.), The Documents of Vatican II (London: G. Chapman, 1966), pp. 199–308.

HV — PAUL VI, Humanae vitae (1968), in AAS, 60 (1968), pp. 481–503. English translation: O. M. LIEBARD (ed.), Love and Sexuality (Wilmington: Consortium Books, 1978), pp. 331–347.

SBF — SYNOD OF BISHOPS ON FAMILY, 43 Propositions (1980). English translation: The Tablet, 235 (1981), pp. 116–118, 141–142, 164–167. The Latin text has been published by J. GROOTAERS and J. A. SELLING, The 1980 Synod of Bishops "On the Role of the Family." An Exposition of the Event and an Analysis of its Texts (Louvain: Leuven University Press, 1983), pp. 345–369.

SCG — THOMAS AQUINAS, Liber de Veritate Catholicae Fidei contra errores Infidelium qui dicitur "Summa Contra Gentiles" (Rome: Marietti, 1961).

ST — THOMAS AQUINAS, Summa Theologiae. Latin text and English translation, edited by Blackfriars (New York: McGraw-Hill; London: Eyre and Spottiswoode, 1964–1976).

AUTHOR INDEX

The author: André Guindon is professor of moral theology at St. Paul University in Ottawa, Ontario, Canada. He is the author of The Sexual Language. An Essay in Moral Theology (Ottawa, University of Ottawa Press, 1976).

DATE DUE